We the People:

Two Hundred Years of the Constitution

Second Edition

Walter Ehrlich

160 Gould Street
Needham Heights, MA 02194

Copyright © 1993 by Ginn Press.
All rights reserved.

Permission in writing must be obtained from the publisher before any part of this work may be reproduced or transmitted in any form or by any means, electronic or mechanical, including photocopying and recording, or by any information storage or retrieval system.

Printed in the United States of America

10 9 8 7 6 5 4 3 2 1

ISBN 0-536-58388-9
BA 1878

GINN PRESS
160 Gould Street/Needham Heights, MA 02194
Simon & Schuster Higher Education Publishing Group

TO SYLVIA

TABLE OF CONTENTS

Preface to First Edition vii
Preface to Second Edition ix
Federalism 1
The Congress 33
The Presidency 73
The Judiciary 99
The Amendments 123
Appendix A: Articles of Confederation 149
Appendix B: Constitution of the United States 159
Bibliography 181
Index 187

PREFACE TO FIRST EDITION

The bicentennial commemoration of the Constitutional Convention and of the great document which the Framers created has justifiably elicited a profusion of materials on the events which transpired two hundred years ago. The bicentennial also is demonstrating, much to our chagrin, how little so many Americans really know and understand about the Constitution.

This volume started in my work as historical consultant for a series of three twenty-minute educational films, one on federalism, one on the presidency, and one on the amendments. People working in the technical areas of those films continuously barraged me with all sorts of questions about the subject matter, so that often our production meetings turned into educational sessions not unlike my classes in American Constitutional History at the University of Missouri-St. Louis. Co-workers on those films suggested how much more valuable the films' textual materials would be if expanded into full-blown essays not limited to the constrictions of a short film narrative. I therefore expanded what I had done on the films and then added two more essays, one on Congress and one on the judiciary.

This volume, then, is intended to give a general overview of five major institutions in our American system, on how they got into the Constitution in the first place, and on how they have developed in our two hundred years of national existence.

These essays are ideal for classes in American history because so often the Constitution and its development are given short shrift in courses which demand so much time for political, social, and economic developments, in addition to what is always so lively and interesting for students, the wars and our international relations. And of course these are all important. Teachers and students in American history courses therefore can fill a large instructional gap through judicious use of the materials in this volume.

These essays obviously fit into courses in American government, problems and issues courses, and similar classroom work in formal school settings.

WE THE PEOPLE

They also can be exceedingly valuable in more informal community or institutional educational courses—such as churches and community centers—becoming ever so popular throughout the country.

Aside from school and institutional courses, these essays are ideal, as we commemorate two hundred years of our Constitution, simply for pastime reading on a plane, a bus, a commuter train, or in the living room. The American people simply need to know more about their Constitution.

If this brief volume can help, then, even a little bit, to better understand the Constitution and how it fits into American society, my efforts will have been worthwhile.

No printed materials reach readers without important contributions by dedicated editorial consultants. I wish to thank especially Kathleen Joyce, Michael McKenna and Lauren Miller of the Ginn Press editorial staff for their most constructive assistance. Any criticism readers may have of fact or interpretation should be directed only to me.

W.E.

University of Missouri—St. Louis
St. Louis, Missouri

PREFACE TO SECOND EDITION

All the premises for writing these essays which I set forth in the preface of the first edition have, I think, proved correct. Friends and colleagues who used the volume found their major problem to be that the book ran out of print and they could not secure enough for classes. Some resorted to duplicating the essays (with my permission, of course, although I suspect others "sort of forgot"), because they found that even used copies were hard to come by.

From communications I received by those who have used this material, the chapter on Federalism received the most accolades. Comments included: "The clearest exposition of federalism I have ever read"; "For the first time my students finally understand the nature of federalism"; "Even though I have taught Government for three years, I never until now really understood why we have had so many problems [understanding federalism]." One colleague wrote me that he took the book with him to a history meeting and found it far more instructive reading on the plane than even the airline's emergency placard! I would be anything but honest if I denied that these statements did not increase my hat size.

Let me emphasize that these essays are not written in a scholarly journal style that only Ph.D. college professors of History and Political Science can understand. They are based upon my own class lectures and discussions. They are written for *students* to understand—students in courses in American history and government who are at the secondary school level, the junior/community college level, and/or the university undergraduate level. This volume is especially appropriate and valuable for discussion sections in college and university survey courses in American history and Political Science. It is excellent also, I am told, for discussion groups in church and community settings.

Let me point out also that one can use any or all of these essays; each stands independently of the others. That is why the reader will find some duplicative

WE THE PEOPLE

narrative. For instance, the issue of Congressional limitations over Presidential war powers is discussed in both the Presidency and Congress essays. So, too, the role of Congress in the amending procedure is discussed in the Congress essay and in the Amendment essay. Because of its unique morphology, the development of the recently adopted Twenty-Seventh Amendment dealing with the salaries of members of Congress is included under Congress and under the Amendments.

This edition does not pretend to include major revisions, although there are some. It is primarily an updated version of the original volume, which was put together during the latter stages of the Reagan administration. This revised edition includes developments during the Bush administration through the election of Bill Clinton and Al Gore in November, 1992. It also includes discussions of some critical constitutional issues that developed since I first wrote these essays. Among others, they include Presidential war powers (especially vis-à-vis the Persian Gulf War); Congressional salary and term limitations; abortion; and impeachment procedures—we have had three challenged House impeachments and Senate trials in just the past few years.

W.E.

University of Missouri—St. Louis
January 1993

FEDERALISM

"The powers not delegated to the United States by the Constitution, nor prohibited by it to the States, are reserved to the States respectively, or to the people." So reads the Tenth Amendment to the Constitution. It embodies a fundamental principle of American government known as "division of power" or "federalism." Simply defined, federalism is the system by which all governmental powers are divided into two geographical or territorial spheres: state (local) powers and national powers.

To understand federalism, one must understand the difficult concept of sovereignty. Sovereignty is absolute, unlimited, unrestricted governmental authority. A sovereign state or country (the terms are used here synonymously) is one which is completely independent and free from external control. For instance, the United Nations consists of sovereign states. (Of course, there is a certain amount of fiction as to the actual sovereignty of some of those states; nevertheless, by international law they are considered to be sovereign.) On the other hand, none of our fifty "states" is really sovereign, even though we often use that term. (Some were at one time: *i.e.*, the original thirteen, Texas, California, and Hawaii.) Canada and other countries avoid the confusion of terminology by calling their local subdivisions "provinces."

The reason we use the term "states" is that when the thirteen colonies declared their independence in 1776, they became thirteen separate and independent states—or countries—each of which purposefully and voluntarily cooperated with the others (through representatives in the Second Continental Congress) to carry out the struggle against Great Britain. Note the plural wording of the Declaration of Independence: "We, therefore, the representatives of the United States of America, in general Congress assembled, . . . do, in the name, and by the authority of the good people of these colonies, solemnly publish and declare, that *these united colonies are, and of right out to be, free and independent states:* that . . . as free and independent states, *they* have full power to levy war, conclude peace, contract alliances, establish commerce, and to do all other acts and things which *independent states* may of right do. . . ." One of those "other acts," as we shall soon see, was to organize themselves into a loose confederation known as "The United States of America." It probably would have been less confusing had they called themselves what they more accurately were: "The Cooperating States of America."

Historically, most governmental forms have been either "unitary" or "confederated," depending upon the location of sovereignty. Great Britain, for instance, long has had a unitary form of government. That means that sovereignty lies in the central government, in the Crown and Parliament. The local governments (comparable to what we call states in our country), whether subdivisions within the

British Isles or in possessions abroad (shires, provinces, etc.), can exercise only those powers authorized by the sovereign central government. (These include powers and authority passed on down to smaller local units such as cities and towns.) That can be illustrated diagrammatically as follows:

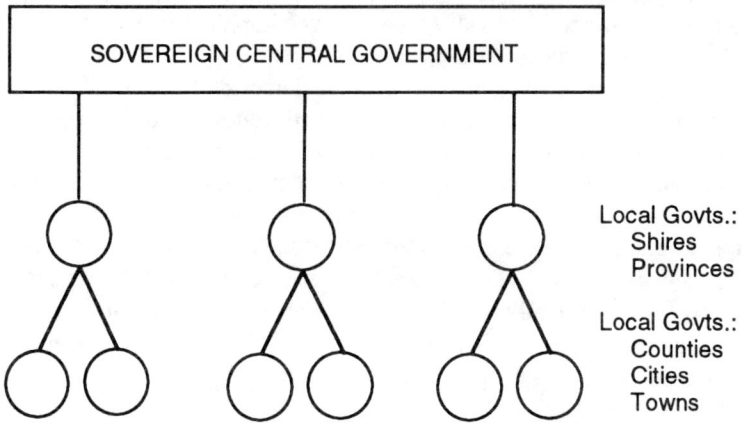

The opposite to a unitary government is a "confederation." There sovereignty lies in the local units. Any central government has only those powers granted to it by the component states or countries, but ultimate sovereignty remains in those units. That means that they have the right, if they wish to exercise it, not to comply with the action of the central government. That is illustrated diagramatically as follows:

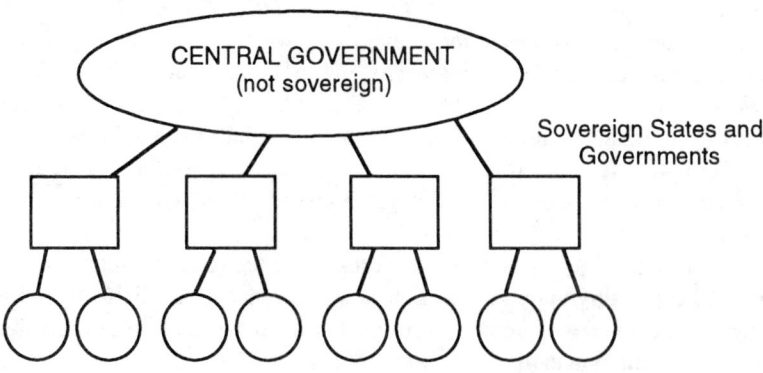

A good example of a confederated structure is the United Nations. It is an organization of sovereign countries which, according to its charter, has a central government known as the General Assembly. Every member state sends a delegation to that General Assembly. At the same time, every member state retains the right not to go along with any action taken by the General Assembly; each state, after all, is a sovereign country and decides for itself what actions it will take. Even the International Court of Justice, or the "World Court," the judicial arm of the United Nations, has no enforcement authority. It must rely on voluntary compliance with its rulings; public opinion (for whatever it is worth) is its only enforcement power.

The same generalizations applied to the government of the Southern Confederacy during the American Civil War of the 1860s.

It was also true earlier of the government established by the thirteen colonies when they broke away from Great Britain. When they declared their independence in 1776, they became not one large independent entity, but thirteen separate and independent countries, which they termed states. They realized, however, that declaring themselves independent was only part of the task; they still had to assure and maintain that independence. And that, they realized, could be achieved only by winning on the battlefield. That, in turn, required extensive and unprecedented cooperation among thirteen political entities in which existed deep roots of separateness and localism, attitudes which had flourished during the lengthy colonial period and which, in 1776, may have been just as strong as the newly-developing vital need for concerted action.

Even though events in the 1760s and 1770s had advanced the argument for unity, when the decision for independence came, two important governmental issues had to be faced. (1) The first was that the Second Continental Congress, the institution through which the colonies had declared their independence, was an *ad hoc* assembly and not a legally-constituted permanent national government. It had come into being in 1774, as the [First] Continental Congress, to respond to the Intolerable Acts, and had then adjourned to await the outcome of its actions. By the time it reconvened on May 10, 1775, fighting had already broken out three weeks earlier at Lexington and Concord. By mere happenstance, this Second Continental Congress was the only body available to carry on the war and implement any effective opposition against the British. For independence to be meaningful, that temporary and provisional institution had to be replaced by a legally constituted permanent organization which incorporated all thirteen new states into some sort of unified political entity.

(2) The second critical obstacle was the deeply-rooted provincialism and separateness which had always existed within the former colonies. Throughout the

entire colonial period, the concept of "American" never really existed. Colonists associated themselves more with their individual colony than with any kind of collective "American" essence. Attempts to unite the colonies (which emanated for various reasons from England) had all failed (*i.e.*, the New England Confederation). In fact, even as recently as during the French and Indian War and in the face of a common Indian danger on the frontier, and even though it originated from within the colonies and was championed by no less a prominent personage than Benjamin Franklin, the colonists still rejected the so-called Albany Plan of Union. That is why cooperative actions in the form of the Stamp Act Congress and the First and Second Continental Congresses and the several economic boycotts were so significant: they showed that by the time of the break from Great Britain the concept of American nationhood was rapidly spreading. Nevertheless, many still thought of themselves more as "Virginians" and "South Carolinians" and "New Yorkers" than as "Americans." Thus, even as they sought to create a new centralized government to ensure their independence, each of the thirteen new states also insisted on maintaining its individuality and sovereignty. The problem, then, was how to create on the one hand a new central government strong enough to achieve and assure independence, but on the other hand one whose centralized powers would not interfere with or impinge upon the independence and sovereignty of the separate states. They did not want to replace a British tyranny with a potential American tyranny.

The result was the Articles of Confederation. (See Appendix A.) Drawn up by a committee of the Second Continental Congress, this new government was formally ratified on March 1, 1781. *It was our first legally-constituted national government.* The thirteen independent states banded together into a confederation which they officially named "The United States of America." The central government consisted of a one-house (unicameral) legislature called "Congress," to which were granted certain specified powers and to which each state sent representatives (from two to seven, the exact number left to the individual state). Each state had one vote in the Congress—logical, since each state was sovereign and therefore equal to each of the others, regardless of acreage, population, or wealth. To ensure that this government in Congress would not be too strong (and therefore not a potential tyrant), the Articles provided for neither national courts nor a national executive. There was a "President," but he was merely the presiding officer of the Congress. Whenever Congress enacted legislation, it would simply designate an individual or a committee to carry out the provisions of that legislation. If any legal questions arose, they would be dealt with in courts which already existed in the various states.

Each of the thirteen states retained its individual sovereignty and could actually decide for itself whether to support Congressional action. Sometimes states did; often they did not, especially if it entailed money. Despite the name "United States of America," we really had thirteen separate countries, loosely united in a voluntary association that the Articles of Confederation itself called (in Article III) a "firm league of friendship." Pointedly portraying that relationship was the dilemma encountered by John Adams, sent to England by the Congress under the Articles to negotiate a trade treaty with our former mother country. Both he and the British fully realized that any or all of the thirteen states could ignore or negate whatever treaty terms Adams might negotiate for Congress. In fact, British foreign minister Charles James Fox was even said to have chided Adams over whether he was expected to make one treaty with Congress or thirteen treaties, one for each of the individual states.

It did not take long for this decentralization of sovereignty and lack of unity to deteriorate into a virtual state of anarchy. The history of the United States under the Articles of Confederation turned out to be one potentially disastrous situation after another, each stemming from weaknesses of the central government: its inability to levy and collect taxes; its inability to regulate interstate and foreign commerce; its lack of a unified court system; its lack of a chief executive empowered to exercise needed powers; its inability to deal with the financial and fiscal needs of the country; its inability to attain necessary cooperation among the thirteen states. As both foreign and domestic dangers threatened the very existence of the new young nation, its leaders readily concluded that a confederation form of government (in spite of some noteworthy achievements) rendered the country too decentralized and too weak. Yet the only other form of central government with which they had any direct experience was the British unitary form—and their concept of that was that it was a most unpleasant tyranny.

When the Framers of the Constitution met in 1787, they established something in between—a federal form of government—which split sovereignty between the states and the central government. For some purposes the *central government* would have sovereign powers; for some purposes the *states* would have sovereign powers. This was not the first time that a federal form of government appeared. Switzerland had had something like it for years, as had the Netherlands, but this was the first time on such a large continental scale. (Variations would be adopted later in Canada, Australia, and South America, among others.)

Without minimizing the creative genius of the Framers, some political theorists have suggested that the federal system that came out of Philadelphia was a logical consequence of the relationship between the colonies and the mother country under the British imperial system. They view that Empire as similar to a federal state. True, it was unitary, with all governmental authority centered in Great Britain. But in actual practice it often resembled a federal system in operation. The British Empire, it must be kept in mind, rested on mercantilism. The government in London exercised strict control over political and economic policies and practices of empire-wide concern. But the British government also allowed colonial governments great leeway in dealing with matters of local concern. Theoretical mercantilism may have dictated the promulgation of certain policies and programs in London; practical considerations and consequences thousands of miles away demanded and were accorded on-the-spot actions which were quite different. English legal theorists went to great lengths to consider the colonies as political units completely subordinate to the Crown and Parliament; but in actual practice those colonies exercised considerable independence and freedom of action, albeit much to the disapprobation of the mother government. Not without some justification have some historians posited that perhaps the major outcome of the American Revolution was merely the transfer of the *locus* of sovereignty from Britain to America, where it became much easier to theorize a philosophy of split sovereignty which had been a reality in practice for many years.

The basic premise of American federalism is that all possible governmental powers fall within two spheres: the national (or federal) sphere and the local (or state) sphere. These can be illustrated by two circles, Circle N for national powers and Circle S for state powers:

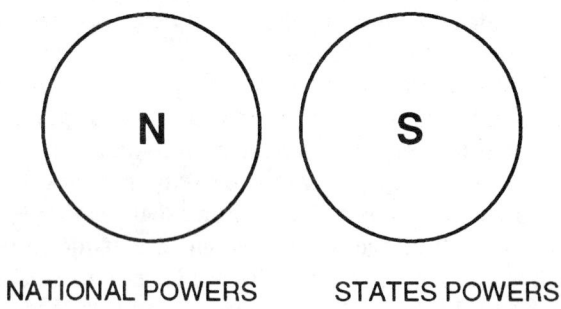

NATIONAL POWERS   STATES POWERS

(For the time being pay no attention to the comparative size of the circles; we shall look at that later.)

FEDERALISM

In actuality, the circles overlap,

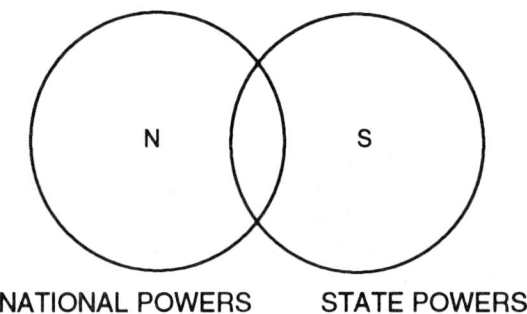

because some powers can be exercised by both state and national governments. For instance, both can tax; both can establish recreational areas; both can prosecute lawbreakers, one for state crimes and the other for federal crimes. Those concomitant powers fall within the areas which overlap, which will be labeled C for "concurrent" powers:

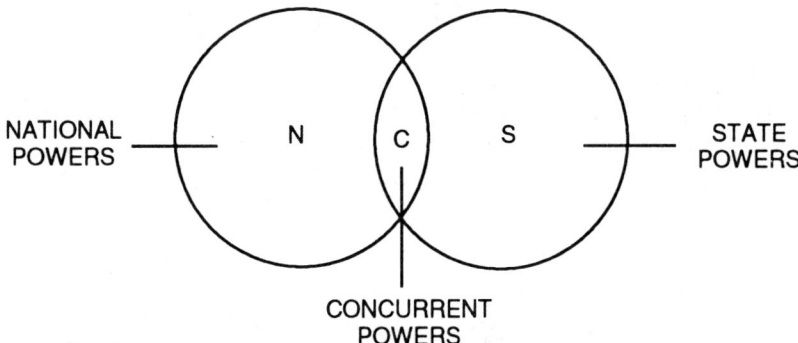

But if the concurrent powers can be exercised by both, might they not conflict? What if a state tax law, for instance, interferes with a federal tax law? What of a state's fishing laws conflict with regulations in a federal park located within that state? No problem: the Constitution takes care of that. Article VI, Paragraph 2 contains the "supreme law of the land" provision, that state law must give way to federal law. So there really is no problem if those powers conflict, even though they are concurrent.

WE THE PEOPLE

In addition to concurrent powers which both can exercise, there are certain powers which *neither* can exercise. Ours is clearly a limited government, with people's rights carefully guarded. For instance, the Bill of Rights—the first ten amendments to the Constitution—forbids the federal government from establishing a religion or censoring the press. Article I, Sections 9 and 10 prohibit states from passing *ex post facto* laws, bills of attainder, or taxes on imports or exports. The Constitution in various places puts limitations on what the national government can do. Furthermore, each state constitution contains its own bill of rights, protecting its people from encroachments by their state government. These we call "denied" powers. Our circles now appear like this, with those denied powers cut out of Segments N, S, and C:

The powers left in Segment N, then, are those exercised only, or exclusively, by the national government; those left in Segment S belong exclusively to the state governments; and those in C can be exercised by both, or concurrently:

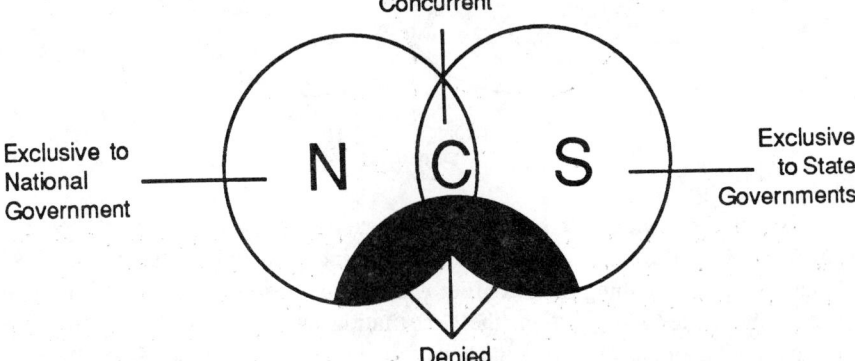

Back now to the basic problem of federalism; that is, the relationship between the powers in N and the powers in S, those exercised exclusively by the national government or those exercised exclusively by the states.

FEDERALISM

How do we know in which segment a particular power belongs?

The Constitution is our guide. The great statesman Daniel Webster once wrote: "We may be tossed upon an ocean where we can see no land—nor, perhaps, the sun or the stars. But there is a chart for us to study, to consult, and to obey. That chart is the Constitution." The Tenth Amendment reminds us also that the federal government has only those powers which are granted to it by the Constitution. What does that mean?

Prior to the Constitution, there was no sovereign central or federal government. Only sovereign state governments existed, and all power rested in them. They and the people created the Constitution, and the Constitution, in turn, created the new federal government. *The only powers the federal government has, then, are those given to it—or "delegated" to it—in the Constitution.* All other powers not delegated to the federal government—the "residual" powers—remained with the states. Let us label those concepts on our intersection circle diagram:

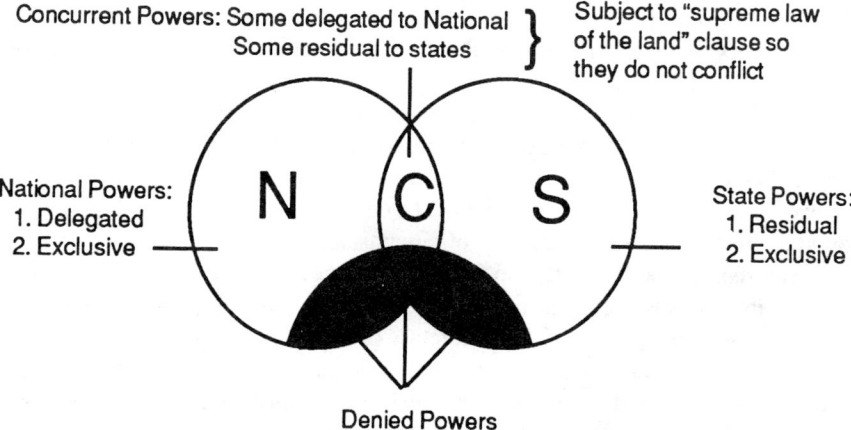

Denied Powers

The powers in Segment N are the exclusive powers "delegated" by the Constitution to the national government. If they are not delegated to the national government, powers are "residual" in Segment S and belong exclusively to the states.

But that still does not tell us which powers belong in each. However, since all the powers of the federal government are *delegated to it,* they should be—they *must* be—spelled out in the Constitution. If they are not there, then, according to the Tenth Amendment, they automatically belong to the states.

The powers granted to the federal government are found primarily in three places in the Constitution. Article I, Section 8 lists the powers of Congress. Article II, Sections 2 and 3 tell us what the President can do. Article III, Section 2 gives the jurisdiction and functions of the federal courts. And of course the Preamble indicates the overall purpose of the Constitution and of the national government which it created. Only one portion of Article I, Section 8 has led to any serious controversy, because of its wording.

Article I, Section 8 lists the powers of Congress in a series of eighteen paragraphs that follow the introductory phrase "The Congress shall have Power. . . ." There is no doubt that all the ensuing powers are *delegated to Congress*. But they are delegated in two ways. The first seventeen paragraphs contain very specifically worded powers, such as the power to levy taxes, to coin money, or to declare war. Their meaning is absolutely clear. In fact, because the wording is so explicit and specific, we call them the "expressed" or "enumerated" powers of Congress and of the national government.

But the eighteenth paragraph—the last of the delegated powers—is worded altogether differently. It is general and even vague, stating that Congress can "make all laws which shall be necessary and proper for carrying into execution the foregoing powers [those designated in the first seventeen paragraphs], and all other powers vested by this Constitution in the government of the United States, or in any department or officer thereof."

The key phrase is "necessary and proper." What does it mean? Certainly what might be "necessary and proper" to some people is anything but "necessary and proper" to others. And what might be deemed "necessary and proper" at one time under one set of circumstances might not be considered "necessary and proper" at another time or under a different set of circumstances.

Surprisingly, nothing exists in the records of the Constitutional Convention to explain that phraseology. But once the new government came into existence in 1789, the issue arose very quickly. Secretary of the Treasury Alexander Hamilton proposed that Congress establish a national bank to handle the government's money, even though state banks already existed, established and regulated under state law. The authority to establish a bank is not expressly enumerated in Article I, Section 8, but Hamilton maintained that it was *implied* by the necessary and proper clause. Thus began an ongoing debate over what we call the "liberal" (or "broad" or "loose") interpretation as against the "strict" (or "narrow") interpretation of the Constitution and of the necessary and proper clause.

The strict interpretation (or construction) has held that Congress could consider a law "necessary and proper" if it met three criteria: (1) the law related to an enumerated power; (2) the objective of the proposed legislation was absolutely vital and indispensable rather than merely desirable or convenient; and (3) it could not be done through the states; that is, there was no credible way to achieve the objective other than through the national government. The strict interpretation became the constitutional basis for those who prefer more direction from and power in the state governments rather than in the national government.

The liberal interpretation (or construction) of the Constitution took a less restrictive view of the necessary and proper clause. Agreeing that states must retain their viable functions and powers, supporters of the liberal interpretation have taken the position that under certain circumstances the federal government could and would serve the American people better than could the individual states. Accordingly, the liberal interpretation has viewed that Congressional authority extended not only to the enumerated powers, but that Congress also had unspecified dormant or "implied" powers which became justified and legitimized when and if they became "necessary and proper." This, of course, would allow much more flexibility than the strict interpretation. Because of this flexibility, some use the term "elastic clause" in referring to the "necessary and proper" clause.

Let us now review our overlapping circles, but this time in outline form. The basic fact of federalism is that all governmental powers are either delegated to the national government, residual in the states, concurrent, or denied:

GOVERNMENTAL POWERS UNDER FEDERALISM

- A. Delegated to national government
- B. Residual to state governments
- C. Concurrent to both national and state governments
- D. Denied to national and/or state governments

Now add that delegated powers are either enumerated or implied:

GOVERNMENTAL POWERS UNDER FEDERALISM

- A. Delegated to national government
  1. Enumerated: Art. I, Sect. 8, Par. 1-17
  2. Implied: Art. I, Sect. 8, Par. 18
- B. Residual to state governments
- C. Concurrent to both national and state governments
- D. Denied to national and/or state governments

As clear as all that might be, it still does not tell us whether some unspecified power should be considered implied or residual. What about wage and hour legislation, or social security, or health care, or abortion? Nothing in the Constitution deals with them. Certainly they do not come under the enumerated powers. But are they implied to the federal government? Or are they residual to the states? They clearly do not come, in the above outline, under A.1. But do they come under

A.2 (an implied power of the national government), or do they belong under B (a residual state government power)?

Based upon the past two hundred years of American constitutional development, the answer consists of two parts. (1) If nothing ties the issue directly to one of the enumerated powers, we assume that the power to deal with that issue *automatically falls under the residual powers belonging to the states.* That was pointedly expressed by Supreme Court Justice Oliver Wendell Holmes, Jr., when he stated curtly: "When the people of the various states want to do something and I can't find anything in the Constitution expressly forbidding it, I say, whether I like it or not: Damn it, let 'em do it." (2) When and if it becomes "necessary and proper," *only then* does the power transfer from the residual to the implied category, or from the states to the national government. Thus, for example, for many years wage and hour regulation and social security and medical programs fell totally within the province of the states. As a matter of fact, federal laws in those areas in the early 1900s actually were declared unconstitutional by the courts on the grounds that the federal government had no such authority. However, as times and conditions changed, more and more Americans concluded that the federal government might serve the people better in those areas than could the individual states. Accordingly, by the 1930s, when their Representatives and Senators in Congress passed laws similar to those disallowed earlier, they were now held to be constitutional. What had not been considered "necessary and proper" at one time and under one set of circumstances had become "necessary and proper" at another time and under another set of circumstances.

That raises two crucial questions. First, what criteria determine if something is "necessary and proper" and whether the federal government or the individual states can better serve the people? And second, who decides?

Nowhere in the Constitution can we find the answer to either question. Instead, they are found by a study of American history.

Let's take the second question first: Who decides? It depends upon one's interpretation of the Constitution. Believers in a strict interpretation feel that the people of the individual states, acting through their state legislatures or their state courts, should make those decisions. This view prefers also that if a residual power is to be transferred, it should be done by a Constitutional amendment, which requires the approval of three fourths of the states. Lacking that widespread support, the particular power in question should remain in the states.

Advocates of a broader interpretation of the Constitution have felt, on the other hand, that the national government is better suited to make those decisions. The national government, particularly in Congress, already represents all the people collectively, and is not subject as much to local vested interests and pressures as are the state legislatures. Besides, this view holds, the right to transfer the power to the national government already exists, in the Ninth and Tenth Amendments. The Ninth Amendment indisputably recognizes that more powers exist than only those expressly enumerated in the Constitution; these would be the implied powers. Furthermore, the word "expressed" was purposefully deleted from the originally proposed text of the Tenth Amendment, again clearly recognizing that there were implied powers which the national government could exercise. The only requisite was to prove that the proposed implied power to be exercised by the national government was "necessary and proper."

Although there have been swings back and forth, the general trend has favored the broad or liberal interpretation, not only by Congress, but also by the Presidents and the courts. That started with the very first Congress when it approved Hamilton's bank proposal. It was stamped into permanent legitimacy in 1819 in the landmark Supreme Court case of *McCulloch v. Maryland*. Referring to the implied powers of Congress under the necessary and proper clause, Chief Justice John Marshall declared: "All means which are appropriate, which are plainly adapted to that end, which are not prohibited, but consist with the letter and spirit of the Constitution, are constitutional." Thus the federal government assumed the authority to decide if something is necessary and proper, the courts upheld it, and the states acquiesced.

That brings us to the other question: What criteria determine whether something is necessary and proper enough to be placed under federal authority rather than under state authority? Again there is nothing in the Constitution, and again we must look to American history for the answer.

Although there are exceptions, the criteria which Congress has followed are mainly two. First, *could* the states adequately provide necessary functions for their citizens? And second, *would* the states provide those necessary functions?

Take, for example, medical care. In the late 1940s and early 1950s, well after Congress had already established the basic social security system, President Harry S. Truman proposed a national medicare program. After reviewing the data, Congress concluded that state-directed medical services were adequate, that the states could do the job and were doing it, and that a federal program therefore was not necessary and proper. By the 1960s, however, when President Lyndon Johnson proffered a similar program, the attitude in Congress had changed. Now Congress felt that the states no longer could provide adequate service and that it had become necessary and proper for the federal government to step in. The result: a national Medicare law was enacted.

The other criterion for federal action has been not whether a state *could*, but whether it *would* perform a certain function. In 1954, for instance, the Supreme

WE THE PEOPLE

Court outlawed racial segregation in public schools as a violation of the Fourteenth Amendment to the United States Constitution. Over the next decade, when a number of states refused to comply "with all deliberate speed," as the Court put it, Presidents Eisenhower, Kennedy, and Johnson used federal troops to enforce the Court's decision. Although this example does not entail Congress passing a law, it does illustrate how the federal government—in this instance the courts and the Presidency—determined that because the states *would* not end segregation, federal action was both necessary and proper. Opponents of federal intervention, whatever else their motives may have been, argued among other things that the constitutionality of segregation should be made by the states and not by the federal government, in this case by state courts rather than by federal courts. Again, though, the broader interpretation prevailed: federal agencies decided, and the schools were desegregated.

Now we can go back to our overlapping circles, having seen how powers get into either segment N or Segment S:

Now, too, we can look at the comparative sizes of the circles. At the Constitutional Convention in 1787, much as the Framers wanted to strengthen the national government over what it had been under the Articles of Confederation, there is no doubt that they intended for Circle S (state powers) to be much larger than Circle N (national powers):

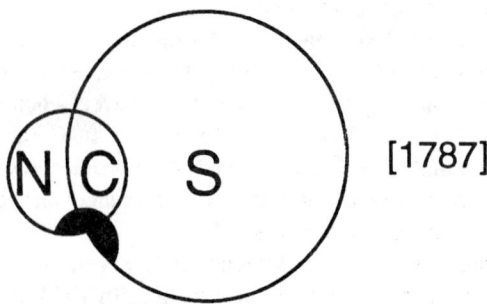

[1787]

16

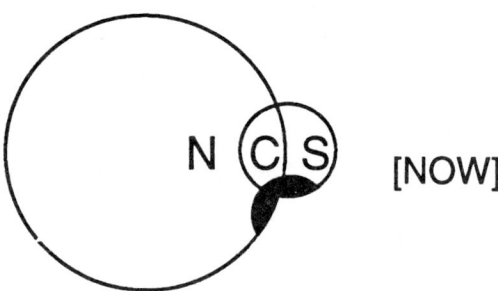

And at first that was the relationship. There is no doubt, though, that today, two hundred years later, the comparative sizes of those circles have changed considerably and the national powers are much broader than the state powers:

We have seen the constitutional rationale. Now let us see historically, albeit briefly, how that anticipated relationship between national and state governmental authority changed.

It started almost at once, in the 1790s, during the first administration of President George Washington. The bank issue, as already noted, precipitated an ongoing debate over the liberal versus the strict construction of the Constitution. That struggle persevered in two separate yet related arenas. One saw the gradual growth of judicial and presidential influence within the framework of the national government. Though this did not affect the institution of federalism directly and immediately, developments in the pre-Civil War presidency and Supreme Court set the stage for those two branches of the federal government to emerge later, in the twentieth century, as much more influential than the Framers of the Constitution probably anticipated. But once they achieved that clout, the Presidency and the Supreme Court would play a major role in the relations between the national and the state governments.

The second arena of debate involving liberal versus strict interpretation of the Constitution focused directly on the issue of federalism. Indeed, it went right to the heart of the problem: Where did sovereignty lie, in the national government, or in the states? What indeed was the nature of the Union and of the federal government as established in the Constitution? At first the issue was not stated that clearly. In the early bank debates the argument was whether the states or the national government provided a more reasonable repository for certain powers. But by the late 1790s, in the controversies involving the Alien and Sedition Acts and the Virginia and Kentucky Resolutions, the concept of "nullification" cropped up—that under certain circumstances a state had the right to nullify (or override) an action of the national government. This raised a fundamental question about the nature of the federal Union, for it seemed to be in direct conflict with the "supreme law of the land" concept. Supporters of nullification argued not only a very strict interpretation of the Constitution, but they also hinted that in the last analysis sovereignty existed in the states. Despite the apparent seriousness of the controversy, nothing was concluded; the matter was pragmatically dropped when the Alien and Sedition Acts that had brought on the debate in the first place expired and the substantive issue became moot.

The issue was resurrected briefly a few years later by New England opponents of the Louisiana Purchase. Led by Senator Timothy Pickering of Massachusetts, the "Essex Junto" talked again of nullification, this time regarding the acquisition of western agricultural lands. Some even considered secession by the New England states and the formation of a new and separate northern confederacy. But again nothing definitive happened; once the Louisiana Purchase became a *fait accompli*, the verbal opposition just faded away.

The War of 1812 produced a new series of constitutional controversies over the nature of the Union, again in New England, where strong opposition to the war existed. Several states refused to allow their militia to be taken over by federal authorities or to engage in military operations outside their state boundaries. Massachusetts and Connecticut interfered with federal enlistment activities. Perhaps potentially most inflammatory was the Hartford Convention, which adopted resolutions aimed at elevating state powers over federal authority. Many historians feel that the only thing which averted an imminent clash between federal and state authorities (in this case, New England states) was the end of the war early in 1815.

The Missouri Compromise controversy of 1820 was a momentous watershed in American history. It involved varied and complex issues, with an important outcome being a realignment of antebellum sectionalism into "The North" and "The South." Considering the importance of the uncertainty of what federalism really meant, it seems surprising that the Missouri Compromise debates focused overtly, at least, on matters other than the nature of the Union. They dealt more with the power structure within the national government and the degree to which it should regulate slavery. True, questions arose over whether the national or state government could do that regulating, but both sides concentrated more on political, social, and economic consequences of that regulation rather than on their constitutional justification.

By the 1830s, however, new social and economic factors came into play, along with westward expansion and slavery, and there emerged clearly what has been called the "states' rights" doctrine. Its foremost proponent was John C. Calhoun, and its greatest advocacy (though not exclusively) was in the South.

FEDERALISM

Now the argument went all the way: that the Union was a compact of sovereign states, and that because the states held sovereignty as a residual power, they had the right to secede. In fact, on at least two occasions extreme states' rights advocates even pushed for secession: in the early 1830s over a tariff conflict (the so-called "Nullification Controversy") and in the late 1840s over western territory and slavery. On both occasions calmer heads and compromise prevailed. But by 1861, with Abraham Lincoln as President and with slavery having grown into a bitter moral as well as political, social, and economic issue, and over which neither side now would compromise, the Civil War broke out.

The Civil War was caused, of course, by more than slavery and the constitutional controversy over sovereignty. Yet four years of trial and bloodshed solved not much more. Nevertheless, the North did win and that, of course, meant that what followed was quite different from what might have happened had the South won. Slavery was outlawed by the Thirteenth Amendment. Then in 1869, in *Texas v. White,* the Supreme Court declared secession by a state to be illegal, holding that sovereignty lay in the national government, not in the individual states. "The Constitution," proclaimed the Court, "looks to an indestructible Union, composed of indestructible States." The Constitution was the supreme law of the land, with sovereignty residing in the people of the United States collectively. The agency of that sovereignty was the national government of the United States.

But still unanswered was whether the states or the national government should decide on whether a power *other than the power to secede* was implied to the national government or residual to the states. For despite the growing acceptance of the liberal interpretation of the Constitution, the prevailing attitude up to the Civil War continued to be that as many powers as possible should reside in the states. True, the national government did eventually decide on slavery. But when Congress in 1830 proposed a massive road and canal program, President Andrew Jackson's famous Maysville Veto placed those projects within the realm of the states. Furthermore, in spite of the early victories of national bank advocates, decentralized banking won out in the 1830s and state regulation of banking prevailed until Woodrow Wilson again established a national presence in the Federal Reserve Act of 1914.

As a matter of fact, if we were to examine our circles about the time of the Civil War, with few exceptions the state circle had not lost too much and the national circle had not grown too much from what it had been in the days of George Washington. Although the President was growing stronger and the Supreme Court was growing more influential, overwhelming sentiment still preferred more powers in the states than in the national government, even though by the end of the Civil War there was no doubt that sovereignty resided in the national corpus.

But a great change took place after the Civil War. From a nation confined originally to the Atlantic seaboard, we expanded westward to the Pacific. Our numbers grew by leaps and bounds. At first mostly white, Anglo-Saxon, and Protestant, increasing immigration made us more diverse and multicultural. The most dramatic changes occurred in the last half of the nineteenth century and early in the twentieth century. The Industrial Revolution transformed us from a rural agricultural society to one that was urban and industrial. Changes in transportation and communication ended isolationism and brought together places and people who formerly had been separated. Technological advances converted American industry from small localized steam-powered and water-powered plants to the massiveness of electrically powered big business. Labor organizations changed from small local groups to huge nation-wide unions, as did farmers' organizations. The years following the Civil War, then—actually some of these changes began even before and during the war—saw the emergence of a totally different United States from that which existed when George Washington was president.

Changed also was how people viewed the role of government. Up to the Civil War, in spite of the liberal interpretation of the Constitution, the predominant view still considered governmental powers more appropriate in the hands of state and local government, with a very limited amount in the national structure. This stemmed from the strong influence of Jeffersonian rural agrarianism and the notion that government is best when it governs the least. It was rooted in the concept that individual freedom meant freedom from government. For government, after all, was the villain against whom the American colonists had revolted—not only national (British) government, but also local colonial government—tyrannical, despotic, oppressive government of all sorts, regardless where the seat of that government happened to be. All we have to do is study the early years of the Articles of Confederation to see that.

But that was life and society and government and governmental philosophy at the time of the Constitutional Convention. By the Civil War and after, American life changed considerably. With it, in the late nineteenth and early twentieth centuries, came a new "Progressive" outlook. It was a natural outgrowth of earlier "Jacksonian Democracy." Simply put, Jacksonian democracy entailed the expansion of social and economic opportunity along with political democracy. Most students of American history associate Jacksonian democracy with the broadening of the franchise and popular participation in government. Just as important, it expanded economic opportunities and engendered all sorts of social relationships. It included educational reforms and improvements in judicial codes; advances in women's rights and egalitarianism; programs for temperance and improved family and domestic environments. Under the leadership of the new Jacksonian-oriented Chief Justice Roger B. Taney, the Supreme Court's decision in *Charles River Brigde v. Warren Bridge* (1837) opened the way for small entrepreneurs and the emerging technology to compete in the economic arena with old-line vested interests and entrenched business monopolies. As a consequence of "The Age of Jackson," more and more people participated in political, social, and economic decision-making processes, and more and more people, acting through their various governments, exercised more and more powers. That, after all, is what the whole idea of democracy is all about, and it was coming into fruition in the nineteenth century in America.

Unfortunately, though, in spite of the many remarkable advances made possible by the Age of Jackson and the Industrial Revolution, the nineteenth century brought also many new problems associated with industrialization and urbanism: problems such as health and sanitation; crowded cities and slums; crime and corruption; inadequacies in transportation and education; and others. Rapidly increasing immigration brought needed labor for the new factories and railroads, but it also exacerbated racial and religious and nationalist prejudices. As the country dealt with those and other problems engendered by the Civil War, a portion of American society generally referred to as "Big Business"—industrial and moneyed vested interests which had prospered so much as a result of the Civil War and the Industrial Revolution—became so powerful and influential that they rather than the masses of the people gained control over state and local governments. John D. Rockefeller, for instance, the great oil tycoon and one of the era's most influential industrialists, boasted that he could do just about anything he wanted with the Pennsylvania state legislature except "refine" it. Graphic cartoons by political satirist Thomas Nast pointed out similar power by other vested interests over state and local governments.

It became apparent that the great threat to people's freedoms came not from government, but from the new powerful private vested interests. Many believed that only a strong national government could compete with them. In contrast with the earlier Jeffersonian view of looking upon government with suspicion—that the only good government was that which did the least—many now felt that individual freedoms needed protection not *from* government, but rather *by* government. That meant placing more and more authority into the hands of the national government.

Doing that, however, kindled a fear that such a radical reform might lead to the abandonment of capitalism and a free enterprise economy for a European-type socialist command economy, and that political democracy might be replaced by a form of governmental totalitarianism. Those solutions—adaptations of Marxist socialism and communism—appealed to many in Europe who saw a strong "proletariat" government as the way to overcome social and economic ills. Quite a few in America concurred, especially among newly-arriving European immigrants. Once more many struggled with the dilemma of a government strong enough to deal with the nation's problems, and yet one which would not endanger individual liberties, and whether that could be done best through national or state governments.

The solution—contested every step of the way—proved to be not less democracy, but more democracy; and not a command economy, but a modified and regulated free-enterprise economy. It hinged upon a new approach to how "necessary and proper" should be interpreted.

It also entailed a new and progressive approach toward interstate commerce. The Constitution expressly granted to Congress the power to regulate interstate commerce; yet during the first hundred years of our national existence, Congress chose, with very few exceptions, not to exercise that power. The prevailing attitude, as we have seen, preferred state authority, and as long as Congress did not act on interstate commerce, state regulation was accepted. But by 1887, to counteract widespread discriminatory abuses in the nation's railroads, Congress enacted the landmark Interstate Commerce Act. Three years later, in 1890, Congress followed with the Sherman Antitrust Act, aimed at overcoming comparable evils in many other businesses engaged in interstate commerce. With the Interstate Commerce and Sherman Acts, Congress began to fulfill the potentials of its power over commerce.

Those two laws opened the door to a spate of unprecedented federal legislation based on the liberal "necessary and proper" philosophy. What followed was the era of Theodore Roosevelt's Square Deal and Woodrow Wilson's New Freedom, of the Pure Food and Drug Acts, of trust-busting and muckrakers, of soil conservation and reforestation, of the Clayton Anti-Trust and the Federal Reserve Acts. Many actions formerly considered within the exclusive purview of state authority now transferred to the federal circle of powers, by virtue of becoming "necessary and proper."

The onset of World War I accelerated the move. Full-scale war mobilization—industrial, agricultural, transportation—saw national power become stronger than ever before. Especially significant was the new role of the national government toward manpower. Not only did it entail conscription to build up the armed forces, but it also included enforcing loyalty and stifling dissent, as a wave of xenophobia and anti-foreignism swept over the land.

With the end of World War I, though, a reaction set in. Many feared that the pendulum had swung too far in the direction of powers for the federal government. They yearned for a return to "normalcy"—for a more strict interpretation of the necessary and proper clause and for the restoration of many activities to state authority. This political atmosphere following World War I blended with other more colorful social and economic phenomena we associate with the "Roaring Twenties."

Then came one of the most traumatic experiences of the twentieth century, the Great Depression of the 1930s. America's economy collapsed—this is not the place to go into the reasons. Millions lost their jobs. Poverty and unprecedented hard times spread throughout the land. Private charities could not stem the avalanche of disasters, and neither could the states. Many despaired even for the continued existence of the American way of life. Indeed, advocates of Marxist solutions became larger in number and louder in advocacy.

Into this breach came Franklin Delano Roosevelt and the New Deal. They picked up the pre-World War I progressivism of Theodore Roosevelt and Woodrow Wilson based on the liberal philosophy of what was necessary and proper. The key again was that American society being what it was in the twentieth century—industrial, urban, multicultural, interdependent—the national government was better suited than the individual states to safeguard the fundamental rights and fulfill the needs of the people. That philosophy prevailed for the next fifty years, under both Democratic and Republican administrations, until the Ronald Reagan era of the 1980s.

The New Deal of the 1930s ushered in an era of legislation aimed at three fundamental objectives. The first was immediate relief from the economic catastrophe that existed. Second was a short-range recovery program to pull the country out of the depression and to start the wheels of industry rolling again. The third was a long-range reform program to insure that such a disastrous economic collapse would never happen again. Historians and economists still argue whether it was the New Deal or World War II which actually pulled the country out of the Great Depression and restored prosperity. For our purposes, though, the long-range reform program is more relevant, for it had tremendous impact on the nature of federalism and on nation-state relationships.

The reason is that under the New Deal the national government took the lead in all sorts of programs aimed at ensuring the economic welfare of the people—programs which hitherto had been considered anathema to American capitalism, or which had been considered within the purview of the states. These included, among other things, social security, wage and hour regulation, codes of labor and industrial behavior, housing and farming policies, and even a variety of cultural programs such as art, theater, music—all of which affected the domestic day-to-day status and behavior of virtually every American citizen.

Regardless of labels, American democracy recognized the suitability and adaptability of many measures heretofore associated with socialism. Just as so-called "radical" programs pushed earlier by various third parties often in time became "respectable" policies adopted by the major parties, so too did the American people incorporate some socialist ideas into the mainstream of everyday democratic thinking, albeit over considerable opposition. Outright government ownership and operation (as exemplified by the T.V.A.—the Tennessee Valley Authority) was a rarity. More widely acceptable, however, was government *regulation* of various aspects of American economic activity. American democracy became an unfamiliar mixture of laissez faire individualism and socialist regulation—not unlike what was happening in some European countries. Since the days of the New Deal, major points of controversy have been not so much *whether* the federal government should regulate, but rather *what* and *how much* it should regulate.

As a result, national governmental powers expanded at the expense of state powers as never before in our history.

Those who have advocated less federal regulation—for whatever their motives, and they have been varied—generally argued that such regulation should be exercised either more by the states or not at all. The term "conservatives" became associated more and more with them. Those who have advocated federal authority—and again for whatever their motives, and they have been varied—have been labeled "liberals." Such labels are, of course, terribly misleading, for so many people, regardless of political party affiliation, are liberal on one issue and conservative on another. And certainly to label one party liberal and the other conservative is equally recklessly misleading and false. Nevertheless, it is not unusual to find people excoriating and denouncing their political opponents as either liberal or conservative, and trying to make those labels the epitome of evil and even un-Americanism.

Up to the end of World War II in 1945, many people considered the vast expansion of national authority to be the natural consequence of the Great Depression and the war. But when the war ended, rather than the usual "return to the good old days" syndrome—as had occurred after World War I—the trend toward continued centralization of domestic governmental power continued. Perhaps one of the most significant pieces of legislation of the twentieth century was the Employment Act of 1946, *enacted with the full endorsement of both the Democratic and Republican parties.* "It is the continuing policy and responsibility of the Federal Government," the law stated, "to use all practicable means . . . to promote maximum employment, production, and purchasing power." Clearly this betokened a much broader view than ever before of the necessary and proper clause, of the liberal construction of the Constitution, and of federal government involvement and participation in the affairs of the American people.

Not surprisingly, then, every administration following World War II, both Democratic and Republican, continued in that pattern, President Truman championed national domestic programs called the "Fair Deal"; President Eisenhower called them the "New Republicanism"; President Kennedy, the "New Frontier"; President Johnson, the "Great Society." No particular catchy title was accorded to the domestic policies of Presidents Nixon, Ford, and Carter, but they continued in the same vein, albeit with different emphases. Thus there came about a strong national government presence in such domestic areas as medical care, urban housing, transportation, farm productivity, and education, all areas formerly considered the exclusive residual domain of the states.

Not only Congress, but the Presidents and the Supreme Court also followed the broad interpretation of the powers of the national government. Nowhere was this apparent as in the field of civil rights. Shortly after World War II, President Truman, by executive order, initiated desegregation in the armed forces, a policy finally completed by President Eisenhower. Equally significant was the famous Supreme Court decision in 1954 in the landmark case of *Brown v. the Board of Education of Topeka.* Under the leadership of activist Chief Justice Earl Warren, the Court outlawed racial segregation in public schools. On several occasions when state authorities refused to desegregate, Presidents Eisenhower, Kennedy, and Johnson used federal troops and marshals to force compliance. Governors Orval Faubus of Arkansas and George Wallace of Alabama argued vehemently and zealously for the residual powers of their states, but federal authority prevailed. Desegregation in the schools paved the way for ending segregation and discrimination in practically every other area of public activity, ranging from swimming pools to hotels to restaurants, all done under the aegis of the federal government.

Along with ending racial segregation, federal action by Congress, the President, and the courts fought other kinds of discrimination against women, racial and religious minority groups, the elderly, the young, and the disabled. Activist court decisions also championed the rights of the criminally accused as well as those already convicted. Concepts such as "Miranda rights" and the "right to privacy" became part of the American legal scene.

Thus by the 1980s the comparable sizes of the national and state circles of power as envisioned by the Framers of the Constitution had changed considerably. The big question was how far it would go. Some even went so far as to suggest getting rid of states altogether, that many of them had artificial boundaries, and that the justification for their existence really was not clear. Others proposed realigning them into fewer states with boundaries that made sense. None of these ideas gained very much popularity, but their mere existence indicates how far the imbalance between state and national governments had grown.

These changes had not occurred without opposition. From the very beginning, as already noted, many championed a stricter and more conservative construction of the Constitution, arguing that the control of various activities should remain in the individual states.

In the 1970s two highly traumatic developments greatly affected the institution of federalism and the liberal versus strict constructionist viewpoints. One was the war in Vietnam; the other was the Watergate Affair. In the former, Presidents Johnson and Nixon persistently continued American involvement in a very unpopular and divisive undeclared foreign war, despite overwhelming pressures to withdraw. In the Watergate Affair, President Nixon resigned the Presidency—he was the first ever to do so—at virtually the last moment to evade certain impeachment for actions which undermined and threatened to destroy basic constitutional values. In both instances, the spotlight was on excesses by instrumentalities of the federal government. Many people became fearful of so much power in Washington, especially when they saw how it could be so badly misused and abused.

At the same time, several highly emotional domestic issues divided the nation, including abortion, rights of women, and separation of church and state. In all instances, it seemed that the outcome might hinge on whether the federal government or the states could exercise the necessary authority. The 1970s also witnessed a wild rise of interest rates and a period of almost runaway inflation, with the federal budget and the national debt spiraling to astronomic figures. Many blamed the difficulties on excesses by the federal government, and wondered whether the system of federalism was too much out of balance.

In 1980 Ronald Reagan was elected President on a platform which in effect said, among other things: "Let's reduce the role of the federal government. Let's get the government off our backs and out of our pockets. Let's bring back some balance to federalism." Once in office, he was responsible for eliminating or decreasing many federal domestic people-oriented programs. He appointed federal judges who were strict constructionists of the Constitution and whose presence in the judicial system (federal judges are appointed for life) portended a long-range trend toward conservatism in the federal courts. He sought a major reduction of federal expenditures and involvement in the everyday lives of the people, cutting spending on housing and urban improvements. He increased outlays for the military—because of fears of Cold War Soviet aggression—but he vetoed measures for road improvements, maintaining these were responsibilities of the individual states.

A critical indication of President Reagan's attitude and policy became evident with the publication in 1986 of a study authorized by him to evaluate the relationships between the national government and the states. Reporting in a document entitled "The Status of Federalism in America," the Domestic Policy Council (a cabinet-level advisory body) asserted that the powers of national and state governments had swung far out of their intended balance, considerably to the detriment of the states. The report further indicated that much of the responsibility lay in United States Supreme Court decisions dating back at least fifty years to the New Deal era, due to the Court's "erroneous judicial reading" of the Constitution. Many of those decisions, said the report, "improperly pre-empted and invalidated the states' legitimate exercise of their sovereign powers," and left them to act merely as "satrapies" or "administrative units" of a "virtually omnipotent national government." The report further accused the Supreme Court of "indifference" to the principle of federalism in some decisions, and of "unprecedented intrusion" into state affairs in others. In so doing, the report continued, the Supreme Court has "undermined the sovereign decision-making authority of the states" and has thereby "acquiesced in improper expansions of Federal power." It was about as strong a condemnation as possible on how and why the powers of the federal government had grown. In a press interview following the publication of the report, one of its authors further asserted that "the national government has been behaving without legitimate constitutional warrant" in usurping state authority.

One immediate outcome of this report (actually it had begun earlier, as though anticipating the report) was a public assault on the Supreme Court led by Attorney General Edwin Meese. (Up to that time [1986], President Reagan had had occasion to appoint only two new members to the Supreme Court, Sandra Day O'Connor [the first woman] and Antonin Scalia [the first of Italian extraction.] Although both represented Reagan's conservative views, the overall composition of the Court did not change that much, as neither of the replaced retirees was a judicial "liberal.") Meese accused the Court of blatant "judicial activism" that dangerously eroded state authority and thereby subverted the intent of the Framers of the Constitution. He argued that Supreme Court decisions should be restricted only to settling the specific case at hand, and should not be viewed as precedents which could become part of public or judicial policy. And those decisions, he maintained, should reflect what the Framers intended ("original intent"), not twentieth-century social or economic forces about which the men at Philadelphia had absolutely no knowledge. This assault by Meese and others seemed to be a clear attempt to reduce the role of the Supreme Court as one of the agencies which has made possible the transfer of state powers to the federal arena.

President Reagan was succeeded by his vice-president for two terms, George Bush. Although Bush did not make as overt and articulated an assault on how federalism had metamorphosed, his words and actions as President, and especially those of his conservative supporters, indicated a determination to continue reversing the trend of federalism, especially in the area of domestic programs.

But beyond the philosophy of which government does what, Bush's presidency was plagued on the one hand by a growing need and demand for more social and economic programs, and on the other hand by a broad revolt against increased taxes. This was one legacy of the Reagan years, when many programs, especially military programs, were financed largely by financial ministrations which amounted to borrowing, thereby increasing the national debt to astronomical figures, far higher than those of the Carter years. Reagan was successful in carrying out this policy largely because of Cold War fears. During the Bush administration the Berlin Wall and the Iron Curtain came down, eastern European and Soviet communism collapsed, and the Cold War came to an end. Many expected the "peace dividend" would see the transfer of spending from military ventures to domestic programs, and thus begin to bring down federal expenditures and make some inroads into the national debt.

But that did not happen. Wars in Panama and the Persian Gulf kept the military budget as high as ever. Those wars over, Bush proposed only modest cuts in military expenditures; but he also wanted reductions of many domestic programs on the grounds that they were wasteful and should be cut in order to bring the skyrocketing budget and debt under control. That immediately brought an outcry to reduce military spending to correct budget and debt imbalances, but to restore domestic programs as legitimately necessary and proper. Aside from Bush's conservative leanings toward such programs, he felt also that many belonged in the states anyway. But resistance to taxes extended to the states too; people objected to higher taxes at the state level as well as at the federal level.

What, then, could be done? What services should the national government provide? The states? Who should pay what taxes?

Adding considerable political controversy—and confusion as to the nature and implementation of federalism—was the volatile issue of abortion. The Constitution says nothing about abortion, and so if any government acted on that issue, it would have to be based on the implied power/residual power authorization. The matter became extremely divisive and acrimonious because it entailed not only politics, but also moral issues with even conflicting religious overtones, not only among faiths, but within them.

Those opposing abortion adopted the label "pro-life," on the grounds that prohibiting abortion saved the life of an unborn fetus. Those supporting the right of a woman to abort became known as "pro-choice," on the grounds that the decision was a private one and that the government does not have the authority to interfere with that right. (This is of course an oversimplified statement of the opposing positions, but this is not the place to go into the complex merits of either side.)

From the point of view of federalism, confusion resulted because of the solution sought by both sides. Political conservatives lined up overwhelmingly on the side of the "pro-life" forces. Although conservatives, they advocate unprecedented power, in this issue, in the hands of the national government, and, as we shall see, even in the hands of the state governments. Their aims include action by Congress to outlaw abortion, or at the very least to place severe restrictions on the practice. They also strongly support a constitutional amendment that would outlaw abortion. They exerted considerable pressure for the appointment of anti-abortion judges to the federal courts, and especially to the Supreme Court of the United States, and to getting that institution to adjudicate abortion as illegal and unconstitutional. Conservatives traditionally have come down on the side of *reducing* the powers of government, especially of the national government, as they pertain to dealing directly with private individuals; yet on the abortion issue their approach has been just the opposite.

"Pro-choice" advocacy, on the other hand, has been overwhelmingly from the more politically liberal elements of American society, who traditionally have looked increasingly to government, and especially the national government, to protect individual rights. Yet on the grounds that morally and legally abortion is a private decision, as well as a medical decision, "pro-choice" advocates argue that Congress has *no* authority to interfere with the individual's decision, and that the Supreme Court exceeds its adjudicative power when it even takes up a case involving such a purely private matter. Thus, those who traditionally have not hesitated to give the national government more "necessary and proper" power if it meant protecting the people, in this issue take the opposite view, that the people are protected best if the national government exercised no power. But if the national government does find it necessary and proper to legislate, say "pro-choice" people, that action should protect the right of women to abort.

Thus the abortion issue confounds the traditional concepts of federalism, *i.e.*, who supports more power to the national government and who would leave those powers to the states.

The same conflicts exist, by the way, at the state level, with "pro-life" advocates strongly supporting state candidates and policies that would prevent abortion, and "pro-choice" advocates strongly supporting no government interference at all, or, if the state government does act, to protect the right of the individual woman in her choice. But as long as it remains at the state level, this problem is outside the purview of federalism. It involves powers exercised only within an individual state—that is, unless the "necessary and proper" process transfers that authority to the national government or to the sphere of concurrent powers. The issue, however, in no less divisive and acrimonious. Indeed, the 1992 elections entailed numerous candidates for all sorts of national and state and local offices—from President of the United States down to local sheriff—and voters demanded to know how virtually all those candidates stood on the abortion issue.

The 1992 presidential election resulted in Democratic Governor Bill Clinton being chosen over incumbent Republican President George Bush. A significant factor in that election was the very strong support shown for independent candidate H. Ross Perot, Texas billionaire businessman. The major and pervasive issue throughout that campaign was the deteriorating state of the nation's economy, choking under an unprecedented four trillion dollar deficit, an international trade imbalance, widespread unemployment, urban decay, costly and inefficient health care, and a badly skewed distribution of the nation's wealth. During that campaign President Bush maintained that the Reagan-Bush philosophy of less federal interference would allow the nation to pull out of those economic doldrums in due time. Both Clinton and Perot pushed for more government action. Focusing on attacking the large deficit first, Perot advocated measures which many considered quite radical and perhaps harmful because they would result in immediate heavy increases in taxes. Clinton's approach was perceived as somewhere in between, less drastic than Perot's but still entailing much more government involvement than Bush advocated.

Clinton won the three-way election, garnering 43% of the popular vote—by the nature of the electoral college, his margin was much larger there—Bush drew 38%, Perot 19%. Thus, almost two-thirds of the electorate (Clinton plus Perot voters) favored a more active role for the federal government in the nation's economy. Presumably, then, the Reagan-Bush philosophy toward federalism will be modified and replaced by one which looks with much less skepticism toward involvement by the federal government. How and in what areas remains, of course, to be seen.

This, essentially, is where we stand after two hundred years of the Constitution and the federal system.

Some fundamental questions immediately stand out:
- Has the federal government become too large and too powerful? If so, where and how should there be a reversal?

- If any federal programs cease or are reduced, should individual states pick them up? Who pays the tab?
- Is the federal government the only agency that can truly protect our constitutional and economic and social rights? Is abortion one of those?
- How should we determine whether a power should be implied to the federal government or residual to the states?
- What is the justification for the existence of our states as they are? What is the justification for their boundaries? Would we be better off under federalism if we combined some states? If we divided some? If we re-draw some state lines? If we had something like "regions" instead of our present states?
- Should we abolish the federal system completely and establish in its place a unitary form of government? A confederation?
- What powers, if any, should be restored to the states? Should the Constitution be amended to forbid the transfer of any specific powers from state to federal authority, regardless of "necessary and proper"?
- What of the role of the Supreme Court and Supreme Court decisions in federal-state relations?

These are only some questions which arise as we examine the American system of federalism after its two hundred years of existence. Can you think of more?

What do you think?

THE CONGRESS

"All legislative powers herein granted," states Article I of the Constitution, "shall be vested in a Congress of the United States, which shall consist of a Senate and a House of Representatives." The Framers did nothing out of the ordinary when they *established* a national legislature; the uniqueness lay in how they *structured* it and in the powers they gave to it.

Governed by Great Britain for a century and a half, the American colonists viewed Parliament as their model. Parliament's own history had been both fascinating and tempestuous. By 1787, when the Constitutional Convention met, the Framers could benefit from many constitutional principles and practices which had developed in the mother country. Some were well-established and clear-cut; some were still in the process of evolving; some were suitable to emulate; some were questionable for the American environment and people. Some which appeared in the Constitution included popular sovereignty, limited government, impeachment, and various legislative procedures and processes.

The Framers benefited from legislative experiences more than those of the mother country's Parliament. From very early on, the colonies had established their own legislatures, beginning with Virginia's House of Burgesses in 1619, and for a century and a half they had experienced at first hand representative government in action. *One cannot over-emphasize the importance of that experience.* Many Americans tend to be very testy with the newly emerging post-World War II Third World nations, unhappy because they are not as democratic as we are. Without in any way condemning or condoning those authoritarian governments, we must realize that popular participation in running a country comes neither automatically nor easily. It takes experience, knowledge, tradition, know-how, individual and group discipline—all things which a society must work at and often hammer out with perseverance and with dedication—and then there is no guarantee that a workable and viable democratic structure will emerge. It is much easier—and historically more likely—for anarchy or mob action to prevail and for a "shining knight" to emerge as a dictator promising to lead his people to a utopian never-never land. Modern history is replete with examples: the "Republic" of France in the 1790s, with its Reign of Terror, and then the Directory and Napoleon Bonaparte; the Russian Revolution and other communist revolutions, with their so-called "dictatorships of the proletariat"; totalitarian governments of both the left and the right in Latin America, Africa, Asia, and the Middle East. Many call themselves democratic and actually believe themselves to be democratic, but they are a far cry from even the modestly representative democracy we had when we became an independent nation, let alone what we are today. That is why 150 years of American colonial experience with representative legislatures looms as so important. When the Constitution was drawn up, we were already partially experienced in making a democratic government work. Even then the task proved very difficult and the product admittedly not perfect.

One feature of that colonial experience is particularly noteworthy in how it related to the legislature. A significant British contribution to the principle of constitutionalism was the concept of *representative government*. Representation as it developed in Britain came to be "virtual" or "national" representation; that is, no matter where one came from physically or how one merited a seat in Parliament, a member of the national legislature represented all of British society. Once in Parliament, that individual stood for all England, not just the narrow geographic or social constituency which sent him there. That concept differed significantly in the colonial legislatures, where "geographic" or "deputy" representation became the norm. Because American communities were separated from each other by hostile Indians and primitive wilderness, only actual inhabitants of those isolated localities could represent with any accuracy the problems and thinking of the people living there. Accordingly, representation in America came to mean that one came from and spoke for a particular geographic region.[1] Over here, provincial or sectional interests merited equal if not more concern than broad national interests. The emphasis on regional interests would reach its peak, of course, in the sectionalism which brought on the American Civil War. In fact, geographic representation and geographic interests still constitute a fundamental characteristic of representation in American legislatures, both in the national Congress and in the state legislatures.

In addition to colonial experiences under the British flag, the Framers looked back upon legislative experiences as independent entities. One kind was local in nature. When the thirteen colonies declared their independence in 1776, one of their first acts was to establish new independent state governments in place of their colonial governments. Because of their unhappy associations with George III, they looked askance upon any strong executive authority. It was no accident, then, that all thirteen state governments focused power in representative legislatures, with very weak governors. Though the state governments differed (*i.e.*, some had unicameral legislatures, some bicameral), they also had many features in common, especially in the internal structure and procedures of their legislatures. Thus the state legislatures provided the Framers with many examples and experiences to emulate.

Like the local state legislatures, national legislative bodies also provided lessons for the Framers. The First and Second Continental Congresses—especially the latter—acted as *ad hoc* national governing bodies and performed appropriate functions. Perhaps more important was the unicameral Congress under the Articles of Confederation, for that organization embodied the first national representative assembly of a legally recognized independent United States of America. Its activities constituted the most recent—indeed, concurrent—experiences from which the Framers drew.

Thus a century and a half as colonies and a decade of independence provided the Framers with many experiences and examples in legislative government. If they were sure of anything, it was that a representative legislature would hold a prominent place in their new government. Less certain, though, was its authority and structure. For in addition to all those experiential precedents, still other forces—philosophic forces—influenced the Framers. They were familiar with recent British political writings, especially those of John Locke, Algernon Sidney, and James Harrington. They were aware, too, of novel concepts of government developed by eighteenth-century European Enlightenment philosophers such as Voltaire and Rousseau and Montesquieu. Some intrigued the Framers; some confused them.

Thus, there was no lack of either experiential or philosophic sources from which the Framers could draw.

Many major questions which faced the Philadelphia convention evolved around the structure and authority of the legislature. What should be the relationship between the states and the new central government, and how should that be reflected in the structure of the legislature? Should the legislature be unicameral or bicameral? Precedent existed for both. If bicameral, how should the two houses relate to each other? Whom or what should they represent? How should the legislature relate to the other branches of the government? And, of course, what could the legislature do and what could it not do?

All those questions, and more, were debated heatedly as the Framers brought together many conflicting ideas, aims, and objectives, as well as varied pressures and interests to promote and protect.

This is not the place to reconstruct the events and debates of the Constitutional Convention. (A number of excellent accounts have been written, based mostly on detailed notes kept by James Madison and others. See Bibliography.) Suffice it to say here, though, that after several weeks it appeared as though all the labors of the Framers might be for naught because of their inability to agree on the nature of the national legislature. True, some tentative accords were reached in fairly short order: three separate branches of government (executive, legislative, judicial); a federal system (separate state and national governments and powers); and a check and balance system. But they could not agree on what all felt was the heart of the whole system—the structure of and representation in the national legislature.

The main differences centered around large state and small state concerns. Under the existing Articles of Confederation, each state retained its sovereignty and each state had one vote in a unicameral legislature; in that way the small states were protected from domination by the larger and more populous states. The small states wanted to retain and safeguard that security in the new government. On the other hand, the larger states viewed that arrangement as a weakness in that it often impeded the will of the majority. They wished more power to the majority through proportional representation in the national legislature. (Coincidentally, of course, it meant more power for the larger states because they would dominate the representation in the national legislature.)

Another way of stating the problem—because it would come up this way again and again later—was whether democracy meant that "all men are created equal" within one large sovereign nation or within each individual state, with all states also being equal. Was the United States one large nation with thirteen subordinate subdivisions, or thirteen separate and sovereign entities with a centralized arrangement for cooperation? Was "democracy" the basis for the "United States" as a whole, or was it the basis for each individual state, which in turn collectively became the basis for the "United States" as a whole? Unless this basic difference between the large and small states could be settled—and the debates became more and more acrimonious and bitter—it appeared the Constitutional Convention might even fall apart. Symbolic of the tension was the suggestion that delegates might even resort to opening each session with prayer: a most unusual as well as divulging proposal considering it came from no less than Benjamin Franklin. Undoubtedly the free-thinking octogenarian feared the consequences engendered by the remark of irascible Gunning Bedford of Delaware, who declared on behalf of the small states: "Gentlemen, I do not trust you!" (Ironically, after the Constitution went into effect, the large state versus small state conflict actually never materialized. Instead, differences developed more along regional and sectional lines.)

The solution came finally through a compromise. As a matter of fact, it might be noted parenthetically that the Constitution itself often is called a "bundle of compromises," and properly so. The large state-small state differences were by no means the only points of contention. There were differences between northern and southern points of view, and not just over slavery; between those who favored a strong central government and those who preferred more power in the states; over the powers of the chief executive and of the Congress; over commercial policies and trade relationships; and especially over seemingly less important items such as the qualifications and terms of office of various officials. In fact, virtually every detail in the Constitution was disputed, and only the willingness to compromise

THE CONGRESS

brought about eventual agreement. There is indeed much merit to the notion that successful democratic government is related directly to the art of compromise. After all, if "all men are created equal" and under the law are equally free to think and to believe, who is to say that only one way is "right" and everything else is "wrong" for everyone? Some sort of reconciliation of differences is absolutely imperative. The difficult art of compromise looms very prominent in making democracy work. Unquestionably without it there would be no Constitution.

In the large state-small state dispute, the two sides were brought together by what is called the "Great Compromise." It was a proposal put forth by the Connecticut delegation and then championed by Benjamin Franklin. When the Convention opened, Edmund Randolph, of Virginia, proposed a bicameral legislature. Simply stated, this "Virginia Plan" called for a "lower" house whose members would be elected directly by the voters of each state. The number of representatives to which each state was entitled would depend upon the population of the state, with each state being proportionately represented. That "lower" house then would elect an "upper" house. Obviously this plan—based on the notion that democracy inferred majority rule—was more beneficial to the larger states, they representing the majority of the total population. William Paterson of New Jersey countered with a proposal—the "New Jersey Plan"—more acceptable to the smaller states: a unicameral legislature (as currently existing under the Articles of Confederation) in which each state still retained equal representation, but a legislature which would have considerably more powers than existed under the Articles. The Connecticut Compromise provided for a bicameral Congress. Representation in the "lower" house—the House of Representatives—would be according to population, a concession to the Virginia Plan and to the large states. In the "upper" house—the Senate—each state would have equal representation, a concession to the New Jersey Plan and to the small states. (As originally proposed, each state was accorded only one Senator; to improve representation, the number was increased to two per state, as it remains today, but with each Senator being entitled to one vote, even though that made it possible for their conflicting votes to balance each other out.) The key to this bicameral arrangement was that *both* houses would have to approve a bill before it became law, thus reconciling both large and small state concerns.

Once the Framers agreed to that compromise, the doors opened, so to speak, to other things falling into place—which explains why historians later called this agreement the "Great Compromise." That does not mean that discord disappeared and all went smoothly. On the contrary, disagreements continued on practically every issue, and debates were as heated as ever. But the atmosphere seemed to be much improved. Having hammered out a compromise on the main point of contention, the Framers found themselves more prone to reconcile other differences the same way. So although heated discussions continued on all issues, the rancor and suspicion of earlier debates gave way to compromise, as the Framers exhibited a determination to come up with a workable and viable document and government. Two centuries and many traumatic events later, we can say that they succeeded.

Article I of the Constitution deals with the national legislature, the Congress. Except for numbers, Congress is structured today as it was when it first met in 1789. It has two branches, the House of Representatives (the "lower" house) detailed in Article I, Section 2 of the Constitution, and the Senate (the "upper" house), set forth in Article I, Section 3.

Representation in the House is in proportion to population. The first apportionment provided for one Representative[2] per approximately 30,000 people. That gave Virginia ten members; Massachusetts and Pennsylvania were entitled to eight each; New York and Maryland six each; North Carolina, South Carolina, and Connecticut five each; New Jersey four; Georgia and New Hampshire three each; and Delaware and Rhode Island one each; a total of sixty-five members of the House of Representatives.[3] As the country grew and the population increased, Congress modified the apportionment by increasing the 1:30,000 formula, maintaining on the one hand a viable representation and on the other a membership small enough to be operable. By the 1900s, however, the House membership exceeded four hundred, and many felt that anything much larger might become unwieldy. As a result, legislation passed in 1911 and again in 1929 fixed the number of members of the House permanently at 435. The number has remained at 435 since then, but the number of constituents per Representative has changed with each decennial census. (United States territories send "delegates" to the House. They were non-voting until 1993. Now they can vote. But if theirs are the decisive votes cast on a measure, a second ballot can be called in which they do not vote.)

The method of implementation is relatively simple, the basic procedure also being defined in Article I, Section 2. Every ten years the Bureau of the Census conducts an official count of the country's population. (Actually the census does more than just count people. All sorts of questions are asked, and compilations of answers create an enormous and virtually endless treasure of statistical data for researchers of all sorts, in both the public and private sectors.) The completed census is turned over to the President, along with a list of the *number* of Representatives to which each state is entitled, figured by simple arithmetic. The President then submits the report to Congress, which duly passes enabling legislation that authorizes each state its proportionate number of Representatives in the ensuing decade. According to the Constitution, even the least populous states must be allotted at least one Representative; how many more depends upon the figures in the census report. By the 1990 figures, the ratio was set at one Representative for roughly every 560,000 people. Seven states—Alaska, Delaware, Montana, North Dakota, South Dakota, Wyoming, and Vermont—have only one Representative; the others have proportionately more.

Once Congress has allocated the numbers to each state, the task of drawing congressional districts within the state falls to the individual state legislature. In the low-population states with only one Representative, that person is elected "at large," as the entire state is in effect one large election district. Elsewhere, the state legislature divides the state into appropriately populated election districts. For a long time the only limiting requirement was that those districts be "compact" and "contiguous," with only a moral obligation that they also be equally populated. Unscrupulous politicians have created extraordinarily shaped districts—at least they were contiguous—but with widely varying population figures and ridiculously questionable compactness, to ensure "proper" majorities within the district. This practice is known as "gerrymandering." The term was coined in 1811 when the Massachusetts legislature, controlled by Governor Elbridge Gerry, apportioned the state into some rather queerly shaped districts. One of them looked like a salamander; to which a newspaper editor commented that it was "not a salamander, but a gerrymander."[4] In the 1960s, at long last, the United States Supreme Court, in a series of landmark decisions which included *Baker v. Carr* (1962), *Wesberry v. Sanders* (1964), *Reynolds v. Sims* (1964), and *Kirkpatrick v. Preisler* (1969), propounded the principle of "one-man-one-vote" and mandated that legislative districts must be reasonably equal in population as well as compact and contiguous in form. In the 1990s, accordingly, each of the 435 Congressional districts averages a little more than half a million people. Though one may wonder about the compactness and contiguity of some, they are at least fairly equal in population.

One of the traumatic consequences of any decennial census is that, with the total number of Representatives fixed at 435, population fluctuations lead to some states losing Representatives and others gaining. Just increasing in population is not enough; what counts is a state's population in relation to the others. For instance, in 1980 Michigan, Pennsylvania, and Missouri recorded population increases, yet lost seats in the House of Representatives because their increases were not in proportion with those of the other states. Florida, on the other hand, gained four seats. In fact, the 1980 reapportionment resulted in seventeen Congressional seats shifting, mostly from New England and the Midwest to the South and West, to the so-called "sun-belt." Similar displacements occurred following the 1990 census. The most "unfair" seemed to have been Montana, which *lost* one of its two Representatives even though the population of the state increased by approximately 10,000 people!

Even as states gain or lose Representatives in Congress because of this proportional balancing, our nation's total population continues to grow. Accordingly, each Representative will be forced to represent more and more people, from the more than half a million as it is now to perhaps a million or more in the decades ahead. (Our total population already has surpassed the 250-million mark.) Concerned that Representatives will lose touch with their constituents—and vice versa—some already are suggesting that the 435 number should be increased. They give examples of legislatures in other democratic countries. In Great Britain, the House of Commons contains 650 members, each representing about 80,000 people. In Germany each member of the national legislature represents about 117,000, and in Japan about 239,000. But proposals to increase the size of the United States House of Representatives have met with stony silence. Many feel 435 is already too large, and that increasing that number, although it might improve the representation ratio, would make governing and governmental operation much more cumbersome than it is.

Article I, Section 2 of the Constitution gives the qualifications for members of the House of Representatives. One must be at least twenty-five years of age, a citizen of the United States at least seven years, and an inhabitant of the state in which he or she is chosen. The Congressional Apportionment Act of 1842 directed states to establish Congressional districts, even though the Constitution does not go that far. Technically, according to the Constitution, one does not have to live within the district, as long as he or she lives in the state; someone living in Kansas City, for instance, could represent a district in the St. Louis area, all the way on the other side of the state of Missouri. However, the tradition of geographic representation is so strong that one who does not actually live within the designated district would stand very little chance of being elected—or for that matter, even being nominated in the first place. A plausible exception would be a situation in which a state legislature, for various reasons, is unable to draw up district lines following the decennial census in time for an election. Under those circumstances, all candidates in the state would be forced to run "at large." That has happened several times.

The term of office of each Representative is two years. All 435 are elected at the same time, on the first Tuesday after the first Monday in the even-numbered years (1992, 1994, 1996, etc.). The Constitution says nothing about how often a Representative can be re-elected, and many have been returned to Congress for term after term, as long as the voters have been willing to re-elect them.

In recent years, and for a variety of reasons, anti-incumbency movements have seen voters in several states amend their state constitutions to limit the number of times their Representatives might be elected to Congress. Most would limit Representatives to a maximum of four or five two-year terms. None of these limitations have as yet gone into effect. Many legal experts feel, though, that these term limitations, even though approved by voters, are unconstitutional because states seek to assume an authority which belongs by the Constitution only to the national government—*i.e.*, to prescribe qualifications for being eligible (or ineligible, as the case may be) to be a member of the House of Representatives. A definitive resolution probably must await an attempt to implement such a limitation and an ensuing litigation brought to the Supreme Court.

At any rate, many Representatives have served for only one two-year term, and many have served for as long as twenty or thirty years. The longest on record is Jamie L. Whitten, Democrat of Georgia, who began his service in the House on November 4, 1941, and as of the time this is written (January 1993) has served his constituency for over fifty-one years.

If for any reason a Representative is unable to complete his or her two-year term, the Constitution provides that the governor of that state may call a special election to fill the vacancy. Common sense suggests that such action would depend largely upon the time left in the unexpired term; there would be very little reason, it would seem, to go to the trouble and expense of a special election if the winner then had little or no time left to go to Washington. But the Constitution leaves that decision to the good judgment of the governor of the state involved.

Article I, Section 2 of the Constitution stipulates several more directives for the House of Representatives. One is that the House shall "chuse" its own presiding officer, identified in the Constitution as the "Speaker." Technically elected by the House at large, in reality he is designated by the majority party. Each party nominates its own candidate for Speaker, but of course the majority party elects its nominee, as the vote is almost always along straight party lines. Among his other functions, the Speaker recognizes members of the House for debate, he interprets rules of parliamentary procedure, and he appoints special committees. To a great extent, then, he controls the operation of the House of Representatives. Ever since the Presidential Succession Act of 1948, the Speaker has been first in line of succession should anything happen to the President and the Vice-President. The Speaker of the House, then, is a very highly esteemed, influential, and important person.

The Constitution provides that the House shall also choose "other officers," but is not specific on what or who they shall be, leaving that to the House itself. Those "other officers" include a doorkeeper, a sergeant-at-arms, majority and minority floor leaders, majority and minority party whips, as well as other House and party officials who perform a variety of day-to-day functions.

Article I, Section 2 of the Constitution contains another brief but very significant provision, that the House "shall have the sole power of impeachment." Impeachment is the first step of a two-stage process that the Constitution prescribes (in Article II, Section 4) to remove "the President, Vice-President, and all civil officers" for "treason, bribery, or other high crimes and misdemeanors."

The two-step process of impeachment and conviction can be compared with the indictment-and-trial procedure in a criminal action. If one is accused of having committed a crime, normal due process of law requires that such accusation be made formally, following a hearing by a grand jury. That person, however, is still not guilty in the eyes of the law. The next step is for the accused to be tried by a "petit" jury, the so-called "twelve person" jury. That jury now hears the case and finds the accused either guilty or not guilty. Only then, and only if the verdict is against the accused, is that individual considered guilty and subject to punishment.

The impeachment process for government officials is very similar. It is not, however, a criminal procedure; it is a *political* procedure provided for in the Constitution as a way to remove from office persons who have committed certain wrong acts specifically designated in the Constitution.

Any member of the House of Representatives may introduce charges. Those charges are duly referred to the House Judiciary Committee. That committee may either dismiss the charges, as it did in 1970 when unfounded accusations were made against Supreme Court Justice William O. Douglas. Or it may draw up articles of impeachment as it did in 1974 against President Richard M. Nixon, in 1986 against federal judge Harry E. Claiborne, and in 1989, in two separate actions, against federal judges Alcee Hastings and Walter L. Nixon. After the articles are introduced on the floor of the House, the Representatives, after due discussion and debate, will vote whether to impeach the particular individual. A majority vote for impeachment means that the individual now is officially *accused* of certain actions violating the Constitution. (President Nixon resigned from office before the House had a chance to debate the articles of impeachment; judges Claiborne, Hastings, and Nixon were all three impeached by the required majority vote.) The next step is a trial in the Senate. There a two-thirds vote is required for conviction; the only penalty which can be prescribed is removal from office. (See below for more on the Senate's role in the process.)

Though impeachment technically is only the *House* action of formal *accusation*, the term "impeachment" is popularly, though incorrectly, used—by scholars as well as by laymen—to refer to the entire two-stage procedure. Thus, President Andrew Johnson was impeached in the House of Representatives in 1868 by a

126-74 vote, but he was acquitted in the Senate, where the vote against him was 35-19, one short of the two-thirds required by the Constitution. President Nixon was not impeached in 1974, however, because, as indicated above, he resigned before the articles of impeachment, approved by the House Judiciary Committee, could be acted upon by the House membership. In 1986 the House approved four articles of impeachment against federal judge Harry E. Claiborne, who had refused to resign his office as United States District Judge in Nevada (and continued to draw his annual salary of $78,700) even though serving a two-year prison term for tax evasion. Later that same year the Senate tried the impeached judge, found him guilty, and removed him from office. Similar impeachments in 1989 of federal judges Hastings and Nixon (as indicated above) were followed by actions in the Senate which found them guilty and removed them too from their offices.

Article I, Section 3 of the Constitution deals with the Senate, the second half of the Connecticut "Great Compromise." Each state, regardless of size or population, is entitled to two Senators. As indicated above, the original compromise to ensure state equality in the Senate provided that each state would have one Senator, but that number was increased to two to give more representation. Each Senator has one vote, however, so it is conceivable that if the two vote opposite ways, a state's vote might actually be canceled out in the chamber where state equality is supposed to be its *raison d'etre*.

This raises a tangential issue, yet one of fundamental importance. Each Representative and Senator has one vote in his or her respective legislative body; how are they expected to vote? Do they vote the way their constituents want them to vote? Do they vote their consciences and vote for what they think is best for the country? Stated another way: do they vote according to the principles of geographic (or deputy) representation, or do they vote according to the principles of virtual (or national) representation? Often issues arise in which local interest and national interest are at odds. Supposing, for example, measures are proposed which might cause hardships for banking or aerospace or defense industries, but at the same time would improve the overall financial picture and the national economy? How should Senators and Representatives who have large and important financial or aerospace or defense constituencies vote? What of the legislators from other states, who might need support from those colleagues for other measures? Or suppose the group which might be hurt by the proposed legislation was unionized workers in the oil fields; how should Representatives and Senators with large union constituencies vote?

We like to think that our Senators and Representatives speak for the people or the area they represent, whether a whole state or a smaller congressional district.

That implies that our legislators place local interests above national interests. But that often is not true. Many times a legislator's vote is in direct opposition to what might be best for the local constituency. Realistically, how does one determine just *what* the local constituency really wants? Legislators constantly distribute questionnaires to their constituents, but not everyone agrees, even within the same party. No legislators can satisfy their entire constituency; even finding some strong consensus is most difficult. Legislators are bombarded from all sides by divergent pressure groups and constituencies. Furthermore, sooner or later they must face their voters if they seek to be re-elected. Seldom are issues and consequences of votes clearly defined. Issues are rarely clear-cut "black or white"; they usually have many shades of gray. But the legislator's vote is different—he or she has to vote "aye" or "nay," one way or the other; there is nothing in between. The legislator cannot vote partially one way and partially the other. It is very easy for people—especially "one-issue" voters—to criticize legislators with whose votes they disagree; but the legislator has to live with both the criticism and the vote. The principles of residency and geographic representation hold fast, then, in how our legislators are *elected*; in *voting*, however, the legislators seem to be guided very often by the principle of virtual representation—that is, they vote their conscience and what they think is best for the nation as a whole.

But even that is an oversimplification. Politics is the art or practice or science of getting things done. In a national legislature consisting of several hundred people representing even more interests and locations, passing a law for a specific purpose encounters many obstacles and differences of opinion. From early on in our history the process known as "log-rolling" emerged as a necessary and practical mode of legislative procedure. In effect it means: "You help me roll my log up the hill, and I'll help you roll yours up the hill." There are more graphic ways to express the same concept: "You scratch my back, I'll scratch yours," or "You vote for my bill, and I'll vote for yours." To ideologues this seems unprincipled and Machiavellian. Yet, with rare exception, it seems to be the best and perhaps the only way to get things done in the legislature. Such practices are unnecessary, of course, in societies where a totalitarian leadership dictates how "legislators" should "vote." But in a democratic society which thrives on multicultural and geographic differences, and where freedom of speech makes possible the expression of such a diversity of views, legislators must recognize the needs and demands of constituencies other than their own. Compromises and trade-offs are an absolute necessity. As we have seen, the Constitution itself could never have been drawn up and ratified were it not for compromises and trade-offs.

It would seem, then, that the key to the success of democratic legislative government is not so much how influential or inflexible a legislator is in representing a certain ideology or constituency, but rather that legislator's honesty and integrity in recognizing *all* legitimate interests, including their commonalties and differences, especially those which differ from his or her own, or those of his or her constituency. Sometimes it means casting a vote that antagonizes powerful and/or influential friends, but that is a risk legislators must take. Certainly the Framers were familiar with that problem, for they constantly referred to "men of virtue" as those who would be involved in government and who would have to make those decisions. On the other hand, some legislators who represent a constituency overwhelmingly homogeneous in population and narrow in its outlook almost always vote that narrow way—and are "rewarded" by being re-elected over and over again. That is one reason for the recent anti-incumbency fervor that has spread across the country and was so evident in the 1992 local and national elections.

Typical of the pressures legislators face was one in 1987 when Congress passed a highway and mass transit bill which President Ronald Reagan then vetoed. Reagan had been outspoken in his opposition to federal spending for domestic programs of this sort. At the same time, many Republicans voted into office in the 1986 elections had won because of their association with Reagan and with that philosophy—they had come into their offices "on Reagan's coattails." Yet after Reagan vetoed the bill, both the House and the Senate overrode the veto, the vote in the Senate being 67-33, just barely the two-thirds majority required for an override. About a dozen "Reagan Republican loyalist" Senators were included in the overriding majority, and had any *one* of them voted for the President, his veto would have been sustained. The White House brought all sorts of pressures on those Senators, but they still voted to override, because the proposed measure called for badly needed road improvements in *their* particular states. As one of those Senators stated in the press: "I cannot vote against my state." It was a sentiment expressed by others too. Instances like this occur all the time. Legislators find it extremely difficult to vote against appropriations which would benefit their district or state. It is, of course, one reason also why federal outlays have mushroomed to such proportions, which many refer to as outlandish.

Article I, Section 3 of the Constitution provides that Senators should be elected to six-year terms, with an overlapping membership. Only one-third of the Senators are elected at a time; two-thirds always remain in office. That means that no matter what happens in any given election year, there will always be experienced Senators serving in the Congress—in contrast with the House, where possibly, though not probably, there might be a complete turnover in personnel. It means, too, that the Senate never starts "from scratch," so to speak; it is, in effect, an ongoing body. Its members, therefore, experience considerable public expo-

and have opportunities to attain national prominence. That explains why, even though some Senators serve only one term, the turnover is relatively slow and many remain for lengthy service. It is not unusual for a Senator to serve three or four or five six-year terms. The longest on record is Carl Hayden of Arizona, whose Senatorial career spanned almost forty-two years—and that after fourteen years before that in the House! No wonder, then, that the Senate is called the "upper" house and that some Senators wield considerable political clout. It also explains why the recent anti-incumbency wave has included attempts to limit terms of Senators as well as of Representatives. Most states which voted to limit Senate terms would limit them to two or three six-year terms. As in the case of the Representatives, however, many question the constitutionality of these state actions, and for the same reasons—that states are trying to interfere with Constitutional qualifications for who can or cannot be elected to the Senate. As with the limitation of the terms of Representatives, a resolution of this issue (as indicated above) probably must also await a Supreme Court determination.

A recent controversy has led to a closer look at the qualifications for an individual to be elected to the United States Senate. In the 1992 Senatorial election in Georgia, incumbent Democratic Senator Wyche Fowler won, but with only a plurality; no candidate received a majority of the votes cast. Georgia law provides, however, that unless a candidate wins with a *majority* of the votes cast, a run-off election must be held. That run-off election duly occurred a few weeks later. This time the winner—and by a majority vote—was Republican Paul Coverdell. A local Georgia citizens group thereupon filed suit in federal court to overturn Coverdell's election and to declare Fowler the properly elected Senator according to the first election, even though he had won it by only a plurality. The group contended that the Georgia law requiring a majority violated the United States Constitution. They claimed that the Constitution sets up only three qualifications for becoming a Senator: age, citizenship, and residency. Any legalized qualification in addition to those three—*i.e.*, the legislative provision that one must win by a majority—added a requirement that had not been imposed by the Constitution, and therefore it was unconstitutional. At issue, of course, was whether an individual state might set requirements and/or qualifications for *its own* Senators over and above what the Constitution requires. The outcome of that Georgia action probably will be determined in the courts, just as will the outcome of the term-limitation requirements mentioned above. Meanwhile, pending that action, Coverdell was duly sworn in tentatively when the House of Representatives assembled in January 1993.

According to the original Constitution, and for many years thereafter, Senators were elected by the state legislatures. That changed with the Seventeenth

Amendment in 1913, which provided that the voters of the state elect Senators directly. That amendment also provided for optional procedures to fill a vacancy should a Senator die or resign. The state legislature can authorize a special election. Or it may empower the governor to make a temporary appointment "until the people fill the vacancy by election as the legislature may direct." In actual practice, governors have made temporary appointments until the next regular Congressional election, at which time voters have chosen a new Senator either to finish the unexpired term or for a full six-year term, whichever happened to be applicable at that election. In the 1992 elections, for instance, California voters elected two Senators—both, coincidentally, women. One was elected to a regular full six-year term. The other was elected for only two years, to complete the unexpired term of a Senator who had resigned.

The Constitution lists only three qualifications to be a Senator. One must be thirty years of age, must have been a citizen of the United States for at least nine years, and must be an inhabitant of the state for which elected. To be a viable candidate, however, one realistically must possess (as must candidates for any public office), other qualities that make one "electable."

Article I, Section 3 of the Constitution contains several more provisions that relate exclusively to the Senate. Just as the Speaker is the designated presiding officer over the House, so does the Constitution provide that the Vice-President of the United States shall preside over the Senate. In fact, other than being in line for the Presidency, presiding over the Senate is the only responsibility the Vice-President has under the Constitution. He is not a member of the Senate, though; he can vote only to break a tie. Although he is Vice-President of the United States, his title as presiding officer of the Senate is "President of the Senate." That explains why under certain circumstances (*i.e.*, a joint meeting of Congress for the State of the Union address) even the President of the United States will address him as "Mr. President" (or presumably "Madame President" should a woman hold that office).

The Constitution also provides that the Senate shall choose a "president pro tempore" who presides in the absence of the Vice President or when the latter succeeds to the Presidency. The President Pro Tem is selected in the Senate as the Speaker is selected in the House; that is, each party nominates a candidate and the Senate as a whole then chooses, the majority party winning. Normally the President Pro Tem attains that position by seniority, being the Senator of his party with the longest service. Furthermore, the President Pro Tem can debate and vote on all measures, even while acting as presiding officer, because he is a member of the Senate, in contrast with the Vice-President who can vote only to break a tie.

As in the case of the House of Representatives, the Senate chooses other officers, some for the Senate as a whole and some purely as party functionaries. Thus there will be a majority leader and a minority leader, a majority whip and a minority whip, party conference officers, and others who carry out many day-to-day functions of the Senate.

It might be pointed out, by the way, that in both the House and the Senate, despite the Constitutional designation of official presiding officer, the *actual* presiding officer may be any member of the body. It is not unusual at any given time to find a Congressman or a Senator other than the Speaker or the Vice-President or the President Pro Tem wielding the gavel. That is because often very few legislators are in the actual sessions for business; most are attending committee meetings or other important official functions. However, when "important" or controversial matters arise, members are present and the designated officials preside. As a matter of fact, one of the main functions of the elected "whip" of each party is to see that the members of his party are in attendance at those "important" sessions to record their votes.

Article I, Section 3 also provides that the Senate shall have the exclusive power to try officials impeached by the House of Representatives. This is the second stage of the impeachment process mentioned above, and a two-thirds vote is required for conviction. The only penalty for such conviction is removal from office and "disqualification to hold and enjoy any office of honor, trust or profit under the United States." Thus in 1986, after the House had impeached U. S. District Judge Harry E. Claiborne, the Senate tried and convicted him. He was found guilty by the required two-thirds vote on three of the four impeachment articles; he was acquitted on the fourth even though a majority voted him guilty. Nevertheless, conviction on any one charge is sufficient for the person to be expelled from office—and that is precisely what happened to Claiborne. It was the first time in fifty years that the Senate had tried an impeachment case; the last had been in 1936 when it had convicted U. S. District Judge Halsted Ritter and removed him from office for judicial improprieties.

Within three years after the Claiborne case, two more United States District Court judges were impeached by the House, Alcee Hastings and Walter L. Nixon. Both were very shortly convicted in the Senate and removed from office. In unprecedented actions, however, both appealed those decisions in separate litigations in the federal courts. They claimed that they had not been tried properly according to the Constitution, which gives to the Senate "the sole power to try all impeachment cases." When the House articles of impeachment were transmitted to the Senate, those articles were taken up by a special twelve-person impeachment trial committee, where all the evidence was presented. That committee then reported to the full Senate. In Hastings' case, the full Senate then voted to convict him on the basis of the committee report. In Nixon's case, the Senate heard arguments and questioned Nixon for three hours, and then deliberated for an additional six hours, before voting to convict him. But the committee laid the groundwork for the Senate action by reviewing the testimony and exhibits, as provided by Senate rules. The committee's meetings were even broadcast live to all Senate offices and videotaped. In 1992 a United States District Court overthrew the Senate conviction of Judge Nixon on the grounds that his impeachment case had not been tried by full deliberation in the Senate—that the Senate has the "sole power to try all impeachments" and cannot give some or all of that power to a committee. The case was thereupon appealed to the Supreme Court, which agreed to hear arguments. Since both Claiborne and Hastings had experienced comparable trial methodology, the outcome of the Nixon case in the Supreme Court should have an important effect upon the lives and careers of all three judges.

But the acceptance by the Supreme Court of Judge Nixon's case could raise an important constitutional issue: checks and balances, or separation of powers. Does the judicial branch have the right to question the legality of an action in which the Constitution places the "sole power" in a branch of the national *legislature*? Does "sole power" include the power of the Senate to prescribe the rules by which the impeachment charges are to be tried—including the role of a special impeachment committee? Does this case fall under the same category as "judicial review" in which, ever since *Marbury v. Madison* in 1803, the Supreme Court has the authority to declare an action of Congress to be unconstitutional? The answers to these and more questions must await the pending action in the Supreme Court.

Although the Senate can only remove a person from office, that person still can be brought to a "regular" court if he or she violated a criminal law. If found guilty there, that individual would be subject to the same punishment as any other criminal. In Claiborne's case, he already was serving a sentence in federal prison for income tax violation, having been found guilty of that offense in 1984. (As a matter of fact, impeachment proceedings were brought in Congress primarily because Claiborne had refused to resign voluntarily after his criminal conviction, and he actually continued to draw his regular salary as federal judge even though he was in prison!) On the other hand, when President Nixon resigned in 1974, the impeachment process came to a halt because he no longer was in office. Many felt, though, that he should be brought into court on criminal charges. But when President Gerald Ford pardoned Nixon for unspecified crimes which he might have committed while in the White House, that criminal judicial procedure was negated. Richard Nixon remained eligible, therefore, to draw full government benefits (pensions, etc.) and to hold "any office of honor, trust or profit under the United States." Presumably he could be appointed to a cabinet post, or as ambassador, or to any other similar government post.

Some have speculated whether Nixon could still have been impeached even though he already had resigned and been pardoned. Why, some have asked; all that Congress could do anyway was to remove him from office—and he was already out of office. What good would a belated impeachment serve, especially since the Nixon issue had so vituperatively divided the country? On the other hand, others have claimed, carrying out the constitutional process would serve at least two important functions. In the first place, it would set the record straight: the truth would come out regarding the various accusations about what President Nixon had or had not done. But more important, it would send a strong message to millions of Americans who had become totally disenchanted with the American political and judicial system—to so many who had come to believe that "equal justice under law" had become a sham, and that a double standard was applied for "special" people. If Nixon had indeed deserved impeachment and dismissal, those people argue, why should he not be punished under the law like anyone else? Instead, he was allowed to remain eligible for numerous government posts and to draw a very lucrative annual pension paid for by tax dollars. Many do not consider this proper "punishment" for one who violated his trust and took the oath as President to "preserve, protect and defend the Constitution of the United States."

Furthermore, those who argued that Nixon still could have been impeached after resigning point to a comparable precedent. In 1876 the House impeached Secretary of War William W. Belknap for corruption and incompetence, even though he resigned just hours before the proceedings began in the House, which many felt was a blatant attempt to avoid the shame of being impeached. The House went ahead with the impeachment charges anyway; they were then forwarded to the Senate, which duly proceeded to try the impeached cabinet member. Although a majority there found the resigned Secretary of War guilty on each charge, it was not the required two-thirds to convict, and so Belknap was acquitted. (He did not, however, regain his cabinet post; President Grant had already replaced him.) After the trial, a number of Senators indicated that they had voted for acquittal because they were not sure whether the Senate actually had jurisdiction once Belknap had resigned. Thus a precedent exists for a post-resignation impeachment proceeding, but its validity under law is at least partially clouded because of the Senate action—or inaction—in the Belknap procedure. As in other instances, no definitive conclusion can be stated unless and until another situation arises in the future that requires a clear-cut determination.

THE CONGRESS

An important provision of Article I applies to both the House and the Senate, but has broader implications. It deals with who elects the Representatives and Senators. The Constitution provides that the qualifications of their electors shall be the same as "the qualifications requisite for electors of the most numerous branch of the state legislature." (Originally, as pointed out above, Senators were elected by the state legislatures, but that was changed when the Seventeenth Amendment provided for direct election by the people.) That means that the qualifications to vote for members of Congress—both houses—are determined actually by each state: if one is eligible to vote for the *state* legislature, one is automatically eligible to vote for the *national* legislature—and for President and Vice-President, it might be added, because the same Constitutional qualifications apply for those who can vote for those two officers. The only restrictions are those stated in the Constitution: that no state can forbid anyone from voting because of race, color, or previous condition of servitude (Fifteenth Amendment); sex (Nineteenth Amendment); failure to pay a poll tax or other tax (Twenty-Fourth Amendment); or age above eighteen (Twenty-Sixth Amendment). Other than those, states can set any qualifications they wish to vote for the state legislature. All states, for instance, require citizenship and some sort of residency and/or registration. Some have educational or literacy tests. Since the Voting Rights Act of 1965 many efforts have been made to prevent abusive state requirements which seem unreasonably discriminatory. In truth, a lot depends not so much on the state requirements as on how that state carries out those requirements. It is one thing, for instance, to require that a person must be able to read and explain what he or she is reading; it is another to require one prospective voter to read and explain something from a first grade primer, and to require another prospective voter to read and explain something from John Milton's *Areopagitica*. Nevertheless (to use an outlandishly frivolous example), if the Oklahoma state legislature passed a law that one must own at least one share of stock in an Oklahoma-based oil company to be eligible to vote for members of the Oklahoma state legislature, and if the courts somehow upheld that requirement as not being discriminatory, that would be a valid requirement for *Oklahomans* to vote for President, Vice-President, and *Oklahoma* Congressmen and Senators as well as for Oklahoma state and local officials. The point is that there is no such thing as a *federal* election law setting forth qualifications for voting. The Constitution indicates what the states *cannot* require; within those limitations, the states set their own requirements.

The rest of Article I (Sections 4 through 10) deals with Congress collectively. (Actually Section 10 deals with prohibitions on the *states,* but many are similar to prohibitions on Congress which appear in Section 9.) Section 4 focuses on times of election and meeting. The Constitution leaves to the states the time, place, and manner of holding elections for Senators and Representatives, but reserves the right for Congress to be the final judge. Congress did not act to systematize those procedures until 1842, and it has followed up with several laws since. Elections for Congress now are held on the first Tuesday after the first Monday in November in the even-numbered years. For many years Maine was allowed to hold its elections earlier (hence the adage "As Maine goes, so goes the nation"); since 1960, however, Maine has voted with the rest of the nation in November.

The time when Congress meets was changed by the Twentieth Amendment in 1933. Originally the Presidential inauguration was on March 4 following a November election. Congress was supposed to meet at least once a year, on the first Monday of December. But the term of the *new* Congress never began until the first Monday of December *after* the March inauguration date, or thirteen months *after* Congress was elected! Any Congressional sessions within that period were attended by the *old* Congress, which often included many "lame duck" members who already had been defeated at the polls, but who nevertheless remained in office for that additional thirteen months. The long delay had been built in originally to allow time to resolve disputed elections or similar problems; but as transportation and communication technology improved, many felt the need for change. That finally came in 1933, when the Twentieth Amendment—the "Lame Duck" Amendment—provided the time-table which now applies. The elections still are held, as before, in November. But now the new Congress meets on the following January 3, and the President is inaugurated on January 20. That leaves only about two months to deal with election problems, but most people feel that is sufficient time. In fact, with recent advances in communication and computer technology, many feel that the time might be shortened even more. On the other hand, many also feel that a transition time is needed for the outgoing personnel to wind things up, and for those who are coming into office to make necessary preparations.

Article I, Section 5 deals with some miscellaneous proceedings in Congress. Each house keeps an official journal, but these records are sketchy and contain only the highlights of each day's activities. Much more important is the *Congressional Record*, which is a daily printed stenographic record of all that transpires in each house. It includes (either in the main text or in an added *Appendix*) also materials which legislators want "on the record" even though they were not stated on the floor of either house.

One extremely important power which each house has is that it is the "judge of the elections, returns and qualifications" of its own members. Even though elected members must meet the Constitutional qualifications of age, citizenship, and residency, each house has at times refused to seat certain elected persons as unacceptable—for various reasons. Thus in 1900, for instance, the House refused to seat Brigham H. Roberts of Utah because he practiced polygamy. In 1919 and in 1920 Victor L. Berger of Milwaukee, Wisconsin, twice was refused his seat in the House of Representatives because of his open opposition as a Socialist to World War I.

Nevertheless, just who is the final judge really remains conjectural. Even though the Constitution gives that power to each house, constituents still can elect the individual of their own choice. That long-standing tradition goes back to eighteenth century England, when the "John Wilkes Affair" determined that no matter how often the legislature may reject an individual, the constituency can turn right around and elect the person it wants. That principle was behind the 1969 decision in the case involving controversial Congressman Adam Clayton Powell of New York, when the Supreme Court declared that *Congress* cannot require any qualifications other than those set forth in the Constitution—even though a *state* may add to those qualifications. Thus, even though the Constitution grants to the House and the Senate the right to be the judge of the qualifications of its members, the constituents can re-elect that person, and that re-election would be upheld by the 1969 Powell decision. (The recent movement for term limitations has nothing to do with qualifications; it deals only with the number of terms to which an individual might be elected. The status of that restriction, however, as indicated above, is far from settled.)

A fascinating episode involving the seating of a member of Congress involved Senator Truman H. Newberry, Republican of Michigan, elected in November, 1918. The Republicans controlled the ensuing Senate session—a crucial time because the Treaty of Versailles was up for ratification—by a bare 49-47 majority. Newberry had won his election over Democrat Henry Ford—not related to the automobile Henry Ford—but Ford challenged the outcome. Newberry subsequently was found to have been elected illegally because he violated Michigan election laws, but he escaped punishment on a technicality. Finally, though, public opinion forced him to resign from the Senate—but that was not until 1922. By that time, however, the Treaty of Versailles had been defeated in the Senate. In 1919 the Senate had seated Newberry pending the outcome of Ford's challenge. Had the Senate speeded up its inquiry and seated Ford instead of Newberry, the line-up in the Senate would have been tied at 48 Republicans and 48 Democrats. The Vice-President, Thomas R. Marshall, a Democrat, undoubtedly would have voted with the Democrats to break ties. The Foreign Relations Committee consequently would have contained a majority of Democrats instead of Republicans, and would have had a Democratic chairman instead of Henry Cabot Lodge, who hated President Woodrow Wilson with a passion. Many feel that a Senate controlled by the Democrats (counting the Democratic Vice-President to break ties) would have ratified the Treaty of Versailles, that the United States subsequently would have joined the League of Nations, and that the whole course of ensuing events which eventually led to World War II and beyond might have been totally different. By such seemingly insignificant occurrences as a state senatorial election is the course of history changed.

In addition to being the judge of the elections and qualifications of its members—their entrance requirements, so to speak—both houses are authorized also to monitor the behavior of their members once they are seated. Each house has established rules to enable it to carry out its business, rules which can be and have been changed from time to time. Any infraction of those rules or any "disorderly" or "unethical" behavior may result in punishment for the offender.

The most severe punishment would be expulsion from the chamber, a measure which requires a two-thirds vote. The impeachment trial of Senator William Blount in 1799 established the precedent that members of Congress do not come under the impeachment provisions of the Constitution. Blount, a Senator from Tennessee, had been impeached by the House, but the charges were dropped in the Senate trial on the jurisdictional grounds that Representatives and Senators were not considered "civil officers" under the Constitutional provision for impeachment, since the Constitution provided for their removal in a different way—by expulsion. After dropping the impeachment charges, the Senate proceeded to expel Blount in a separate action, by the required two-thirds vote, exercising its authority under the Constitution to expel a member for "disorderly behavior." The outcome was, of course, the same—that Blount was removed from office. There have been a number of additional expulsions in ensuing years.

More common than expulsion (because expulsion is such a severe penalty and requires a two-thirds vote) is the "censure." That is a resolution, by a simple majority vote, in which the particular house publicly and officially airs its disapproval or condemnation of the activities of one of its members. Such was the case with the censure of Senator Joseph R. McCarthy of Wisconsin in 1954 for his reckless and irresponsible character assassination of numerous innocent victims in the guise of a Senatorial investigation presumably to root out communists in government. A public censure does not physically punish an individual; its effect is more in the realm of arousing public sentiment. In the case of Senator McCarthy, for instance, almost overnight he lost whatever personal power and influence he had wielded prior to his censure.

Annual salaries of members of Congress are set by law, by each house separately. Normally Representatives and Senators receive the same pay, but occasionally they may differ. In 1982, for instance, the House salary was $69,800 a year compared with $60,600 for the Senate. By 1986 both were the same, at $75,100. Salary increases have been voted several times since; by the end of 1992 they were both $129,500, with provisions for annual cost of living increases.

Members of Congress have many expenses and their cost of living is quite high. Nevertheless, every once in a while they come under criticism for voting themselves what some feel might be too much financial benefit. One such criticism was triggered by events of the summer of 1991. Already under considerable fire for being the recipients of many "perks," especially large sums from PACs (political action committees), the Senate voted itself a sizable and immediate salary increase. One reason was to bring Senate salaries up to those in the House, which had voted to increase its salaries in 1989, but not effective until the next session began in 1991. Another "trade-off" was that Senators would no longer accept honoraria for outside speeches—which were often no more than random observations and usually merited little or no compensation—as a "speech," that is. Sometimes, too, PACs "purchased" large quantities of books or pamphlets authored by members of Congress. Many felt that these large "honoraria" were merely ruses to circumvent restrictions on how much money could be contributed to legislators for political purposes. It did not help that the Senate salary vote came without the usual prior publicity and was squeezed in during a late night session in the middle of the summer, and, as one national news magazine reported, "with a swiftness usually reserved for national emergencies."

Coming at a time when the nation's economy was experiencing painful job layoffs and increasing unemployment, the Senate vote to increase its salaries by a whopping $23,200 led to widespread demands to limit Congressional pay. (It apparently mattered little that many in both houses of Congress actually refused to accept their latest increase. Some returned it; others contributed it to charity. Still, the outcry against the Congressional "salary grab," as many dubbed it, resulted in many incumbents being defeated in the 1992 elections.)

Little known to many people, a constitutional amendment to limit Congressional pay already was "in the pipeline," so to speak. Incredibly, it was one of the twelve amendments written by James Madison and proposed by Congress *in 1789!* Ten had been duly ratified and became the Bill of Rights. Two were not ratified. One dealt with numbers in the House of Representatives. The other provided: "No law, varying the compensation for the services of the Senators and Representatives, shall take effect, until an election of Representatives shall have intervened." In other words, salary increases could not take effect in the current session (as the Senate had done in 1991); they had to await the *next* session of Congress (as the House had done in 1989 and as both houses have done historically). No time limit for ratification had been placed on Madison's proposed amendment. While the Bill of Rights amendments were ratified by 1791, only six states ratified this proposal. By 1873 only one more state had ratified. Not until the 1980s, influenced by "Reagan conservatism," did any more states ratify, usually bestirred by some Congressional excess—but not really knowing whether their ratification actually meant anything, since the amendment had been lying around in the state legislatures for such a long time. The Senate action in the summer of 1991 aroused a new interest in this "lost amendment," and states which had paid no attention to it for a long time suddenly found reason for action. On May 7, 1992, Michigan became the thirty-eighth state to ratify, bringing the total over the Constitutional requirement of three-fourths of the states.

That raised the question, of course, whether a Constitutional amendment proposed in 1789 could remain viable and be ratified more than two hundred years later. Although many felt that the answer was in the negative, two events seemed to confirm that the Madison proposal had indeed become a valid amendment to the Constitution. One was the certification by the Director of the National Archives that since no time limit existed in the 1789 proposal, it now had been duly ratified according to the Constitution. (Section 106b, Title 1 of the United States Code empowered him to make this determination.) He therefore ordered the text of the amendment to be published in the *Federal Register* in which are printed official legal notices and other regulations of the United States government.

The second event was the affirmation by resolution by both the House and the Senate that the amendment was indeed ratified and approving the action of the Archivist. The purpose of that Senate action, however, according to one of the Senators who introduced the resolution in the Senate, was more than just to agree with the Archivist; it was also to assert that Congress, and no other agency of the government, has the final say over whether an amendment has received the required votes for ratification if no time limit has been stipulated. By confirming what the Archivist had done a few days earlier, Congress indicated that *its* approval removed any doubt of the validity of the Twenty-Seventh Amendment. As one Senator stated at the time, the "action by Congress will ensure the soundness of the amendment and protect congressional prerogatives."

Supporting the 1992 affirmation by Congress is a Supreme Court decision in 1939 (*Coleman v. Miller*, 307 U.S. 433) that although amendments must be ratified within a "reasonable" time, it is up to Congress to decide, if no time limit is specified in the proposed amendment, what is meant by "reasonable." That apparently is precisely what Congress did in 1992 when it affirmed the Archivist's action as valid. It would seem, then, that in spite of the negative views of some constitutional scholars, the 1789 Madison proposal—that Congressional salary increases cannot go into effect until the next session—has now become the

Twenty-Seventh Amendment to the Constitution. It would not apply, of course, to any increases voted prior to when that Amendment went into effect.

In addition to their salaries, members of Congress receive other perquisites. They are allocated funds for clerical and administrative staffs as well as office space in House and Senate office buildings. Congressional budgets include funds for telephones, telegraph, postage, and stationery. Gymnasiums, dining rooms, health facilities, and similar perks are provided either at no cost or at a very reasonable cost. Legislators have the "franking" privilege; that is, they may use the mails free for official business. They receive liberal travel allowances and tax benefits for having to maintain residences in both Washington and their home districts. Legislators also enjoy substantial retirement and pension benefits, far better, some say, than what is available to those in private life.

In addition to these forms of compensation, members of Congress also are granted others privileges and immunities. The most important, perhaps, is freedom from arrest going to or from, or during their attendance at, sessions of Congress—except for treason, felony, or breach of the peace; and absolute freedom of speech or debate at those sessions. This is to protect members of Congress from unwarranted interference with their legislative activities. The Framers were aware that British kings had interfered with Parliament by summarily arresting its members, and wanted none of that in the new country. This does not protect a legislator from prosecution if he commits a criminal offense, nor does it protect him from being summoned as a witness. On the other hand, this Congressional immunity can shield an unscrupulous demagogue by allowing him to make unsupported and even damaging allegations—case in point: Senator Joseph McCarthy mentioned above—but it is very likely that a free press and fellow legislators sooner or later will set the record straight.

Article I of the Constitution does more than establish the legislative branch of our national government; it also implements the principle of separation of powers, or checks and balances. The procedure for impeachment illustrates Congressional restraint on executive and judicial abuses. That Congress must meet at least once a year clearly prevents an imperious executive from attempting to govern alone, as earlier British monarchs had done. One house even checks the other, since any bill must be approved *in toto* by both houses. That means that even minor differences must be ironed out, and the houses must approve exactly the same bill—including the exact wording—before sending it to the President for his signature and approval.

Among the most evident provisions for checks and balances are those which deal with the Presidential veto. Once both houses approve the same bill, it goes to the President. He may then choose one of several courses of action.

(1) He may sign it into law.

(2) He may veto it—refuse to sign it. If that happens, the President must return the bill to the house where it originated, and give his reasons for vetoing. Those reasons usually are stated briefly and tersely. Sometimes they occasion masterful and philosophic state papers; Andrew Jackson's famous veto of a bank bill in 1832, for instance, contains a classic essay on Jacksonian democracy.

If both houses pass the bill again, this time by a two thirds vote, it becomes law without the President's signature. This is known as "overriding a veto." If the measure fails to get the necessary two-thirds override in *either* house, the President's veto is upheld and the bill does not become law.

The override becomes a very highly controversial political issue especially when the President is of one party and Congress is controlled by the other. That was the case during the presidency of Harry S. Truman in the immediate post-World War II era; of Richard M. Nixon in the late 1960s and early 1970s; and of Ronald Reagan and George Bush from 1980 through 1992. Indeed, many observers of the 1992 election surmise that one reason why President Bush failed to win re-election was his almost ongoing battle with Congress and the ensuing "gridlock" in government resulting from the override situation: Congress would pass a bill, Bush would veto it because he disagreed with portions of it, Congress could muster a majority but not the required two thirds to override—and the bill would die from the veto. At least thirty-six measures thought by Congress to be necessary were thus vetoed by President Bush; lacking the line-item power, he vetoed the entire bill rather than approve it with provisions that he disagreed with. In only one instance was Congress able to muster the required two-thirds vote to override.

In recent years, Congressional action of overriding a veto has come under critical scrutiny because of its deliberate use to limit Presidential powers. This technique could be used only because Congress was confident it could muster enough votes to override a veto. A good example came out of the Nixon-Congress confrontations of the 1970s and clearly in reaction to the broad malaise which existed over the Vietnam war. In 1973 Congress passed the War Powers Act requiring certain actions by the President when he assumed the responsibility to commit American forces overseas. Nixon vetoed the measure; Congress overrode it by the required two-thirds vote. Among other things, the law provided that any time American forces were engaged in hostilities without a formal declaration of war, Congress, under certain circumstances and by concurrent resolution—which does not require Presidential approval—could direct the President to disengage those troops. The key here, of course, was that those who opposed the President felt confident they could muster the two-thirds necessary to override. Under those circumstances, they included in the bill provisions which clearly limited Presidential actions—which by the Constitution became law when Congress overrode the President's veto. The 1973 War Powers Act was only one of several anti-executive measures which became law under similar legislative circumstances. This device has been labeled a "congressional veto" or a "legislative veto," because it can restrict or even negate powers of the President. Is this a valid expression of checks and balances, or is in an unwarranted infringement by the legislature on constitutional executive powers? Valid arguments can be made on both sides. Presumably a definitive answer will come from the Supreme Court in an appropriate case.

(3) A third possible action by the President when he receives a bill from Congress is to neither sign nor veto the measure; if ten days (excluding Sundays) pass and Congress is still in session, the bill automatically becomes law even without the President's signature. This was placed in the Constitution to prevent a President from defeating legislation by delay or inaction. On the other hand, Presidents often use this technique to show their dislike for a particular measure but find it politically unwise to veto it; at least they can say that the measure became a law without their written approval. (Often that dislike is aimed at only a small portion of the measure, but the President must approve the bill entirely or veto it entirely. Many governors have the "line-item veto" authority; that is, they can veto part of a bill and still approve the rest. The President lacks that luxury. Many proposals have been introduced to grant the President the line-item veto, but as yet none have been approved. More on the line-item veto below.)

(4) The President may neither sign nor veto the bill—as in (3) above—but if Congress adjourns before ten days pass (Sundays excluded), then the bill automatically dies. This is known as a "pocket veto"—the President puts the bill in his pocket, so to speak, and forgets about it. The President does not have to return the bill to Congress to face a possible override, because that body is no longer in session. The only way to resurrect the measure is for someone to re-introduce it from scratch in the next session.

Mention was made above of the "line-item" veto. Although Presidents long have desired that authority, Congress has always opposed granting it to him. The central fact is that often authorizations for "pet" projects of Representatives and Senators, even though they serve the interests of only a particular group, industry, or region, are added to major appropriations bills as the only way to get them approved. The rationale is that the President would not veto a major bill just because of these relatively "insignificant" things added to it. In that way, many such projects are funded by the national government which otherwise, if they had to stand individually on their own merits, would never be approved by Congress, and certainly not by the President. And the funding for all those projects accumulates into a very large sum.

Those who favor the line-item veto argue that it would enable the President to eliminate billions of dollars of "pork" from federal expenditures and thereby make it possible to: (1) reduce the horrendous national debt and deficit, and bring some semblance of responsibility to government spending; and (2) cut down on the excessive national government role in the everyday life of the people by forcing states to pick up a more equitable portion of governmental responsibility, thereby restoring a balance to the system of federalism.

Those who oppose the line-item veto also present two major arguments. (1) Granting the need for fiscal restraint, a line item veto would make it possible for a President to veto many measures which are absolutely vital to local areas, measure which provide jobs, housing, health care, educational facilities and materials, transportation needs, and similar everyday and continuing necessities for a better life; and the fear that partisan Presidents—and is there ever a President who isn't partisan?—would make those decisions too often for political expediency rather than for the legitimate needs of the local area or group. For in truth, in a democratic society such as ours, what may constitute "pork" from one point of view is a genuine and absolutely legitimate need from another point of view. (2) The line-item veto would give the President such inordinate powers over Congressional action as to completely undermine the spirit of checks and balances. He could, in effect, exercise complete control over one of Congress' most important responsibilities and functions: how the government's money is spent.

In addition to the purely substantive nature of the pros and cons of the line-item veto, yet another question must be answered: how to actually implement the line-item veto. Can it be done by an act of Congress? Would it require an amendment to the Constitution? Could the judiciary be involved in any way, as in pending court action relative to the impeachment process? These, and probably others, are questions which will require answers when and if the line-item veto for the President becomes a viable matter.

In addition to bills which eventually become statute law, Congress also passes many resolutions, some of which have the effect of law, some of which only express Congressional opinion. Joint resolutions require the President's signature; others do not. Though not as binding in the courts as law, resolutions still greatly influence public policy and action; they do, after all, represent the sentiment and bent of Congressional opinion.

Many Americans lack a clear understanding of how all these bills and resolutions are enacted. Visitors to both the House and the Senate galleries often are shocked to see so few members on the floor discussing pending legislation.

Most bills are passed by voice votes—and usually only a few voices are heard—but the floor leaders (majority and minority leaders and whips) make sure that the outcomes accurately reflect the legislators' feelings. In actual fact, the legislators spend much more of their time at hearings and committee meetings, where the "nuts and bolts" work is done, or in getting information first-hand by on-site visitations and inspections. Each house has its own internal organization, which includes party leadership and committees, and most of the work is done through them. Committees issue a multitude of reports, and legislators and their staffs must read voluminously to acquire necessary information. At the same time, they are bombarded from all sides by constituents, lobbyists, and vested interests, all seeking favorable votes on pet measures or individual favors of many kinds, ranging from jobs for themselves or a friend to tickets for some athletic or social function. The work-load of a member of Congress is tedious, long, highly pressured, highly demanding—and very important.

A singular Constitutional recognition of the principle of no taxation without representation is found in the provision in Article I that *all* bills for raising revenue must originate in the House of Representatives. The Representatives, after all, are elected directly by the people. (Even though the Seventeenth Amendment later brought direct election for Senators, the original procedure for money bills continues in effect.) The Senate may propose changes—and often does—but the House still must approve those changes. In actual practice, such changes—as well as modifications in any other bills—usually are ironed out by a conference committee consisting of members of both houses. The results are compromises which then go back to each house for final approval and submission to the President.

The Constitution establishes a uniquely American system of federalism that divides government authority between our national government and our state governments. Fundamental aspects of that arrangement are found in Article I provisions dealing with the powers of Congress—what it can do and what it cannot do. More specifically, Article I, Section 8 details the powers that Congress can exercise; Article I, Section 9 lists the things that Congress cannot do; and Article I, Section 10 sets forth what the states cannot do. All other powers, as clarified in the Tenth Amendment, belong residually to the states. That, in essence, is the principle of federalism: certain powers belong to the national government and certain powers belong to the states. (See essay on Federalism.)

In setting up this federal system of government, the Constitution in Article I also implements another very important principle: that ours is a limited government. Even though it constitutes the legislative body of the national government, Congress does not have unlimited inherent powers. Its powers are only those granted in Article I, Section 8. True, one of those is the grant of implied powers in the "necessary and proper" clause (or the "elastic" clause as it is often called); yet even that broad exercise of potential powers clearly is limited by the prohibitions found in Article I, Section 9. No matter how broadly one might interpret the necessary and proper clause, Congress cannot (unless exceptions are authorized by the Constitution) suspend the writ of *habeas corpus*; pass a bill of attainder or an *ex post facto* law; levy direct taxes (except an income tax) other than in direct proportion to the population; tax exports; give preferential treatment to the seaports of one state over another; appropriate money except by law; or grant titles of nobility. In addition, the Bill of Rights (the first ten amendments) contains additional prohibitions on Congress and on the national government, adding to our protection and instilling further the principle of limited government.

Just as the national government is limited in its power, so too does the Constitution limit the state governments, in Article I, Section 10. No state may make a treaty or alliance with a foreign power. No state may grant letters of marque and reprisal. No state may coin money, pass bills of attainder, *ex post facto* laws, or laws impairing the obligation of contracts. Nor can any state grant titles of nobility (honorary titles such as "Kentucky Colonel" or "Oklahoma Admiral" or "Missouri Squire" are not considered titles of "nobility"). In addition to these prohibitions, each state has its own state bill of rights, either in statute form or as part of the state constitution. They comprise additional evidences of the principle of limited government in our system.

Thus the Constitution goes far beyond merely establishing the national legislature. It does so in a way that achieves the fundamental principles of American constitutionalism: federalism, checks and balances, limited government, and popular sovereignty. Perhaps that explains why Congress has been right in the midst of so many important historical developments in American history. It was there that many heated constitutional debates occurred over the *locus* of sovereignty in our federal union, a conflict which carried over into the bloody battlefields of the Civil War. It was there, too, in Congress, that fundamental changes in the character of our country—from rural, agricultural, and homogeneous to urban, industrial, and multicultural—were reflected in the evolution of legislative programs which saw the federal government become more and more involved in the lives of the American people.

It was there, too, that emerged some of the great political figures in American history. Some served in Congress with a distinction that matched or even exceeded their achievements later as Presidents; they included James Madison, Lyndon B. Johnson, and Gerald R. Ford. James K. Polk was Speaker of the House prior to becoming President. John Quincy Adams and Andrew Johnson served in Congress both before and after their experiences as President; in fact, many consider Adams' post-Presidential years in Congress the most productive part of his career. Most Presidents whose earlier public careers included service in Congress were probably no more than average Representatives or Senators. They included mostly nineteenth-century Presidents: Jackson, Van Buren, Tyler, Fillmore, the two Harrisons, Pierce, Buchanan, Lincoln, Hayes, Garfield, and McKinley. In fact, two who later became outstanding Presidents—Jackson and Lincoln—left very bland records in Congress which scarcely foretold such later greatness. Only six Presidents of the twentieth century had any prior Congressional experience: Harding, Truman, Kennedy, Johnson, Nixon, and Ford. (The route to the White House in the nineteenth century often went through Congress; in the twentieth century it seemed to travel more through a state governorship or some other executive position.)

Many have served in Congress with considerable distinction and perhaps aspired to the Presidency, but never made it. Our history books recount manifold praiseworthy contributions by the likes of Daniel Webster, Henry Clay, John C. Calhoun, Thomas Hart Benton, Joseph T. Robinson, Robert LaFollette, George W. Norris, Sam Rayburn, Robert A. Taft, and many, many more—outstanding legislators, but never elected President.

An important and fascinating part of the history of Congress has been its constant up-and-down contention with the Presidency in the ongoing confrontation that is inevitable in a check and balance system. Who has the power to do what? Where does one of them cross the line? The Framers of the Constitution went only so far in trying to answer that question. They established basic principles and defined minimal powers, enough to solve the problems of their times, but they left it for future generations to meet their own problems. Since then the Presidency and the Congress have of course cooperated for the good of the country, but they also have vied with each other over many issues.

The result has been an almost roller-coaster relationship, sometimes the President prevailing, sometimes Congress. For the student, a general rule of thumb might be to identify the "great" Presidents; when they were in the White House, Presidential leadership held sway. Thus the eras of George Washington, Thomas Jefferson, Andrew Jackson, Abraham Lincoln, Theodore Roosevelt, Woodrow Wilson, and Franklin D. Roosevelt witnessed Presidents leading and Congress following. The periods in between generally saw Congressional ascendancy. One cannot be sure that resulted from weak Presidents or strong Congresses or Congressmen; nevertheless the ups and downs did occur. Perhaps the greatest expression of Congressional supremacy occurred during the Reconstruction period following the Civil War. Even before that war ended, Abraham Lincoln had set into motion a program of Reconstruction under the direction of the

President; then he was assassinated. Andrew Johnson continued Lincoln's program of "Presidential Reconstruction," but very soon Congress reacted vehemently to the change in Presidential leadership. The result is what historians call "Congressional Reconstruction," climaxed by the impeachment and trial of President Johnson and the failure by only one vote to remove him from office.

Beginning in the 1930s, with the Great Depression, the New Deal, and then World War II, there has been a steady increase in Presidential domination of governmental power at the expense of Congress. That has resulted from forces both foreign and domestic that created what many referred to as an "Imperial Presidency." (See essay on The Presidency.) Matters reached a tumultuous climax in the 1970s during the administration of President Richard M. Nixon, precipitated by the Vietnam conflict and the Watergate affair. Even though Nixon repeatedly denied any wrongdoing and insisted that he was doing nothing basically different from what many of his predecessors had done, Congress determined that it must "blow the whistle" on what to many seemed flagrant violations of his Constitutional trust as President.

Presidential power had grown excessively and abusively, many legislators claimed, because Congress had abdicated its responsibilities and allowed Presidents to exercise authority and influence which should rightfully belong to Congress. Nixon's flagrant and outrageous excesses triggered the need to revitalize checks and balances. The American public was deeply and passionately divided over the President, many viewing very favorably some aspects of his vigorous foreign policy, yet utterly appalled and shaken at domestic activities which seemed to make a mockery of American Constitutional liberties. With Congress on the verge of impeaching him, Nixon resigned in 1974—the first person ever to resign the Presidency—and Vice-President Gerald R. Ford succeeded him. (Ford had become Vice-President only shortly before, under the operation of the Twenty-Fifth Amendment, when Nixon's first Vice-President, Spiro T. Agnew, had himself resigned rather than confront almost certain impeachment for irrefutable criminal and malfeasance charges.)

During the administrations of Nixon, Ford, Jimmy Carter, Ronald Reagan, and George Bush, Congress regained some of its lost prerogatives. This was due overwhelmingly to public reaction to the "imperial Presidency" and Nixon excesses. Another contributing factor was that Ford and Carter were philosophically less aggressive as Presidents than their predecessors. Reagan and Bush also believed idealogically in lessening federal powers, and advocated and supported reducing many domestic programs—not only from the Presidential milieu, but also from the Congressional sphere of authority.

But it was in the area of foreign affairs—fueled by the consuming fear that a President might involve the country in another Vietnam-type undeclared war—that Congress boldly asserted itself. In 1973 Congress passed the War Powers Act over President Nixon's veto. The stated purpose of the measure was to "insure" that the President involved the "collective judgment" of both houses of Congress any time he committed American forces to hostile situations abroad. Three procedures were outlined: Presidential consultation with Congress, Presidential reports to Congress, and possible Congressional termination of the military action. Although the intent of the act seemed clear, the impreciseness of many provisions created confusion in actual practice as to who could do exactly what, as succeeding events were to show.

During the post-Nixon years, the nation was convulsed by numerous overseas developments which focused on the Middle East and Iran, on Central America, and on nuclear arms limitations negotiations with the then Soviet Union. Unscrupulous and bloody terrorist depredations exacerbated already tenuous scenarios. Yet, despite giving lip-service to the fact that the President normally leads in foreign affairs, many in Congress often differed with Presidential approaches to those matters, especially those taken by President Reagan. The result was a series of Congressional acts, invariably passed over Presidential vetoes, which further monitored the President and his dealings abroad. They included, among others, the National Security Act (1980), the Arms Export Control Act (1985), and the Intelligence Authorization Assistance Act (1986). All were aimed at reasserting that Congress, as the elected representatives of the people, should have more of an input into American foreign affairs.

At the same time, well aware of the Vietnam and "imperial Presidency" syndromes, all Presidents since Nixon have been reluctant, if only for domestic political reasons, to employ American forces in troubled areas of the world unless they had overwhelming public support behind their actions. Yet as commander-in-chief and guardian of American national security, their responsibilities inevitably brought about confrontations with Congress over those Congressional acts which seemingly tied the Chief Executive's hands. These events included President Ford's use of forces to evacuate refugees from Vietnam and Cambodia and to rescue the American merchant ship *Mayaguez* from Cambodian pirates; President Carter's attempt to rescue American hostages in Iran; President Reagan's deployment of troops in Lebanon, Grenada, and Central America; and President Bush's use of armed forces in Panama and the Persian Gulf. Undoubtedly the most controversial, because it raised the specter of another possible Watergate-type scandal, was the so-called "Irangate" incident—clandestine and illicit sales of arms during the Reagan administration to terrorist Iran and secret transfers of money from those sales to anti-communist "contra" forces in Central America. (Indeed, the revelation of Vice-President George Bush's alleged association with that scandal in the mid-1980s proved to be a significant factor, after Bush himself became President, in his losing bid for re-election in 1992.)

Some sort of clarification of the relationship in foreign affairs between Congress and the Presidency came close to a showdown in 1990, when Iraqi forces invaded and conquered oil-rich Kuwait. United Nations intervention, orchestrated largely by President Bush, resulted in international sanctions being imposed by the U.N. in an effort to force Iraqi dictator Saddam Hussein to withdraw his forces. When it began to appear that those sanctions might not be effective enough, the U.N.—again with President Bush in a key leadership role—began to prepare for military intervention. Large and powerful American forces deployed into the Persian Gulf area, prepared to be a part of the U.N. operation.

At that point a most impressive debate occurred in Congress. Seeking to convince Iraq that the American people fully supported his willingness to use force and that the country was not divided by a "Vietnam malaise," President Bush sought from Congress a statement of its support. At the same time, those who preferred to continue sanctions rather than resort to force also sought a national forum to express that view. The result was a type of substantive foreign policy debate in Congress unlike anything which had occurred for a long time. Several points became quite clear: (1) The United States strongly supported President Bush in opposing Saddam Hussein. (2) There existed a difference, though, whether we should continue to apply economic sanctions against Iraq or whether we should proceed at once with military force. Although some argued against force unless Congress first declared war, Congress nevertheless approved the President's use of military force, albeit by a close vote. Indeed, once the debate concluded and the President ordered American troops into action, both sides—the pro-sanctions people and the pro-force people—united solidly behind the President. Operation Desert Storm—the Persian Gulf War of 1991—proved to be a very short and very successful military operation. The remarkably low number of casualties—far fewer than even the most optimistic predictions—helped make it also a very popular war and helped to reverse much of the bitterness of Vietnam.

But one very significant factor stood out. During the great debates in Congress, at no time were any of the Presidential war powers limitations invoked. The debates focused on the substantive issue of sanctions versus immediate force. Although some members of Congress equated the use of force with war and argued that only Congress can declare war, their only challenge to the President's power to deploy American forces was that they felt he should try sanctions longer. The implication seemed to be that if sanctions did not do the job and if the President then asked for a declaration of war, they would vote in the affirmative.

Left up in the air, however, were the actualities of the various Presidential war powers limitations. None were invoked. About fifty Democratic members of Congress asked a federal judge to force the President to seek a formal declaration of war before instituting military action, but their request was denied—but their request was not made under the aegis of any of the war powers acts. Was that because Congress did not want to tie the President's hands in the Persian Gulf situation? Was it because, as some have suggested, those Congressional limitations on the President, if invoked by Congress and then challenged in court, might be found unconstitutional? Did a Democratic Congress seek to push a non-military alternative so that, if the military operations advocated by the President proved disastrous, Congress could then turn that against him politically? Or was there a genuine desire not to force a President-Congress conflict over war powers? The answers remain for the future.

For the present, though, one thing is certain. Even after the Gulf War came to a successful military conclusion, constitutional scholars disagree on whether the President has the authority to employ American forces in a shooting war without the prior consent of Congress and its accompanying formal declaration of war. In spite of two hundred years of precedents in which many Presidents have done just that, an attitude has grown that warfare in modern times is unlike any military operations that ever existed in the past. According to this point of view, modern technology makes any use of force potentially nothing less than all-out war—and therefore, according to the Constitution, such decisions should rest with Congress.

Meanwhile, superimposed over these developments was a series of court cases in the 1980s and early 1990s which raised, among other issues, the questions of separation of powers, the conduct of foreign affairs, and the legitimate role of checks and balances in those areas. Traditionally the Supreme Court has viewed the conduct of foreign affairs as a political rather than a judicial matter, and has steered away from any litigation which, as one scholarly observer put it, "challenged the legality, the wisdom, or the propriety of the Commander-in-Chief in sending our armed forces abroad to any particular region." At the same time, in other cases dealing with domestic matters, the Court did not hesitate to strike down either Congressional or Presidential interference with practices rooted in the constitutional tradition of the separation of powers and supported by our history.

Some political observers have posited that the unsettling appearance of the President-Congress checks and balances arrangement may be nothing more than the by-product of normal American politics. During the post-Vietnam years, both houses of Congress have been dominated by the Democratic party; the Presidency, on the other hand, except for the one four-year term of Democrat Jimmy Carter, has been in the hands of the Republicans. Partisan politics, these observers suggest, has been at the root of so much of what has been called government "gridlock"—a term popularized by President Bush in decrying his own problems in getting along with Congress. The 1992 election resulted in the selection of a Democrat, Arkansas Governor Bill Clinton, along with a Congress in which Democrats controlled both the House and the Senate. Whether this will end "gridlock" and clarify some of the President-Congress checks and balances developments remains to be seen.

Nevertheless, the post-Vietnam years do seem to illustrate the need to clarify the responsibilities and limitations of both Congress and the Presidency in their ongoing check-and-balance relationship. Louis Fisher succinctly summarized the issue in his first-rate *Constitutional Conflicts Between Congress and the President* (Princeton University Press, 1985):

> Congressional influence depends on its willingness to act and take responsibility. A failure to act creates a vacuum into which Presidents can enter. . . . Presidential authority reaches its highest level when the President acts pursuant to congressional authorization. His power is at its lowest ebb when he takes measures incompatible with the will of Congress. But in between these categories [lies] a zone of twilight in which Congress neither grants nor denies authority. In such circumstances congressional inertia, indifference or quiescence may sometimes . . . enable, if not invite, measures on independent presidential responsibility.

Much, then, depends on the President and on who is in Congress, on who is willing and able to take responsibility, and in whom the people of the United States are willing to place their trust and confidence.

And so, after two centuries of Congress under the Constitution, a number of questions seem to beg for answers.

- Is Congress responsive enough to the needs and desires of the American people?
- What changes might be instituted to improve representation and representative government?
- How effective are the internal institutions of Congress—committees, legislative procedures, seniority, etc.?
- How well does our checks and balances system work?
- What have two hundred years of Congressional history taught us?

These, and many more, are questions which need to be further investigated and answered.

What do you think?

NOTES

1. Note, for instance, the outcry of "no taxation without representation" at the time of the Stamp Act in 1765. Since no Americans sat in Parliament, the colonists claimed that Parliament was violating a basic principle that no Englishman should be taxed without representation. Members of Parliament who understood representation to be "virtual" saw absolutely no merit to colonial protestations; as Parliament saw it, members who came from London represented Englishmen in Virginia and Massachusetts just as much as they represented their fellow countrymen in the British isles.

2. Along with the title "Representative," we also use the term "Congressman" or "Congresswoman" to apply to a member of the House of Representatives. One could argue that technically we could apply the latter titles to members of the Senate as well—but we use only the title "Senator" for those who are members of the "upper" house.

3. The Framers included all thirteen potential states. Rhode Island and North Carolina did not ratify the Constitution until after the new government had already gone into operation; but these numbers applied to their first allocation.

4. Sometimes, though, a popular candidate can win in spite of a gerrymander. William McKinley, for instance, overcame five different attempts by unfriendly Democratic-dominated Ohio legislatures to gerrymander his Congressional district. Not only did local voters sympathize with his plight, but it is also possible that the resultant publicity boosted his career to eventually becoming President of the United States.

THE PRESIDENCY

No person in our country wields more power than the President of the United States. Yet all the Constitution says in Article II is a simple: "The executive power shall be vested in a President of the United States of America."

That power derives from several sources; or, as some put it, the President wears several hats.

(1) He is first and foremost the nation's *chief executive.* Though Congress alone may pass laws, the President is responsible for carrying them out. Therefore the President's attitude toward a particular law becomes very important. This could be reflected in how he carries out Congressional legislation; for instance, he might emphasize some things and place not as much priority on others. Just because Congress passes a law—and even if the President signs it—doesn't necessarily mean that the President will implement the law fully the way Congress intended. He may have signed the law only to get some of its provisions; he might simply de-emphasize those parts which he doesn't care for.

In addition to wielding so much power in carrying out the laws of Congress, the President also has the authority, as chief executive, to issue what are called "executive orders." This generic term includes any rule or regulation issued by the President (or an office or administrator under his authority) which interprets or implements a provision of the Constitution or a law or treaty. Thus, Congress may create a particular agency, but its implementation and operation will depend upon the President and his agents.

(2) As *chief of state* and *ceremonial head of the nation,* the President is the only individual elected official who represents all Americans. (Of course, Congress *collectively* also represents all the people.) As the Supreme Court stated in *United States v. Curtiss-Wright Corporation* (299 U.S. 304 [1936]): "The President alone has the power to speak or listen as the representative of the nation."

(3) The President plays a prominent role in the *legislative process.* Through his annual State of the Union address and other messages, he recommends laws and programs for Congress to enact. Though only members of Congress can actually introduce bills, the impetus for most comes from the White House, and the President's influence over members of Congress largely determines the fate of those legislative proposals. The history of Congress is replete with instances of how Presidential leadership and lobbying—or lack of it—influenced the votes of individual members of both the House and the Senate, regardless of their party affiliation. Presidents who can get along with Congress, even if the Congress is controlled by the other party, and regardless how partisan each might be—and we have had many highly partisan Presidents and highly partisan Congresses—those Presidents demonstrate true political leadership in the legislative process. The President's veto power, or even the mere threat of it, often discourages action on

laws he does not want. He can summon Congress into special session to push for legislation he deems necessary. Though only the House of Representatives can introduce "money bills," the President proposes the annual budget, which by the 1990s had grown to astronomical figures. Our entire tax structure comes from Congressional laws, but the contents of those laws often reflects Presidential proposals and relations with Congress. Since budgetary and tax programs so strongly affect the American social and economic scene, the President's role in the legislative process assumes increased importance.

(4) The President has a role in the *judicial process*. He can issue pardons for certain offenses. Through his power to appoint all federal judges—from the lower district courts all the way up to the Supreme Court—he has a tremendous impact on the judicial and legal make-up of our country. Whether courts take a liberal or conservative stance often depends upon who the judges are, and the judges often reflect the political—and even the social and economic—bent of the President who appointed them. Federal judges hold office for life, and generally remain on the bench for many years after a President's term has expired. Thus, even after the President leaves office, his judicial appointees often continue to influence the law of the land for many years afterward. *U. S. News & World Report*, a credible and reputable weekly news journal, commenting on the large number of federal judges Presidents Ronald Reagan and George Bush had appointed in the 1980s and early 1990s—almost 70 percent of all sitting federal judges—reflected that their conservative appointees probably would influence American jurisprudence well into the twenty-first century.

(5) The President is the *chief administrator* of our government. He appoints the heads of the major departments, not only those of cabinet level but also many more who are responsible for the operation of almost every facet of the government and who affect the livelihood and living style of millions of American men, women, and children. The executive branch includes more than two million civil service appointees responsible for the day-to-day and person-to-person implementation of enormous numbers of federal rules and regulations. They range from forest rangers who protect our fish and wildlife resources, to air traffic controllers who watch over the flights of our jet airliners, to medical personnel who deal with nutritional problems of new-born infants.

(6) The President is *commander-in-chief of the armed forces*, in peacetime as well as in war. Presidents have utilized those forces to carry out both domestic law and foreign policy. Presidents Eisenhower, Kennedy, and Johnson, for instance, enforced racial integration with federal forces. Presidents have dispatched military forces abroad nearly two hundred times since 1789, sometimes after Congress declared war, but much more often in times of peace, without any declaration of war, to back up American foreign policy all over the world.

(7) The President is also the *chief diplomat* of the United States, and thus bears the responsibility of carrying out all of American foreign policy. Only he, or someone designated by him, can make treaties, although they must be ratified by two-thirds of the Senate. As nineteenth and twentieth century changes converted America from international isolationism to world leadership, the President's role and power in foreign affairs grew enormously, since it involved our crucial relations with the whole world, and especially (since World War II) the awesome responsibility for nuclear war.

(8) Presidential authority stems from still more sources, which many refer to as "unofficial" or "informal" or "extra Constitutional." As the leader of his political party, he wields immense influence in domestic affairs, including even matters of purely local concern. Presidents have endorsed candidates for governor or mayor or state treasurer, and often that support affected a purely local election. The President's informal influence over America's citizenry is virtually immeasurable. Some look to him as a father figure. Some look to him for moral leadership. Since the advent of radio and television, Presidents have used "fireside chat" techniques to come into millions of living rooms all over the country. Presidents and their families have influenced even hair styles, clothing styles, and entertainment patterns.

How have these powers and that influence developed? The starting point has to be the Constitution. What did the Framers intend when they drew up the Constitution in 1787? And are those intentions and concerns still valid two hundred years later?

The men who drew up the Constitution faced a serious dilemma. Colonial experiences which had brought on the American Revolution demonstrated the dangers of a central government and a chief executive so strong as to become a tyranny. George III and the British unitary form of government exemplified for the Framers all that could be evil in government. That is why when the colonists achieved freedom and set up their own independent state governments, they placed very little power in the state executives (governors). That is also why, when they established a national organization—the Articles of Confederation—they decentralized into a confederated form of government with no chief executive and with most authority in the individual states. True, there was a "President," but that was merely the title given to the presiding officer of the Congress. He had no real executive authority. Any measures passed by the Congress of the Articles of Confederation were put into effect not by the "President," but instead by either individuals or committees designated *ad hoc* for just that one purpose. Americans soon learned to their dismay that a central government with too little power resulted in national weakness and virtual anarchy. One extreme proved to be just as bad as the other.

The Framers of the Constitution therefore sought something in between: a central government with a strong executive—but not too strong. He must have sufficient power to do what had to be done. Wrote Alexander Hamilton in *Federalist No. 70*: "Energy in the executive is a leading character in the definition of good government. It is essential to the protection of the community against foreign attacks, ... to the steady administration of the laws, ... and to the security of liberty against the assaults of ambition, of faction, and of anarchy." But a "vigorous Executive" also must be subject to limitation lest he go too far. The Framers achieved this by incorporating into the Constitution the principle of "separation of powers," or, as it is commonly known, "checks and balances."

This principle allows the three branches of the government—the executive, the legislative, and the judicial—to operate harmoniously yet independently of each other. Governmental responsibilities are spread among all three, so that no one branch can exercise excessive power. At the same time, each branch is empowered by the Constitution to check the others if there is a threat to upset that balance. For example, Congress passes a bill, but the President might veto it (*i.e.,* Andrew Jackson's famous vetoes of the Maysville Road bill in 1830 and the bank bill in 1832.) Even if a President signs a bill, the courts still exercises "judicial review" to ensure constitutionality. Again there are many examples. In 1803 the Supreme Court, in the landmark *Marbury v. Madison*, declared part of the Judiciary Act of 1789 unconstitutional and thereby established the principle of judicial review. Half a century later the Civil War was pushed a step closer when the Supreme Court in the Dred Scott Case declared part of the Missouri Compromise unconstitutional. The President is empowered to make appointments and treaties, but they are subject to approval by the Senate. Illustrating this scenario is the Senate's rejection of the Treaty of Versailles following World War I, even though President Woodrow Wilson was one of that treaty's principal authors and had already signed it on behalf of the United States. And certainly a constant safeguard against executive abuse rests in the power of the House and Senate to impeach and convict a President for "bribery, treason, or other high crimes and misdemeanors." These are but some examples of how one branch of the government can prevent excesses by the others. The ultimate check, of course, lies in the people and the democratic power of the ballot box, to vote officials into or out of office.

With the check and balance principle incorporated into the Constitution, the Framers felt they had solved the dilemma regarding the chief executive; that is, a President with enough power to do what was necessary, but a mechanism under the separation of powers principle that ensured that he could not abuse his constitutional authority.

Even as the Framers incorporated that precept into the 1787 document, they did so within the parameters of yet another constitutional principle—the principle of flexibility. Indeed, perhaps one of the wisest decisions made by the Framers was not to try to solve all problems for all times. They knew the situations they faced then, in 1787, and what had brought them about. Of course they had to plan for the future, but they did so within reason; they made no pretentious attempts to anticipate all governmental relations which might arise in the future—because they did not know what the future might bring. They set down the basic principles and framework of government, but left it for future generations to adapt their specific situations to those principles and that framework—and to make whatever changes might be necessary when necessary.

From the very beginning, then, it became incumbent to define and re-define what Article II of the Constitution meant by the simple yet cryptic expression: "The executive power shall be vested in a President of the United States." As a result, over the past two hundred years that executive power has broadened considerably and that Presidency has grown proportionately stronger. Two important forces contributed.

(1) The first was the prevailing view of the role of the Presidency. Some saw it primarily as a "stewardship"; that is, once Congress passed the laws, the President carried them out, strictly according to the letter of the law. The Congress, after all, collectively represented the people and the states, and their wishes should prevail; the President's role was to carry out their collective wishes. He would employ the veto power only when absolutely necessary. Some felt, too, that a President might exercise only those powers expressly granted to him, and that to go beyond that violated his trust under the Constitution. According to this "stewardship" view, although the President was the leader of the country, his leadership must be exercised in somewhat modest and unassertive ways; anything more than that might tend toward executive tyranny. Calvin Coolidge, Herbert Hoover, and to a degree Dwight Eisenhower are good twentieth century examples of that "stewardship" view of the Presidency.

Much more prevalent, however, has been the broader and more flexible "leadership" view, that the President could exercise virtually any legitimate powers as long as they were not denied, either specifically in the Constitution or through the operation of the check and balance system. Since Washington's time, that "leadership" interpretation of the term "executive power" has resulted in a continuous increase and expansion of the powers of the Presidency.

(2) A second contributing factor, closely related to the first, has been what the courts and scholars often have termed as "times have changed." When Washington took the oath of office in 1789, he presided over a relatively small country consisting of the original thirteen Atlantic seaboard states and the trans-Appalachian wilderness extending to the Mississippi River. The nation's total population was about four million, predominantly homogeneous (white, Anglo-Saxon, Protestant), an overwhelming majority comprising a rural agricultural society physically isolated from the rest of the world. Since 1789 those circumstances changed gradually but drastically. Succeeding governments and Presidents faced conditions and problems altogether different from those which existed in Washington's time. To meet those new problems, powers once universally rejected became instead acceptable, on both the local and national levels, and especially in the Presidency. More on this later.

First, though, who can be President of the United States? The Framers mulled over many possible qualifications, because of their determination to prevent any chief executive from becoming a despot. Some thought a multiple executive advisable, each to deal with separate matters, and thus divide power. Some thought a life-time term advisable, to ensure stability. Some even considered creating an American monarchy and inviting friendly European royalty to the position. Most had no doubts, though, that George Washington would be the first chief executive—even those who preferred a king. Undoubtedly he was the role model for many of the Framers as they envisioned the office. But who would follow? In the end, the Framers listed only three qualifications: age, residency, and citizenship. They left it for future generations to add any others.

To be President, according to the Constitution, one must be at least thirty-five years of age. That ensures a certain maturity and experience. (At least it seemed to ensure those qualities in the late eighteenth century.) In actual fact, most Presidents have been in their fifties when they assumed office. Theodore Roosevelt and John F. Kennedy were in their early forties; six others, including recently elected Bill Clinton were in their middle or late forties. Dwight Eisenhower was the first to reach age 70 while still President. (William Henry Harrison was 68 when elected, but he died shortly after his inauguration.) The oldest person elected to the Presidency was Ronald Reagan, elected in 1980 at age 69 to his first term, and in 1984 at age 73 to his second term. He therefore holds the record, so to speak, as the oldest to serve as President. Somewhere in the fifties, though, seems to be the most preferable age.

Article II of the Constitution also requires that the President shall have been fourteen years "a resident within the United States." Does that mean fourteen *consecutive* years? Must that residency have been *just prior* to his election? And what does "within" mean? Both John Adams and Thomas Jefferson had been abroad in the 1780s, but in official capacities as ambassadors to England and France; obviously that did not disqualify them from being elected. All doubt disappeared in 1928 with the election of Herbert Hoover. He had been out of the country a good deal of that fourteen years (1914-1928) directing relief agencies in war-torn Europe. His election made it clear that the fourteen year residency did not have to be either consecutive or immediately prior to election.

The third stipulation in Article II is that the President must be "a natural born citizen, or a citizen of the United States at the time of the adoption of the Constitution." Most people have taken the term "natural born" to mean "native born"; in fact, a reading of the records of the Constitutional Convention seems to justify that. Still, some have wondered—and not by any means frivolously— whether so-called "test tube babies" or persons born by cesarean section are "natural born." Questions have been raised too about a baby born to American parents in a foreign country. Such a person would be an American citizen, but could that person become President? Those questions really are unanswerable and probably would have to await an actual situation in which such a person is actually elected—and some sort of case is brought to the Supreme Court challenging that person's right under the Constitution to the office. The chances are much more likely that because of the Constitutional question involved, no political party would take the chance of nominating such a person in the first place.

Equally fascinating is the eligibility requirement that one must have been a citizen at the time of the adoption of the Constitution. Today, of course, two hundred years later, that provision is moot; all Presidents since William Henry Harrison have been native born in the United States. All before him, though, were born here before there was a United States; they were at least "native born" (or "natural born"). Many historians feel, though, that the provision was put into the Constitution specifically so that Alexander Hamilton would be eligible one day to become President. Though many at the Constitutional Convention resented Hamilton's imperiousness and almost anti-democratic attitudes, they nevertheless recognized in him, as had George Washington during the Revolutionary War and after, a man of great ability. But Hamilton had been born in Bermuda, the illegitimate son of a spirited and beautiful bar-maid, the father reputed to have been a British officer. By making someone qualified who was a citizen of the United States when the Constitution was adopted, the Framers made Hamilton eligible.

Though the Constitution still contains only those three qualifications, the American people have from time to time established other informal and extra-Constitutional requirements. For years one had to be a Protestant white male. His

Catholic religion was a significant factor—although certainly not the only one—in Al Smith's defeat in 1928. In 1960, however, an election year in which religion played a very prominent role, John F. Kennedy became the first Catholic to win the Presidency. A Black, a Jew, a Hispanic, a Native American (Indian), or a woman have yet to attain that position. In 1984 Geraldine Ferraro was nominated as the Democratic candidate for Vice President; although she lost, many feel that at least the sex barrier now has come down. Following the debacles of the post Civil War Grant era, public opinion insisted that no professional military man should ever again be President. That changed in 1952, when the American electorate chose the extremely popular Dwight D. Eisenhower, military hero of World War II. "Political availability" includes characteristics such as a photogenic family, a good speaking voice, and especially (in this age of electronic communication) a good television presence. Observers have even suggested, perhaps cynically but certainly not without some justification, that what counts most now in getting elected is not who or what one *really* is or believes, but rather how one communicates to the voters a favorable *image* of who or what he (or she) is or believes. Not without some justification was President Ronald Reagan, one of the most popular Presidents in modern times, called "the great communicator."

In addition to concern over the qualifications of the President, the Framers deliberated at great length also over the length of his service. Proposals ranged from a brief two-year term to election for life; they settled finally on the four-year term. The Constitution says nothing, however, about the number of terms, leaving it up to the people to re-elect a President as often as they wish. But George Washington chose to retire after a second term, and when his successors chose to do the same, a two-term tradition became as established as though written in law. Several Presidents later challenged the tradition, but unsuccessfully. Ulysses S. Grant was denied the nomination for a third term. Theodore Roosevelt also sought a third term, claiming correctly that his "first term" really had been only the completion of the unexpired term of assassinated William McKinley. Roosevelt was nominated, but the voters nevertheless refused to break the two-term tradition. Finally, in 1940, with World War II under way in Europe and many Americans fearful that we would be drawn into it soon, voters elected Franklin D. Roosevelt to a third term, and in 1944 to a fourth term, primarily because they did not want to "change horses in midstream." But after Roosevelt died and the war ended, the Twenty-Second Amendment was proposed (1947) and ratified (1951). It was clearly a reaction to Roosevelt's four elections, which many felt violated the spirit of the Constitution although certainly not its actual provisions. Since 1951, then, the President has been limited by the Constitution to just two terms. (In 1986 a move began in several Republican circles to repeal the Twenty-Second Amendment and thereby pave the way for Ronald Reagan, a very popular President, to run for a third term. The movement never really got off the ground, because of the widespread innate sympathy for the two-term tradition.)

This essay intentionally omits two important events in the saga of the Presidency: how that person is nominated in the first place and how that person is elected. Though they are consummate democratic procedures, both nomination and election are exceedingly complex and at times confusing processes—involving such institutions as caucuses, primaries, proportional representation, direct and indirect voting, the electoral college, and other diverse and poorly-understood political institutions. Just to add to the confusion is the following: a presidential election is not really a national election; it is fifty different state elections plus another in the District of Columbia. Our country goes through a quadrennial journalistic and educational exercise every election year when virtually every newspaper, news magazine, radio and television news organization, and any other agency which feels up to it undertakes to explain, with diagrams and illustrations, just how the process unfolds. The reader is directed to any of them. One who follows these activities step by step cannot but help wonder how something so complicated can work. But it does! Every four years we hear that something must be done to simplify the procedure or make it more fair—but every four years nothing happens. And for good reason: the American people have been satisfied with their Presidents—even when some have been elected (as is often the case) with fewer than a majority of the popular vote. So if many do not understand *how* the system works, they are at least satisfied that it *does* work. Why, then, tamper with success? Or, as that great American sage Casey Stengel once said—or was it Yogi Berra—"If it ain't broke, why fix it?"

What has been the record of Presidents produced by this complex and confusing electoral procedure? The metamorphosis in presidential power began almost at once, during the administration of the very first President. George Washington stamped permanently upon the office the mark of his own personal dignity and respect. He could have adopted a monarchy-type configuration comparable with other chief executives of his time; instead, he never stretched the constraints of democratic constitutionalism. As President he prescribed and was accorded proper deference; yet he remained personally no more than an American gentleman. He rode in a yellow carriage adorned with gilded cupids and his own coat of arms, a ritual pomp commensurate with his rank as chief of state. His executive mansions—first on Cherry Street in New York and later on High Street in Philadelphia—were staffed by fourteen white servants and seven Black slaves, all duly powdered and liveried. This patrician aristocrat icily stared down anyone who presumed to open a conversation without proper introduction, or dared express excessive cordiality. Yet this same patrician aristocrat also insisted upon weekly afternoon receptions and levees so he might have the opportunity to hear from the "common man." So, too, did Mrs. Washington hold periodic open house receptions for females.

No precedent set by George Washington ranks more important than his use of federal troops in 1794 to put down the so-called "Whiskey Rebellion." Defiant farmers and distillers in western Pennsylvania refused to abide by a new federal excise tax on whiskey. Although himself a colonial revolutionist only a decade or so earlier, President Washington looked with alarm at what he now considered an unreasonable anarchist insurrection. Encouraged by Secretary of the Treasury Alexander Hamilton, Washington called up the militia of several states. Nearly 15,000 volunteers responded—more than Washington had ever led for most of the American Revolution! The President even accompanied the troops part of the way—Hamilton led them all the way. Overawed by the staggering response to Washington's willingness to use force, the Pennsylvania resistance collapsed. With an eye to conciliation and peaceful settlement, Washington wisely minimized punishment and retribution.

The Whiskey Rebellion made patently clear that the President, as commander-in-chief, could and would use armed forces, if necessary, even in peacetime, to enforce domestic policy. That precedent legitimized similar Presidential action in many ensuing domestic crises. In 1861, for instance, Abraham Lincoln called up federal troops to suppress secession and to preserve the Union. Indeed, the Civil War never was a declared "war." When the Confederates fired on Fort Sumter, President Lincoln proclaimed that the execution of federal law was being obstructed "by combinations too powerful to be suppressed by the ordinary course of judicial proceedings." Therefore he called for militia to suppress insurrection just as Washington had done in 1794. Both Congress and the Supreme Court later legitimized Lincoln's action. In 1894, President Grover Cleveland quelled union activities which interfered with the United States mail. In the 1950s and 1960s Presidents Eisenhower and Kennedy marshaled federal forces to ensure court-ordered racial integration. Many more examples could be cited.

Presidents used their power as commander-in-chief not only to enforce domestic policy. They did the same *vis-à-vis* foreign policy and American interests abroad, not only in war time, but also in peace time. Thomas Jefferson sent American forces to North Africa to counter aggressive action there by Barbary pirates and terrorists endangering American interests and citizens. No declaration of war was made. Certainly we are aware of American westward expansion and our relations with the Indian inhabitants of our continent. Many wars were fought; not a single one was declared. Presidents Taft and Wilson sent Marines into

Central America to protect American interests there. Since World War II every President has stationed troops virtually all over the world—in Europe, in the Far East, in Southeast Asia, in the Mid-East, in the Caribbean—to support American foreign policy, and especially to "contain" any further spread of communist influence. One of the most volatile and divisive experiences in American history resulted from our involvement in Vietnam in the 1960s and 1970s. Though some bitterly protested against an "illegal war," most opponents of our military intervention objected not to the legal authority of the President to take such action, but rather to the wisdom of doing so—that it was an unwise foreign policy, that human and other expenditures being poured into the conflict could be much more beneficially and profitably utilized to meet a variety of domestic problems, etc. Nevertheless, as commander-in-chief, the President has the responsibility and authority to employ the armed forces, in peace as in war, to carry out American policy.

Presidents have committed American forces not only because of American foreign policy, but also to support United Nations policy. (Of course, no President would take such action unless he felt strongly that such action was also in accord with our own national interests.) Thus in 1950 President Harry S. Truman ordered American armed forces to repel Communist North Korean invasion of South Korea, and in 1990-1991 President George Bush sent American troops into the Persian Gulf area to reverse the Iraqi conquest of oil-rich Kuwait. In both instances our armed forces fought full-fledged wars. In both instances, however, these were not wars declared by Congress, but American forces sent by the President to implement United Nations policies—which were also considered as being in our national interest. (In both instances, although Congress did not declare war, it took other measures indicating strong support for the Presidents' actions.)

As a matter of fact, Congress has declared war only five times in American history: the War of 1812, the Mexican War (1846), the Spanish-American War (1898), World War I (1917), and World War II (1941). All other uses of force to implement American foreign policy—ranging from John Tyler's dispatching a warship to defend Texas even before it was part of the United States to George Bush ordering a huge military machine into full-fledged action in "Operation Desert Storm" against Iraq emanated solely from the President's power as commander-in-chief.

Executive power expanded from much more than the early precedents of our chief executive as commander-in-chief. Political parties were not too clearly defined during the years that Washington and John Adams served as President. But under Thomas Jefferson and his successors up to the Civil War, especially Andrew Jackson, the political potentialities of the office emerged and grew dramatically. Historians have labeled the first half of the nineteenth century as the age of "Jeffersonian and Jacksonian democracy." It was an era of expansion into the frontier, of population amalgamation, and of conflicting forces of both nationalism and sectionalism. It was an era, too, of romanticism, of reform, and of rapidly expanding democracy—social democracy, economic democracy, and political democracy. Eighteenth century society dominated by upper-class aristocracies gave way to a new society characterized by a democratically oriented middle class, the farmer, and the laborer. Political parties thrived in such an environment, and Presidents from Jefferson on utilized their office as a strong force in American partisan politics. Much though Jefferson was a partisan-oriented President, it was probably Andrew Jackson, more than any others, who molded the political power of the Presidency through institutional innovations such as the spoils system and rotation in office. But others, including Jefferson, Martin Van Buren, John Tyler, and James Knox Polk, were also astute party powers. With the growth of the frontier spirit of democracy, with the development of the national party conventions, and with the proliferation of newspapers, Presidents associated themselves directly with the masses of the people and with a national constituency. Andrew Jackson showed so much executive strength that his opponents dubbed him "King Andrew I." His enormous popularity enabled him to prevail over such diverse opposition as powerful banking interests and nullification sectionalists.

Two more purely executive actions in the early nineteenth century merit attention in how they added to Presidential power and prestige. One was the Louisiana Purchase in 1803, when Thomas Jefferson added a huge territory to the United States, almost doubling it in size. It started out as an offer to Napoleon to purchase New Orleans in order to alleviate shipping burdens of western farmers; it suddenly became an unprecedented bargain when the French government offered the whole of French Louisiana. Jefferson's supporters, overwhelmingly strict consructionists of the Constitution, questioned the legality of his proposed action, and urged the passage first of a constitutional amendment specifically granting to the President the power to purchase land. But the rapidly deteriorating relations between England and France predicated that time was running out on this unusual bargain, because amending the Constitution would take too long. Strict constructionist Jefferson readily adopted a broad and liberal interpretation of the term "executive power." His action opened the door for later Presidents to do the same.

The other landmark executive action of the early nineteenth century was the Monroe Doctrine. It consisted of a series of separate but related foreign-affairs policies enunciated by James Monroe in his 1823 message to Congress. The Western Hemisphere was closed to new colonization by any European power, declared the President, and "we should consider any attempt on their part to extend their system to any portion of this hemisphere as dangerous to our peace and safety." In addition, we would look upon any interference by a European power in the internal affairs of existing countries in the Western Hemisphere "as the manifestation of an unfriendly disposition toward the United States." For our part, continued the President, we would not interfere in the internal affairs of European countries. In 1823 the United States lacked the power to enforce the non-colonization and noninterference dicta, and even President Monroe realized that any realistic restraints depended almost wholly upon British policy and the British navy. By the end of the Civil War, however, that changed, as the United States burst onto the world scene as a potent military power. As the directors of American foreign policy, Presidents of the late nineteenth and early twentieth centuries utilized the Monroe Doctrine to broaden executive authority far beyond anything James Monroe had ever conceived.

The Civil war was a major landmark in American history for many reasons. One was its impact upon the Presidency. As we have seen, the power of the Presidency already had grown from Washington's time to Lincoln's. Now it reached a new peak. Undoubtedly the crisis of secession and civil war created unusual and extraordinary circumstances which called for drastic measures. Nevertheless, Lincoln viewed the role of the President almost simplistically: his job was to preserve the Union. He had sworn—the President's oath of office is found in Article II of the Constitution—not only to "faithfully execute the Office of President of the United States," but also, to the best of his ability, to "preserve, protect and defend the Constitution of the United States." That he did. And in the process he created a newer and more powerful Presidency. To some he was a virtual dictator who exceeded his authority, often violating constitutional rights behind the pretense of preserving the Union—as, for instance, when he suspended the right of *habeas corpus*. Some view the landmark Emancipation Proclamation as a great and glorious beacon of freedom; others see it as cynical political fluff that was all proclamation and no emancipation, an instrument of expediency for purely political motives.

Yet Lincoln did develop new powers through creative and imaginative interpretations of existing constitutional authority, adding to powers and precedents which previous Presidents had exercised—as, for instance, his use of the confiscation power and his centralization of so much authority in the hands of the federal government. Ironically, John Wilkes Booth inadvertently may have helped the historic justification of Lincoln's use (or abuse) of Presidential power. Most Americans think of Lincoln as the paragon of liberty and human rights, the noble "father of freedom" glorified in marble in the magnificent Lincoln Memorial in Washington, D. C. They overlook that the living President Lincoln faced harsh criticism and extremely bitter opposition throughout his entire Presidency. Opposition political cartoonists had a hey-day thanks to the President's tall and gangly physique; they often caricatured him as a long-legged and long-armed baboon type. But the brutal assassination at Ford's Theater suddenly made Lincoln a martyr. It stilled the detractors and critics of his questionable constitutional practices, and indelibly glorified Lincoln and justified his measures as savior of the Union.

In the period following the Civil War—the Reconstruction Era—there was an effort to restore the earlier balance between Congress and the President, to reduce Presidential authority, and to increase Congressional power. Much of that resulted from the fact that Lincoln's successor, Andrew Johnson, was a southerner (Tennessee) who sought to reconcile North and South as painlessly as possible—as Lincoln had hoped to do—in the face of a Congress controlled by the so-called "Radical Republicans" whose motives verged very close to revenge for the past four years of bloodshed. The high point here was the impeachment of Andrew Johnson in the House of Representatives and the razor-thin failure (by only one vote) in the Senate to remove him from office.

But during that same post-war era of the late nineteenth century, other developments altered the overall role of the national government, and with it the role of the Presidency.

Most fundamental was the transformation of the United States from its earlier small eastern seaboard, rural agricultural society. The westward movement—"manifest destiny"—created a nation from the Atlantic to the Pacific. By 1890 the Superintendent of the Census announced the disappearance of the frontier as our population expanded from its original four million to about seventy-five million, and would exceed a hundred million by World War I. A population and way of life that had been overwhelmingly rural agricultural became more and more urban industrial. The mass immigration of the late nineteenth century converted a population which had been predominantly homogeneous into a multiethnic and multicultural people. By the beginning of the twentieth century, the Industrial Revolution and all its ramifications inexorably and dramatically had transformed the United States from what it had been at the time of the adoption of the Constitution into something quite different.

With those outward physical changes came a major modification in the American view toward government. It was an outgrowth of the broad liberal progressive thinking that emerged to meet some of the negative aspects of the Industrial Revolution—the overcrowding, the poverty, the inequitable distribution of wealth and resources, health and education problems, and similar social and economic inequities. Thomas Jefferson's contemporaries and political philosophy had viewed oppressive government as the greatest threat to human freedom. Freedom to live the fullest life meant that people must be free from government restriction. Government should exercise only those delegated powers which were absolutely necessary, and it should never stand in the way of individual interests. That was at the core of eighteenth century Enlightenment thinking. The Industrial Revolution, however, created new forces which threatened human liberty, forces such as unbridled industry and wealth, big business and labor monopolies, and similar vested interests. Believers in democracy came to feel that a democratic government controlled by the people was the only institution capable of dealing with such powerful industrial forces. Where before freedom inferred freedom *from* government, now it became freedom *through* government. And since the President was the elected head of that government, his position demanded concomitant power and authority.

Thus a Theodore Roosevelt intervened dramatically in the coal strike of 1902, and he and William Howard Taft involved the Presidency and the government in a series of widely publicized activities ranging from antitrust suits to national parks and conservation projects. Roosevelt and Taft and Wilson spearheaded a progressive movement which instituted socio-economic reforms ranging from working hours and conditions to food and medicine labeling to major federal reserve bank reforms. Out of the Industrial Revolution, then, came fundamental modifications in domestic America, including a new role for the national government as well as for the President as the head of that government. Practices and powers which nineteenth century Presidents would never have exercised became more and more acceptable as the country moved into the twentieth century.

The same was true in American foreign policy. During the nineteenth century American foreign relations, directed by the President, were based primarily upon a triad of three interrelated concepts:

(1) First was isolation. We were separated physically from the rest of the world by water, and because of the time and distance between us and other countries of the world, we would have as little as possible to do with them—outside of normal trade relations—and their political problems. By the "rest of the world" we meant mainly Europe, or "western" civilization. Africa, Latin America, and Asia were still considered backward areas with whom our relations centered almost entirely on trade—sources of raw materials and markets for our manufactured goods. Isolationism was a policy enunciated and recommended by George Washington in his famous "Farewell Address"—that we should make no foreign alliances and steer clear of any foreign entanglements—and it made good sense for a long time, considering our physical separation from the rest of the world.

(2) Second was westward expansion, or "manifest destiny." Impelled by the Louisiana Purchase, American efforts aimed at a nation extending from the Atlantic to the Pacific. We had lots of land that could be filled by lots of people who could grow and raise lots of products. That focused American foreign energies toward Mexico and the Indians. Thus, except for trade and immigration, we virtually turned our backs on Europe and faced westward.

(3) Clearly related to isolationism and "manifest destiny" was the third leg of America's nineteenth century foreign policy, the Monroe Doctrine. As indicated above, it meant that European states should not interfere with the western hemisphere and that we would not interfere with Europe's problems.

Thus nineteenth century American foreign policy, except in the areas of westward expansion, remained fairly passive, and Presidents could devote most of their efforts to matters within the country, while their secretaries of state dealt with foreign affairs.

That changed by the end of the nineteenth century, as a result of the same Industrial Revolution which transformed domestic America. Technological changes in transportation and communication reduced the time and space barriers that the oceans had once provided. American industries expanded rapidly after the Civil War. More than ever they needed resources and markets abroad, not only in Europe but everywhere else in the world. What had been an isolated United States began the inexorable movement toward becoming part of a global village.

The Spanish-American War in 1898 signaled the beginning of that change, and within two decades World War I brought it home forcefully. In 1796 George Washington's Farewell Address had extolled the virtues of isolationism and warned against the dangers of entangling alliances. In 1919 Woodrow Wilson personally led the American delegation to Europe, where he advocated American leadership in both the Treaty of Versailles and in the international association it created, the League of Nations.

But the United States nostalgically clung to the century-old dream of isolationism. Rejecting Wilson's leadership, we refused to join the League of Nations. The decade of the 1920s also saw Presidents Harding, Coolidge, and Hoover abandon the domestic leadership of the progressive Teddy Roosevelt, Taft, and Wilson, hoping instead to revive the "normalcy" of earlier less complicated times, with Presidents who were stewards rather than leaders.

Then came the traumatic 1930s, with the Great Depression and the onset of World War II. Forces in both domestic and foreign affairs converged in the Presidency of Franklin Delano Roosevelt, and solidified earlier developments to expand and strengthen the role of both the national government and of the President.

Domestically, the New Deal became the forerunner of decades of programs through which the federal government championed a variety of causes such as social security, minimum wages, public housing, and numerous other social and economic benefits programs.

In foreign affairs, the threat of American survival brought on by European military dictators, culminating in World War II, saw more and more power exercised by the President as commander-in-chief to preserve the nation. Some equated Roosevelt in World War II with Abraham Lincoln in the Civil War. By the end of the war in 1945, especially with the development of the atom bomb, the United States had emerged as the most powerful country in the world. Many considered the President, as leader of that country, the most powerful individual in the world.

During earlier crises, especially in the Civil War and World War I, the country had accepted—even demanded—expanding executive leadership and authority. But once those crises had passed, those powers dissipated, and the Presidents' roles had reverted more toward stewardship than strong leadership. Thus we find in the post-Civil War 1870s and 1880s Presidents such as Grant, Hayes, Garfield, and Arthur, none of whom are known as dynamic leaders. The same applies to post-World War I Harding, Coolidge, and Hoover.

But it was different after the Great Depression and World War II. There were two main reasons, one related to foreign affairs and the other to domestic affairs.

The United States emerged from World War II as one of the great powers of the world. Isolationism became a thing of the past, as we became a founder and one of the leaders of the United Nations, and a leader in fostering world-wide recovery from the trauma and horrors of the war. But so, too, did the Soviet Union emerge as a major world power. The two had been allies during the war against a common enemy, Nazi Germany. The war over, the deep differences between the United States and the Soviet Union became apparent, in their domestic philosophies and in their foreign policies. The result was the division of the world into what was called the Free World, with the United States as its leader, the Communist World, with the Soviet Union as its leader, and the Third World, whose countries attempted to remain neutral and non-aligned, at least nominally.

This confrontation between the United States and the Soviet Union since 1945 was called the "Cold War," in contrast with a "hot" or "shooting" war. In this Cold War both sides confronted each other on numerous issues, but none so hazardous and potentially dangerous as armaments. Since both sides possessed huge arsenals of nuclear weapons, the fear of a nuclear holocaust prevented the outbreak of war directly between the two major powers. But it did not prevent war among their surrogates. Bloody fighting erupted in Korea, Vietnam, Afghanistan, the Middle East, Central America, and Africa, all referred to as "conventional wars" because nuclear weaponry was never employed. Yet the fear that nuclear weapons might become involved remained a constant nightmare.

With the international scene in such an unstable condition and the fate of the whole world almost always in a precarious balance, it became imperative that the Presidents have the authority to make necessary decisions and take appropriate actions for American defense. Accordingly, following World War II, rather than experiencing a regression of Presidential power and influence (as after earlier crises), we saw them expand during the Cold War. Virtually every President since the end of World War II faced serious international crises: Truman with a Europe and Japan which had been decimated by World War II, then the Berlin Blockade and war in Korea; Eisenhower with Mid-East and Lebanese crises; Kennedy with the Cuban missile crisis; Johnson with Vietnam; Nixon in Vietnam and the Mid-East; Ford in the Mid-East; Carter and the Iranian hostage crisis and the USSR-Afghanistan war; Reagan in Lebanon, Grenada, and Central America; and Bush in Panama and the Persian Gulf. Additional crises were instigated periodically by the spread of international terrorism through ruthless and unscrupulous political and religious groups.

Hanging over all these was the constant danger of a nuclear holocaust should someone make a mistake in judgment or action, whether on our side or the other side. Accordingly, more and more responsibility fell on the Presidents, not only to make the right decisions, but to have the authority to enforce that responsibility. Thus, instead of the Presidency tending toward a stewardship, it assumed more and more leadership and authority due to an almost constant state of international crisis. (What the collapse of communism and the breakup of the Soviet Union might bring about—well, that is in the future and no one could possibly predict what the future might bring.)

In one area of foreign relations especially did Presidential authority expand at the expense of both Congress and the check and balance system. Prior to the twentieth century our relations with foreign countries usually were conducted through treaty arrangements. Treaties, according to the Constitution, are made by the President but must be ratified by two-thirds of the Senate. In the twentieth century, however, the device known as the "executive agreement" became more and more popular. Especially since the 1920s, Presidents found executive agreements to be just as binding as treaties, much more expedient to negotiate, and without the political roadblocks of Senate constraints. Executive agreements are simply agreements made between heads of state, many of whom (in other countries) are not at all responsible to a legislature. This procedure allowed Presidents unprecedented freedom and latitude in conducting foreign relations. The result has been more Presidential power and influence in foreign affairs than ever before, especially since a President can often bypass the Senate.

The Cold War and related international crises were not the only factors which contributed to increasing Presidential power after World War II. Also significant were the many domestic crises which demanded strong Presidential leadership.

The New Deal of the 1930s merely opened the door to the progressive notion that the federal government must help raise the socio-economic level of the great mass of America's citizenry; or, as the Preamble to the Constitution states, to promote the general welfare. That philosophy became codified national policy with the passage of the Employment Act of 1946, passed with the overwhelming approval of both parties, which declared "that it is the continuing policy and responsibility of the Federal Government to use all practicable means . . . to promote maximum employment, production, and purchasing power." The Fair Deal, the New Republicanism, and the Great Society represented programs of both Democratic and Republican Presidents that built on the New Deal and affected the social and economic relations of millions of American citizens: social security programs, programs involving medical care, housing, education, farm production, factory output, forest and river usage, programs involving the infant and the aged—programs which affected virtually every community in the land. The decades following World War II also saw unprecedented changes in civil rights, race relations, and human equality, including desegregation, women's rights, and equal employment opportunities. In all these areas the national government played a prominent role, with Presidential leadership and influence leading the way, as states either could not or would not assume the costs and burdens of carrying out those functions. For these reasons in domestic matters, as well as the international developments, Americans looked for and welcomed leadership and strength in the Presidency.

All this expansion of Presidential power was not without its critics. Many felt Congress should have more of a say in making policy and in setting priorities, whether domestically or in foreign affairs. A spreading conservatism argued that the states should direct the many domestic programs which the federal government and the Presidency were pushing, or even that many programs were not even the responsibility of any government. At the same time, liberal and pacifist elements feared that Presidents were pushing too aggressively in international matters and they sought to constrict their foreign powers.

Nevertheless, the decades of the 1950s and 1960s produced achievements that can be described only as remarkable. In medicine they included polio vaccine and organ transplants. Microchips revolutionized computer technology. Human beings walked in space and on the surface of the moon. So much seemed within reach: the end of hunger and poverty, universal human dignity, world peace. Yet they remained elusively unattainable, and hope gave way to frustration. Perhaps nothing burst the bubble of optimism more than the assassinations of President John F. Kennedy, his brother Robert Kennedy, and civil rights champion Dr. Martin Luther King, Jr.

Matters came to a traumatic head in the 1970s during the Presidency of Richard M. Nixon. Once more developments in both foreign and domestic fields proved critical.

The key factor in foreign affairs was the war in Vietnam. Although successful in avoiding a direct nuclear confrontation with the Soviet Union and with Communist China, the United States had become involved, since the end of World War II, either directly or indirectly, in other forms of conflicts, including so-called "conventional" wars. In none of these was war ever declared by Congress; nevertheless, Presidents (as commander-in-chief) sent troops into combat (as did Truman in the case of Korea) or into near-combat (as did Eisenhower in Lebanon).

But the most controversial was the use of American forces in Southeast Asia, in the so-called Vietnam War. Lacking a declaration of war by Congress, Presidents who sent troops into combat always risked criticism at home from both friend and foe. But never was the country more divided than over our involvement in Vietnam—and there had been considerable opposition in earlier days during the War of 1812, the Mexican War, and World War I. Our involvement in Vietnam can be traced as far back as the 1940s and World War II, but it reached its peak during the administrations of Lyndon Johnson and Richard Nixon in the late 1960s and early 1970s. More than half a million members of the American armed forces engaged in full-scale combat, with extremely heavy casualties—and yet no consensus existed to explain why. Because American war aims were so muddled and unclear, public pressure forced President Johnson finally to institute peace moves in preparation for withdrawal; he even decided not to run for a second term so he could bring the fighting to some sort of end. But when his successor directed certain actions which convinced large numbers of Americans that he was not disengaging, a ground-swell of anti-war dissent soon became a concerted movement to impeach President Nixon.

Coinciding with the impeachment movement that stemmed from President Nixon's handling of the Vietnam situation was another ground swell for impeachment over an explosive domestic crisis. The detailed facts of the "Watergate Affair" cannot be told here; suffice it to say that many accused Nixon of exceeding and abusing his powers as President and of undermining basic constitutional freedoms and processes. One of his severest critics, historian Arthur Schlesinger,

Jr., author of *The Imperial Presidency,* likened the growth and misuse of American Presidential power to the evils of the ancient Roman imperial system. The term "imperial presidency" vividly expressed the widespread fears that Nixon had finally crossed that invisible line drawn by the Framers of the Constitution. When the House Judiciary Committee approved articles of impeachment in 1974, Nixon resigned, the first and only President ever to do so.

Nixon's resignation was a watershed in the development of Presidential powers. Critical issues in foreign and domestic affairs did not disappear after 1974, but Presidents have acted with much more restraint and discretion. The mere threat of impeachment apparently had its effect. Also, in the 1970s Congress passed the War Powers Act and the National Emergencies Act, measures which struck at the root of the imperial presidency by involving Congress more directly in foreign affairs. These measures later were augmented by others, including the National Security Act (1980), the Arms Export Control Act (1985), and the Intelligence Authorization Assistance Act (1986), among others, all intended to restrain a President from actions which might involve the United States in unpopular or unwanted overseas adventures, and to give Congress a more important voice in our foreign relations.

Interestingly, though, considerable controversy exists whether those acts are indeed constitutional. Two hundred years of American history have piled up considerable precedent that the President, as commander-in-chief, has the authority to dispatch American armed forces to carry out our foreign policy. One may disagree with the *wisdom* of such foreign policy—but does that make it unconstitutional? Presidents since Nixon have taken steps in foreign affairs, but none have invoked any of those acts which would require the President to report to or seek permission from Congress; indeed many—Presidents and others—have expressed the opinion publicly that they consider those acts to be unconstitutional. Nor has Congress invoked those acts to limit the hands of the Presidents. The nearest we came to that was in late 1990 and early 1991, right after Iraq conquered Kuwait in the Persian Gulf and we were poised to institute hostilities against Iraq. A remarkable debate occurred in Congress then, over whether we should follow a policy of immediate hostilities or first an economic blockade to force Saddam Hussein to back down from his conquest. Although the close vote endorsed the use of force, at no time did the debate specifically entail the issues raised in the above-mentioned resolutions and laws. (This might suggest that even those who opposed the immediate use of force in the Persian Gulf did so from the point of view of policy disagreement rather than over constitutionality.)

All Presidents since Nixon have had to face the harsh realities of international developments. The Cold War continued unabated until 1990, when communism dramatically collapsed in the Soviet Union and its satellites, and that super-power almost overnight retreated from what we considered its international adventurism. Arms control remained as tough an issue as ever, however, especially with the advent of laser and space technology which brought about so-called "Star Wars" possibilities. International terrorism continued, and activities associated with countries like Iran and Libya, and perhaps others, led many to believe the notion of state-sponsored terrorism.

Well aware of the Vietnam and "imperial presidency" syndromes, American Presidents still had to face their responsibilities. Thus President Ford used armed forces to evacuate refugees from Vietnam and Cambodia, and to rescue the American merchant vessel *Mayaguez* from Cambodian pirates. President Carter dispatched a military mission in an unsuccessful attempt to rescue more than fifty Americans held hostage for several years by Iranian extremists. President Reagan deployed troops into Lebanon, even in the midst of a bloody civil war raging there, and those troops sustained extremely heavy casualties at the hands of suicide terrorists. Reagan also sent American forces into the Caribbean island of Grenada, to overthrow a Marxist government there. When he became convinced that Libya was behind certain acts of international terrorism which resulted in the loss of American lives, President Reagan authorized a bombing mission against Libya in retaliation.

A highly controversial development in foreign affairs—because it was considered by many serious enough to raise the specter of another Watergate-type scandal—was the so-called "Irangate," an incredible series of clandestine happenings involving illicit sales of arms to terrorist Iran and secret transfers of money to "contra" anti-communist forces in Central America. A storm of controversy threatened to convulse a Reagan Presidency from one of almost unprecedented popularity into one hampered seriously by loss of integrity and confidence. Reagan survived the near disaster, but his Vice-President and successor, George Bush, later had to face some fallout.

Most foreign problems which plagued post-World War II Presidents were underscored by the Cold War and our determination to prevent the spread of communism and communist influence: our policy of "containment" instituted under President Truman. But in 1990, after almost seventy-five years of police state power, the communist dictatorship collapsed in the Soviet Union. (This essay is not the place to evaluate whether that collapse resulted from external American pressures or from internal domestic forces; probably both contributed.) The Soviet Union itself broke apart into a number of newly-proclaimed and newly-named sovereign states. The Berlin Wall came down, and communist governments collapsed throughout the former Soviet satellites in Europe—although those in other parts of the globe, including China and Cuba, remained intact.

Nevertheless, President George Bush found it necessary to use armed forces in foreign affairs even though now no longer focused on containing communism. In 1989 he unilaterally ordered the invasion of Panama to overthrow dictator Manuel Noriega, reputedly responsible for widespread drug traffic. In 1990 Iraq conquered oil-rich Kuwait. With dictator Saddam Hussein threatening the world's Mid-East oil supply, the United Nations took measures to expel Iraq from Kuwait. President Bush led in organizing the United Nations coalition which in 1991 undertook "Operation Desert Storm," an all-out military operation which drove Iraqi forces from Kuwait. Just prior to the outbreak of hostilities, Congress engaged in an unprecedented debate over whether military force or economic sanctions was the desirable immediate approach to deal with Iraq. The consensus, although by a narrow margin, was force; yet Congress did not declare war. In fact, neither Congress nor the President formally invoked any of the above-mentioned legislation limiting the President's power to take military action without Congressional approval. The great success of "Desert Storm"—especially when casualties proved to be far fewer than feared—undoubtedly quelled any potential post-war criticism of excessive use of Presidential power in handling foreign affairs. From the constitutional point of view, then, President Bush's handling of "Desert Storm" was no different from the action taken by President Truman in Korea: the United States, as a member of the United Nations, carried out the mandate of the United Nations—which was to liberate Kuwait from Iraq—and the President helped carry out that mandate through his authority as commander-in-chief of the armed forces of the United States. The issue of the role of Congress versus the war powers of the President (in time of peace lacking a Congressional declaration of war) still remains in limbo.

Foreign affairs was not, of course, the only concern of Presidents since the Nixon era. All Presidents continued to face the many domestic issues which had inexorably grown during the twentieth century—health care, housing, innumerable urban problems, racial discord, education, drugs, all sorts of economic matters such as unemployment and trade, and even issues of morals and values. The "Reagan Revolution" undoubtedly forced the question of whether less government—including Presidential leadership—was the best way to solve those domestic problems. As those problems proliferated during the Bush administration, especially those which related to a troublesome economy, the role of government (state and national) and of the President became a central feature in the Presidential election of 1992. The election of Democrat Bill Clinton over incumbent Republican George Bush seemed to signal a desire for a return to a more effective national government leadership, including Presidential leadership. At the same time, though, unprecedented voter support for independent candidate maverick billionaire Ross Perot seemed to indicate also a strong feeling that many changes were needed in *how* that government leadership should be effectuated—that reform *within* the operation of the government was long overdue, especially in the Congress and in the administrative agencies which were a part of the Congress or of the executive branch.

In two hundred years, then, the Presidency has changed. Its functions and activities have broadened far beyond what the Framers dreamed. So too have its powers and influence. Yet in 1974, when President Nixon provoked perhaps the most dangerous threat to American constitutionalism since the Civil War, the system worked and Nixon was forced from office.

Some observers of the American Presidency have suggested that the real power of any President depends on three things: (1) his legal powers; (2) his support by the public; and (3) his skill as a politician in combining the first two. There is much truth to that observation. In fact, some argue, since television communication has become so important, what may count most is not what a President really is, but rather how he "comes across" to the American people and the resultant perception they have of him.

As we embark on the third century of our Constitution, the American people can look back at the past two hundred years and ask themselves several important questions about the Presidency:

- Has the Presidency served those functions which the Framers intended?
- Has the Presidency grown too big and too strong?
- Have the other branches of the government kept pace with the Presidency so that the check and balance system still works?
- Does our history suggest the need for any institutional changes in the Presidency—the length of the term, the methods of nomination and election, for example?
- Is the job too big for one person? Should the Vice President have more responsibilities?
- Would we be better served by a parliamentary system, similar perhaps to the British system, with the President a part of the legislature and responsible to it, instead of being independent of the legislature?

These and other questions face us in the future, if they do not face us already. What do you think?

THE JUDICIARY

Article III of the Constitution establishes our national judiciary as follows: "The judicial power of the United States shall be vested in one Supreme Court and in such inferior courts as the Congress may from time to time ordain and establish." Accordingly, Congress has established a three-tiered hierarchy of basic federal courts plus ancillary tribunals that handle customs, claims, and patent litigations.

In reality, we have fifty-one court systems in our country, a complicated hodge-podge often misunderstood by many people. The confusion is compounded by ordinary nomenclature: many courts designated with the same name—a "circuit" court or a "district" court, for instance—but which perform different functions, and many which perform similar functions but are known by a variety of names. Each state has its own court system, established and empowered by that state's constitution and statutes. The jurisdiction of each is confined to that state and to that state's laws. Thus, fifty separate state court systems deal with the judicial problems of their respective states. The federal judiciary established in the Constitution—the fifty-first, if you will—deals with federal law and with national and interstate issues that transcend any one state. This essay deals only with the federal court system.

The federal judiciary came into existence to correct a major weakness of the Articles of Confederation. During the Revolutionary War era, widespread antagonism and suspicion prevailed against both strong and centralized government. It was an understandable reaction to the despotism of British authority which had brought on the American Revolution in the first place. Many Americans were convinced that part of that tyranny derived from excessive and abusive powers exercised over them by British imperial courts. Consequently, when our first independent national government was established in 1781—the Articles of Confederation—one way to ensure weak central authority was to reduce any centralized judicial power over the people. Not surprisingly, therefore, and especially since each state already had its own courts, no national tribunals were created. All law, including congressional law, was enforced and interpreted by existing state courts. The result proved to be both confusing and chaotic, as state judges interpreted laws inconsistently and even conflictingly. This in turn was a major contributor to the overall malaise that gripped the nation and eventually precipitated the calling of the Constitutional Convention in 1787. When the Framers finally met in Philadelphia, there was no doubt in their minds that they must establish a national court system. Indeed, the question was not whether there should be such courts; the issue instead was how to structure them and what powers and jurisdiction they should have.

As in the case of the executive and legislative branches of the new government, the Framers had many examples to emulate. Basically, though, both American law and the American legal structure were English in origin.[1] As a result, the numerous colonial laws and legal systems had much in common, not only with England but with each other, whether they emanated from English common law, English local law, church law, or local colonial law. However, since few lawyers resided in the colonies at first, laws and courts tended to be somewhat in disarray, with judicial authority in the hands mostly of governors and their councils. But as the colonies produced and trained more professional lawyers, that picture gradually changed. By the mid-1700s legal practice and, to a large degree, local colonial governments had come under the sway of American legalists and jurists, steeped strongly in British law to be sure, but with adaptations and modifications influenced by the uniqueness of conditions in America.

As already indicated, early judicial authority in most colonies resided in the governors and their councils. In time, as circumstances demanded, local courts came into existence. Generally, those new courts exercised original jurisdiction, and governors and councils became appellate courts. In some instances (*i.e.*, Massachusetts, New York, Virginia) the upper chamber of the legislature acted as the colony's supreme court. Thus, there existed a variety of structures, but one could find in all of them some arrangement containing institutions of both original and appellate jurisdiction.

It is important to keep in mind too that the colonies were part of a world-wide imperial system whose central authority was in Britain and whose economic outlook embraced mercantilism. Not surprisingly, therefore, considerable supervision of colonial enterprise emanated from various English administrative agencies, which included from time to time such bodies as the Lords of Trade, the Board of Trade, and different committees of the Privy Council. Especially pertinent was the Committee on Appeals of the Privy Council, which reviewed colonial court decisions. In effect, that Committee constituted a supreme court for the whole empire, including obviously the American colonies. Among its other purposes, the Committee tried to maintain uniformity and consistency in how British law was interpreted and implemented throughout the Empire so that the law was applied the same way, no matter where the litigation occurred. That the Committee's decisions often evoked discontent from American commercial and business interests is here immaterial; what is important is that *the concept of an empire-wide supreme court was familiar to the Framers* when they met in Philadelphia. They were thus well aware of the notion of one local court system, including a supreme court (governor and council) in a given colony, and another supreme court whose authority encompassed the entire empire. As indicated earlier, their greatest concern was not *whether* to establish a national supreme court, but rather *how* to structure it and what powers and jurisdiction it should exercise.

Somewhat surprisingly, therefore, one does not find too much deliberation at the Constitutional Convention over the court system. Perhaps two reasons explain why. One was the widespread consensus that a national court system should be created, especially a national supreme court; hence no need for much discussion and argument. The other reason was more important: the inability of the Framers to agree on how to structure a national court system. One group—those who sought to maintain as much power in the states as possible—felt that existing state courts should be utilized and incorporated into the new national system. Another group—those seeking greater authority in a new national government—urged the creation of a judicial system totally separated from the state courts. The Framers decided, therefore, to include in the Constitution what they could readily agree on, and leave the rest to the new government. So Article III provided for a national judiciary with one Supreme Court, but left the rest of its structure for Congress to determine. The basic framework of jurisdiction was included, but its implementation also was left to Congress. Though no one minimized the importance of the new court system, there appeared to be greater urgency to create the new executive and legislative branches and to get them into operation, as no comparable bodies existed to perform their function. State courts, after all, already existed and were functioning, and if need be they could continue to perform necessary judicial functions until the new court system was implemented by the government created under the Constitution.

In providing for one Supreme Court to handle all categories of litigations, the Framers had no way of foreseeing, of course, the overwhelming work load that eventually would devolve on that one tribunal. Otherwise they might have established more than one supreme court (perhaps each to deal with a different type of litigation), or at least provided a way to do so in the future. As the Constitution is worded, however, Congress can create as many *other* kinds of national courts as it deems necessary, but there can be only *one* Supreme Court.

That could be changed, of course, by constitutional amendment. Considering the difficulties of such a procedure, it does not seem feasible. Indeed, during most of his tenure as Chief Justice in the 1970s and 1980s, Warren E. Burger publicly deplored deleterious effects the heavy case load was creating for the Supreme Court, but no movement developed for an amendment to establish more than one body. That may be because a different approach to meet the problem seems more acceptable: improve the screening process that determines which cases eventually reach the highest tribunal. That could be done in several ways. Congress might create more intermediary courts. Or the Supreme Court might be reorganized internally, utilizing its personnel differently and presumably more efficiently. Neither of these approaches is a sure-fire panacea, but at least they would not entail altering the two-hundred-year-old Constitutional proviso of only one Supreme Court, a change probably very difficult to bring about.

The Constitution provides, then, for one Supreme Court, leaving it to Congress to determine which and how many other national (federal) courts we should have. Nothing is said about the size, personnel, procedures, or internal organization of either the Supreme Court or the other federal courts; those also were left for Congress. The Constitution does provided, though, that all federal judges shall hold their offices during "good behavior." Accordingly, appointed by the President (with the consent of a majority of the Senate), federal judges serve for life and can be removed involuntarily only by what is known as "for cause." Expressed in terms of what the Constitution says, "for cause" means that federal judges can be removed involuntarily only by impeachment and conviction for "treason, bribery or other high crimes or misdemeanors." In providing for life tenure for the federal judges, the Constitution made them independent of both the President and the Congress. It is a classic example of the separation of powers principle. Federal judges are free to do their jobs; they know that as long as they maintain "good behavior" they have no fear of either executive or legislative harassment. In fact, in two hundred years of our history, only seven federal judges have been removed through the impeachment process, the first in 1804 (John Pickering) and the most recent in 1989 (Walter L. Nixon). (All have been lower court judges; the one attempt in 1804-1805 to remove a Supreme Court justice, Samuel Chase, failed. He was impeached by the House, but not convicted by the Senate.)

Although the Constitution establishes eligibility requirements for who can be President, Vice-President, and members of Congress, it states no qualifications for national judges. Most are appointed for their judicial experience and legal record; but some have had little or no experience as judges and have been named for purely partisan political purposes. Often an appointment reflects a President's political or judicial philosophy, and since judges are appointed for life, such appointments can result in a President's views and beliefs being perpetuated through judicial decisions long after he has vacated the Oval Office. A recent study publicized by *U. S. News & World Report,* for instance, noted that Presidents Ronald Reagan and George Bush have appointed nearly seventy percent of all currently sitting federal judges, suggesting a conservative bent in our national court system well into the twenty-first century, long after they have been out of office. Nevertheless, despite the lack of prescribed qualifications and despite the fact that Presidents tend to appoint persons of their own political and philosophical persuasions, most federal judges, lower court as well as Supreme Court, have been capable individuals, have exercised considerable judicial independence, and have performed their duties creditably. Indeed, if history is any guide, commented *The Christian Science Monitor* (February 11, 1987), upon the elevation of a staunch conservative to be Chief Justice, "the court under new Chief Justice William Rehnquist may . . . prove to be less conservative than President Reagan hopes and many Americans fear."

Most of Article III deals with the jurisdiction of the national courts. The Constitution establishes that jurisdiction in two ways. The first is by designating the types of cases which come into the federal courts; the second is by identifying in which of those cases the Supreme Court has original jurisdiction and in which it has appellate jurisdiction. Although Article III does not specifically say so, all other cases fall within the purview of the states. That was later confirmed by the Tenth Amendment which clarified the relationship between the national and state governments by indicating that all powers not granted to the national government nor denied to the states resided within the authority of the states. Yet, (as if legal procedures are not confusing enough to the average citizen) the Judiciary Act of 1789 also provided for dual jurisdiction by both national and state courts in some instances (see below).

Article III stipulates that federal courts have jurisdiction over cases involving the interpretation or meaning of the Constitution, of any law of Congress, or of any treaty made by the authority of the government of the United States. In addition, federal courts handle cases involving ambassadors or other "public ministers and consuls" representing a foreign country. Cases involving "admiralty" or "maritime" issues also come to the federal courts; those are disputes dealing with matters arising on the high seas or on navigable lakes and rivers. Cases in which the United States is one party, either plaintiff or defendant, also litigate in the federal courts. (A long-established principle of law holds that "a sovereign cannot be sued in his own courts" without its consent. Theoretically, then, the United States government cannot be sued without its prior approval. Congress has enacted a complex legal formula, however, which grants that approval under certain conditions.) A case brought by a citizen of one state against a citizen of another state is brought in a federal court; this is commonly referred to as a "diversity of citizenship" suit. An action in which one of the litigants is a foreign country or a citizen of a foreign country also is handled in the federal courts. All the above cases are referred to generically as "federal cases" or cases involving a "federal question."

The Constitution as originally promulgated also provided that the federal courts would handle a suit between a state and a citizen of another state. Many objected, concerned about state finances if states could be sued too readily. Many feared also that allowing a state to be sued by an outsider might infringe upon that state's sovereignty. (Note the above principle about a sovereign being sued.) Matters came to a head in short order, in 1793. In one of its earliest cases, *Chisholm v. Georgia* (2 Dallas 419), the Supreme Court ruled favorably for a citizen of South Carolina who had sued the state of Georgia. The decision stirred states' rights people to change the Constitution to protect the states. Accordingly, in 1794 the Eleventh Amendment was proposed (the first ten, the Bill of Rights, already had been approved), and in 1799 it was ratified. It provides that a state cannot be sued in the federal courts by either its own citizens, a foreign country, or citizens of another state or foreign country, unless that state gives its prior consent. Lacking that consent, such suit must be brought in the state's own courts, which also requires the state's consent. A state still can be sued in the federal courts without its prior consent, though, if the party plaintiff is the United States or one of the other states.

In addition to designating the types of cases which come into the federal courts, Article III specifies in which cases the Supreme Court has original jurisdiction. The number is relatively few: only those involving "ambassadors, other public ministers and consuls, and those in which a state shall be a party." In all other federal cases the Supreme Court has appellate jurisdiction. Congress, though, is authorized to make exceptions. Thus in 1868, in the midst of the turbulent Reconstruction era, Congress withdrew from the Supreme Court the right to hear certain appeals arising under the Habeas Corpus Act of 1867. Although the law was blatantly partisan, it still was a power authorized under the Constitution. The Court had no choice but to obey it, as exemplified in 1869 in the case of *Ex Parte McCardle* (7 Wallace 506).

The major point on jurisdiction, then, is that except for a few instances, the Supreme Court's docket is overwhelmingly cases appealed from the lower federal courts.

In addition to setting forth the jurisdiction of the federal judiciary, the other major focus of Article III was to create a structural framework for the national courts. As already indicated, the Constitutional Convention, unable to come to an acceptable agreement, deferred most of that to the new government. It became one of the priority tasks undertaken by the first Congress and resulted in one of its most important achievements, the Judiciary Act of September 24, 1789.

The brainchild mostly of Senator Oliver Ellsworth of Connecticut—who later would be the second Chief Justice of the United States Supreme Court—the act made two momentous contributions to the constitutional framework of our government.

The first was to establish the machinery for a federal litigatory system: three layers of judicial bodies ranging from the local district courts to the highest Supreme Court. The lowest level consisted of thirteen United States District Courts of one judge each—one district for each of the eleven states (North Carolina and Rhode Island had not yet ratified the Constitution) plus one additional district in Virginia (for Kentucky) and one in Massachusetts (for Maine).

The country then was divided into three appeals areas, with a United States Circuit Court for each, to which appeals could come from individual member district courts. Each circuit court consisted of two Supreme Court justices and one district court judge. (For many years the docket of the Supreme Court was so sparse that most of the responsibility of the Supreme Court justices entailed "riding circuit" in those appeals districts to hear appeals there. Although modified in 1869, it was not until 1891 that that practice finally ended. Supreme Court justices today still exercise administrative supervision over a particular circuit, but at least they do not physically attend those courts.)

At the apex of the federal court system the Judiciary Act created the one Constitutionally-specified Supreme Court consisting of a Chief Justice and five associate justices. (Note the custom of referring to a Supreme Court member as a "justice" and to the other federal court members as "judges.")

In addition to basic organization, the Judiciary Act spelled out in great detail the jurisdiction of the federal courts as well as their internal organization and procedures.

With relatively minor exceptions, the federal litigatory system as established in 1789 retains the same basic structure today. A major difference is in numbers, not surprising considering how the country has grown in the past two hundred years. By the 1990s the original thirteen district courts have increased to over a hundred, with more than seven hundred judges (many district courts are broken down into "divisions" to accommodate the heavy volume of cases). The original three circuit courts have become eleven, plus one more just for the District of Columbia. The one Supreme Court has remained one Supreme Court, as specified in the Constitution, but the number of justices has changed from time to time, from as few as five to as many as ten. It has been nine since 1863, although several unsuccessful attempts have been made to change the number, at one time (by President Franklin D. Roosevelt) to as high as fifteen.

In addition to the changes in numbers, the name of the middle layer of courts has been changed from United States "Circuit Court" to United States "Courts of Appeals," to avoid confusion with so many state courts which use the term "circuit." Occasional changes have been made too in various court practices and procedures, as well as in the creation of needed ancillary courts. They have included the so-called "legislative courts," those established by Congress under powers given to it elsewhere in the Constitution (Article I, Section 8). Among them are the Customs Courts, the Court of Customs and Patent Appeals, various territorial courts, the Tax Court, and the Court of Military Appeals.

Yet with all the above modifications in the past two hundred years, the basic structure and functions of the federal court system have remained essentially as they were set up in the Judiciary Act of 1789.

As indicated above, the Judiciary Act of 1789 made two momentous contributions to the constitutional framework of our government. The first was to establish the machinery for the federal litigatory system, as just described. The second was to establish the principle of *national* supremacy in our judiciary, thereby paving the way within our federal system for the gradual and inexorable growth of the national government and the concomitant diminution of power of state government.

In spite of the Framers' desires, the actual sovereignty relationship between state and national authority had never been clearly settled at the Constitutional Convention, because the Framers thought of the new federal system as one of *split* sovereignty. The problem that never seemed to be clearly defined was where and how it was split. That was particularly true as it applied to the state and national court systems. It is quite clear that the men at Philadelphia wanted a national system which would render more *uniform* justice than the state courts were providing under the Articles of Confederation. Thus they readily concurred in one Supreme Court at the peak of a layered system, but, as already noted, they differed on whether those layers should utilize state courts or should consist of separately created new federal courts—and they decided, therefore, to leave the decision to the new government. Hence the provision in Article III that Congress could establish whatever courts it deemed necessary.

The first Congress dealt with the impasse by incorporating both views in the Judiciary Act of 1789. Separate national courts were created, as noted above, with well-defined jurisdiction. At the same time, state courts were granted concurrent jurisdiction in specified "federal cases." That was a signal concession to states' rights advocates. But the provision of the Judiciary Act with by far the most significant long-range ramification proved to be Article 25, which authorized appeals from the state courts to the national judiciary when the ruling of the state went against national authority or prerogative. That provision—Article 25—was to become, as some constitutional historians categorized it, the "very heart of the American federal system of government." The Constitution in Article VI asserts that it (the Constitution) and all federal laws were to be "the supreme law of the land." For that to be true, some mechanism must assure that state courts and legislatures could not supersede or override national action, as they had so often done under the Articles of Confederation. If appeals could be taken from the states to the federal courts, then the latter, as an integral part of the *national* government, could enforce the "supreme law of the land" doctrine.

States' righters, nullifiers, and then secessionists contested that notion philosophically, politically, and even by violence and force, but in the long run the final determination resided in the people of the nation rather than in the people of the individual states. A tragic and bloody civil war was necessary, though, before the Supreme Court could conclusively pronounce that doctrine in the case of *Texas v. White* (7 Wallace 700 [1869]). Yet even today some deny the authority of the federal courts, including the Supreme Court, to declare such sweeping powers for the national government. *Texas v. White*, they say, did nothing more than invalidate secession: "This Constitution . . . looks to an indestructible Union, composed of indestructible States." Despite Article 25 of the Judiciary Act, goes the argument, states still retain sovereignty in certain areas of residual powers as incorporated in our federal system, and state courts—not federal courts—should decide those cases—segregation being one of those categories of cases. But federal authority prevailed.

How did that happen in the past two hundred years?

The federal courts played an inauspicious role in the early years of our history. During the 1790s, the dockets of the new national courts were relatively sparse. That was especially true of the Supreme Court. In fact, its justices spent most of their time "riding circuit" in their appeals districts, enduring miserable and untoward travel and living conditions. Indeed, several early justices, including Chief Justices John Jay and Oliver Ellsworth, resigned because they concluded that the position lacked sufficient import.

A major turning point came with the appointment in 1801 of John Marshall as Chief Justice. When he died thirty-four years later, he left a Court honored for its jurisprudence and growing in power and influence. Historians have accorded him the distinction of being probably the greatest jurist in our nation's history.

A strong nationalist, Marshall and the "Marshall Court" took several monumental steps toward implanting and implementing the "supreme law of the land" principle and national supremacy. First, though, it was necessary to clearly establish judicial review and the power of the Supreme Court as the unchallenged arbiter over all constitutional issues. That came in the famous case of *Marbury v. Madison* (1 Cranch 137 [1803]), in which the national tribunal declared part of a law of Congress unconstitutional. The concept of judicial review was not new to American law; as noted above, it had existed even in colonial days in the judicial relations between the colonies and the mother country. (Strong precedent existed also in the British legal system, going back at least to 1610 to the great Chief Justice Sir Edward Coke and the famous "Dr. Bonham's Case.") But in specifying the powers and jurisdiction of the federal courts and of the Supreme Court, the Constitution says nothing about judicial review. Scholars generally conclude that the men at Philadelphia assumed it as part of any organized legal structure; yet some Framers' disposition would have limited judicial review only to state courts. Nevertheless, in the 1790s the federal judiciary in at least two instances—*Champion v. Casey* (U. S. Circuit Court, Rhode Island, 1792) and *Ware v. Hylton* (3 Dallas 199 [1796]) —invalidated state actions, and in one case—*Hylton v. United States*, 3 Dallas 171 (1796)—the Supreme Court inferred—but only inferred—a similar power over Congressional law. In *Marbury v. Madison*, however, the Supreme Court actually exercised that power. Although some resisted, judicial review became an instrument of paramount importance in the Court's contribution to the rise of national supremacy. Perhaps it was fortunate that fifty-four years passed before the Court has occasion to declare another act of Congress unconstitutional—in the famous *Dred Scott* case—but by then no one seriously challenged the Court's authority to exercise that power. It had become firmly accepted. (Of course, many did disagree with the Court's substantive reasoning in *Dred Scott*, but that is quite different from challenging its authority to exercise judicial review.)

Having established the role of the Court as final arbiter, Marshall gradually consolidated that authority.[2] In a series of landmark decisions, he inexorably strengthened the power of the national government *vis-à-vis* state legislative and judicial authority. In *Fletcher v. Peck* (6 Cranch 87 [1810)], not only did the Court declare a state law void under the Constitution, but it also added new dimensions to the economic role of the national government in relation to private property and the contract clause of the Constitution. *Dartmouth College v. Woodward* (4 Wheaton 518 [1819]), popularly known as "The Dartmouth College Case," broadened that role, as the Court dealt with both contracts and corporations. In 1824 the Court's interpretation of the commerce clause in *Gibbons v. Ogden* (9 Wheaton 1) opened a new vista for national authority, in the first of many commerce clause decisions that constituted a vehicle even into the twentieth century for the expansion of national authority over the states.

But perhaps no decision of the Marshall Court stands in long-term import as its 1819 pronouncement in *McCulloch v. Maryland* (4 Wheaton 316). From the very first session of Congress in 1789, no constitutional issue seemed more fundamental than liberal versus strict interpretation of the Constitution. It entailed more than the immediate issue of a national bank. It involved even more than the important matter of delegated and residual powers. In the long run it raised the issue also of the locus of sovereignty in the American system of federalism. Where was the line between state and national powers? And more specifically, what was the meaning of the "necessary and proper" clause in the Constitution? In a decision that had incalculable ramifications for the constitutional development of our federal system, the Supreme Court in *McCulloch* upheld and confirmed the liberal interpretation of the Constitution. It solidified the foundation upon which national authority would grow. Obviously that national power did not come into being overnight; it grew gradually, but inexorably, over the next century and a half. John Marshall played a singularly prominent role in getting it started. (More cases could be cited, but a brief essay does not permit going into that kind of detail.)

The Marshall era was followed by the Taney era, which lasted through the Civil War. Unfortunately Roger Brooke Taney is usually remembered for probably the most infamous pronouncement ever made by the Supreme Court, the majority opinion in *Dred Scott v. John F. A. Sandford* (19 Howard 393 [1857]). Yet Taney still ranks as one of our greatest jurists because of so many positive accomplishments of the "Taney Court," achievements which actually extended the foundation established by John Marshall.

Taney was a consummate Jacksonian—an aristocrat who inherited conservative tidewater traditions (especially toward slavery), but who believed strongly in the new West and in democratically-oriented economic growth and competition. One might expect that especially because of his views toward slavery, Taney would be a strong states' righter. Far from returning judicial supervision over economic growth to the states—as many expected a Jacksonian southern slaveholder would do—Taney maintained federal authority and even broadened it. In the landmark *Charles River Bridge* case of 1837 *(Charles River Bridge v. Warren Bridge* [11 Peters 420]), the Taney Court faced up to the basic dilemma of American democratic capitalism: the conflict between the rights of private property and those of society. Without destroying the former, the Court upheld the latter. It paved the way for building onto the Marshall legacy a strengthened nation-centered view of the contract and commerce clauses of the Constitution, albeit recognizing a role for the states. In a series of momentous cases extending from the 1830s into the 1850s, the Court asserted a concurrent federal-state jurisdiction which allowed a degree of state supervision of economic growth as long as it did not interfere with federal statute. That freed new industry from monopolistic restraints of established corporations and outmoded charters formerly secure under the Marshall Court's doctrine of protecting property rights under the contract and commerce clauses of the Constitution. The Taney Court was able to broaden competition and economic growth, basic to the new

Jacksonian concept of economic democracy, and thereby allow new technology to lead the nation into the future. In spite of the sectional strife which brought on the Civil War (with which Taney is so often remembered), the Taney Court actually refined Marshall's constitutional law to open new economic opportunities for many Americans. Taney also retained a strong national power, re-defined to accommodate a judicious dual sovereignty. What must not be overlooked is that whenever a state threatened to upset that "judicious" relationship, Taney was quick to resurrect John Marshall and national supremacy. And in the end he did that also with slavery, when he asserted in *Dred Scott* the authority of the *national* government to protect slaves as private property in the territories. (Many incorrectly assume that only states' rights advocates favored slavery.)

The Supreme Court did not escape the disastrous impact of the Civil War. In one sense it was "business as usual"—that is, cases of all sorts filled the docket and the Court continued to deal with them as it always had.

But at least two important changes took place during the Civil War and Reconstruction which must be noted.

The first was a direct consequence of the *Dred Scott* decision. To weaken the impact of that decision, opponents of slavery in the North launched an unparalleled assault to discredit Chief Justice Taney and the justices who had concurred with him in that nefarious pronouncement. The attack was *not* on the *institution* of the Court; it sought rather to destroy public confidence in the Court's *personnel*. It was an attack on the justices, not on the Court. And it was successful. Many Americans lost confidence in the Court's ability to deal justly with matters in which sectional interests might be at stake. Prior to *Dred Scott* many had viewed the Supreme Court as the legitimate arbiter of divisive constitutional issues; indeed, many, both North and South, had long anticipated that only that tribunal could finally put to rest those controversial issues—especially slavery. But for more than a decade after *Dred Scott*—and what a traumatic decade!—the Court's esteem and veneration built up under Marshall and Taney eroded, due to those unprecedented personal attacks. It proved to be only temporary, however, and the Court's prestige returned later; but during the era of the Civil War and Reconstruction the Presidency and the Congress dueled for power and authority, with the Supreme Court placidly on the sidelines. That is not to say that the Court was out of the picture completely; it still had plenty to do, and it became involved in a number of controversial cases, especially several which involved important issues of civil rights. Nevertheless, the major power struggle was between the Presidency and the Congress. And it should be pointed out also that that conflict was within the parameters of the *national* government. For by its very nature, the Civil War resulted in the expansion of national authority at the expense of the states. Thus, though the mid-nineteenth century Court played a minimal role, *non*-Court events which transpired during the Civil War and Reconstruction reaffirmed and added to the earlier judicial achievements made by the Marshall and Taney Courts in aligning national-state relationships under American federalism.

In addition to the short-range change in the Supreme Court's status during the Civil War and Reconstruction era, a second change occurred that proved to have significant long-range consequences. It related directly to the association of the newly dominant Republican party with the emerging business and industrial interests in the radically reorganized American economy. In the latter half of the nineteenth century the United States changed from a rural agricultural to an urban industrial society. Its population also changed, and became a multi-ethnic and multi-cultural pluralism. Whereas the pre-Civil War *Democratic* power structure had benefited politically through allying with landed and agrarian interests, the post-Civil War *Republican* power structure tended to associate itself with the new industrial and commercial economic interests.[3] Furthermore, and for a variety of reasons (not the least of which stemmed from the political and economic corruption rampant during the post-Civil War era) "big business" found it relatively easy to dominate individual state and local governments. Accordingly, once the secession issues of the ex-Confederate states were resolved (Reconstruction Acts, etc.), political thinking in Washington, albeit dominated by Republicans, viewed federalism with a perspective somewhat reminiscent of the Jeffersonian view that more governmental power should be exercised in the states. Supreme Court appointees reflected that political philosophy, falling back on the Taney Court prescript that had legitimized state authority as long as it did not interfere with authorized federal prerogative. Thus the *Slaughterhouse Cases* (16 Wallace 36 [1873]) and the so-called "Granger Cases," especially *Munn v. Illinois* (94 U.S. 113 [1877]), not only suggested a re-evaluation of federalism, but also had broad implications for such diverse areas as civil rights and commerce. The Supreme Court, then, played a very important role during the so-called "Gilded Age" in slowing the flow of economic oversight (with all its concomitant social ramifications) toward the national government and in restoring much of it to the states. Some even feel that the Supreme Court, by virtue of the almost sanctity of its decisions, may even have been in the forefront of this move.

At the same time, though, the unprecedented transformation of American society gradually revolutionized the attitude of America's populace toward government, and especially toward the role of the national government. In spite of the almost century-long growth of national authority over that of the states—the result of the liberal construction of the Constitution, the expansion of presidential prerogative, the jurisprudential interpretations of the Marshall and Taney Courts, and the constitutional configuration of the Civil War—most mid-nineteenth century Americans still thought of federalism as empowering more state jurisdiction than national, and still preferred the Jeffersonian "least government" doctrine. Freedom, after all, had always meant freedom *from* government, especially national government. But by the post-Reconstruction era, in the new urban, industrialized, and pluralistic American society, government was no longer the greatest threat to individual freedom. Many viewed the relentlessly growing and seemingly untrammeled power of big business as the major threat. Influenced by the emerging "progressivism," more and more Americans felt that the only power capable of dealing with that threat, and still able to preserve our basic American way of life, was a strong national government, but one that must be controlled through the democratic process by the masses of the people. Freedom *through* government replaced freedom *from* government. It entailed a radically different view of the role of the federal government—and its component branches—from what had prevailed in the first century of our national history. With only brief interruptions, that philosophy has prevailed down to the present time.

That new notion of the role of the national government inexorably embraced Congress, the Presidency, and the national judiciary, ranging from the lower district court level all the way up to the Supreme Court. Beginning in 1887 and 1890, with the Interstate Commerce and Sherman Anti-Trust Acts, Congress unveiled a new interpretation of its delegated powers, especially over interstate commerce, thereby triggering new actions and programs that ranged from pure food and drug legislation to antitrust and wage and hour reforms. Presidents Theodore Roosevelt, William Howard Taft, and Woodrow Wilson championed causes that included re-forestation projects to breaking up big business combinations to overhauling the national banking structure.

The Supreme Court also reflected this new role of the national government in overseeing and protecting the freedoms and liberties of more and more people. Oliver Wendell Holmes, renowned for his legal learning and humane interpretations of the law, created new concepts in judicial thinking and inspired future generations of lawyers to recognize that law must change with society's needs. Louis Dembitz Brandeis, first as a brilliant lawyer and then as one of the most distinguished jurists to sit on the Supreme Court, revolutionized legal thinking by utilizing medical and sociological data to interpret the needs of society. New approaches were made toward both state and federal police power, and with them came progressive concepts such as the "stream of commerce" and the "rule of reason."

In all these developments, the Supreme Court not only helped advance social and economic life for "mainstream America," but it did so, along with Congress

THE JUDICIARY

and the Presidency, through expanding interpretations of national governmental powers over those of the states. This transition occurred slowly, of course, between the 1890s and the 1930s, and sometimes in almost roller-coaster fashion, as the Court interpreted narrowly in some instances and broadly in others. It was part of the saga of how federalism developed: whether states would or could carry out certain responsibilities, or if it became "necessary and proper" for the national government to step in. Especially during the post-World War I "Roaring Twenties," the prevailing philosophy in America's national leadership in Washington tended to back away from the type of activism characteristic of earlier progressives.

Then came the Great Depression of the 1930s and the Franklin D. Roosevelt-New Deal era. Those familiar with American history know that Roosevelt's policies not only championed the progressive notion of strong federal involvement in the country's economic life, but that the New Deal called for considerably more national government participation than had ever existed before. Then came a startling setback: the Supreme Court declared several key New Deal laws unconstitutional. Roosevelt's reaction was to try to change the Court, and a judicial crisis of almost unprecedented proportions came into being. Accusing the "nine old men" of obstructing critical policies necessary to lift the country out of its most devastating depression, Roosevelt proposed sweeping changes in the Supreme Court that would enable him to appoint enough new justices (presumably favorable to his political philosophy) to virtually ensure endorsement of his programs. This occurred right after the election of 1936, in which Roosevelt won reelection by the greatest landslide victory since James Monroe had run unopposed in 1820. Roosevelt was riding a wave of unprecedented political popularity. Furthermore, the programs which the Court had knocked down had elicited considerable public support. Nevertheless a nation-wide reaction set in against what was called Roosevelt's "court packing scheme." Many indicated that attaining his political objectives by other means was acceptable, but not by "fiddling with the Constitution." The result was a stunning defeat for an exceptionally popular President.

As events turned out, though, Roosevelt succeeded after all, through what some of his implacable supporters liked to describe as "divine intervention." Old age and poor health forced several Supreme Court justices to resign, and within a very short time new Roosevelt appointees created a pro-New Deal majority on the Court that now upheld programs of strong government involvement.

That new Court, though, accurately reflected the growing popular sentiment for a more active role by the federal government in American life. The progressivism that had evolved half a century earlier became, in the 1930s and following, the prevailing view of an overwhelming majority of the country, as reflected in election returns and in executive and legislative programs. "Liberal" or "moderate" candidates and programs predominated, under the aegis and leadership of both major political parties. With the executive and legislative branches embracing that philosophy, inevitably the judiciary, appointed by moderate Democratic and Republican Presidents, reflected that same point of view.

Perhaps the pinnacle of twentieth century liberalism on the Court came under the leadership of Chief Justice Earl Warren, appointed in 1953 by Republican President Dwight D. Eisenhower. Most people quickly associate the Warren Court's activism with the 1954 case of *Brown v. the Board of Education of Topeka* (349 U. S. 294). That landmark decision overturned the sixty-year-old "separate but equal" doctrine in *Plessy v. Ferguson* (163 U. S. 537 [1896]) and asserted that racial segregation in public schools violated the "equal protection" provision of the Fourteenth Amendment. Extended soon by more Court decisions and by abetting legislative and executive actions to other phases of American life, the *Brown* principle revolutionized American society, bringing an end—although not without considerable opposition and strife—to segregation in all sorts of public institutions that included housing, restaurants, hotels and motels, transportation, parks, theaters, sports arenas, concert halls, swimming pools, and many more.

But the Warren Court dealt with much more than segregation. In a series of landmark decisions which included *Baker v. Carr* (369 U. S. 186 [1962]), *Wesberry v. Sanders* (376 U. S. 1 [1964]), and *Reynolds v. Sims* (377 U. S. 533 [1964]), the high court advanced the "one-man-one-vote" principle, which brought extensive reforms in both election and representation procedures throughout the country. Many agreed with Justice William O. Douglas that "the conception of political equality from the Declaration of Independence to Lincoln's Gettysburg Address" finally seemed to be coming into fruition. These Court decisions became even more meaningful as the Twenty-Fourth Amendment outlawing the poll tax was ratified in 1964, and Congress passed two momentous civil rights laws, the Civil Rights Act of 1964 and the Voting Rights Act of 1965.

Another significant area of Warren Court activism dealt with reform in judicial procedure. Among other decisions, the Court's pronouncements in *Escobedo v. Illinois* (378 U. S. 478 [1964]) and in *Miranda v. Arizona* (377 U. S. 201 [1966]) brought new meanings to the Fifth and Sixth Amendments and the rights of individuals accused of a crime. Indeed, one can hardly watch any of the numerous crime stories which saturate television programming without hearing reference to the accused's "Miranda rights."

During the 1950s and 1960s the activism of the Warren Court matched and reflected the national trend of liberal politics, as the Court delved into areas its predecessors had cautiously avoided. "Acting with breathtaking boldness," wrote constitutional historian Herman Belz, "the Court undertook sweeping reforms of the electoral system and the nature of political representation, the administration of criminal justice in the states, school desegregation and race relations, the law of freedom of speech including the local regulation of obscenity, and the status of religion in public life." And superimposed over all these almost revolutionary substantive reforms was the unmistakable expansion of national authority over the states, as well as of the role of the Supreme Court as a powerful spokesman for that national authority.

In spite of this liberal bent of the general population, in 1968, by the vagaries of Presidential politics, conservative Richard M. Nixon was elected as chief executive. By the early 1970s he was able to appoint a new Chief Justice, the "strict constructionist" Warren E. Burger, and four new Associate Justices to the Supreme Court. Many expected this new presumably conservative alignment to inaugurate a marked reversal in the Court's direction. Except for some criminal and non-race-related civil matters, however, members of the Burger Court, old and new alike, manifested a decided judicial independence and maintained much of the jurisprudential tack of the earlier Warren era. Although many cases were decided by close margins, libertarian principles were upheld—or at least not struck down—in areas such as affirmative action, women's rights, freedom of the press, and (probably the most emotional and controversial) abortion. That, of course, upset many conservatives, especially when they had anticipated just the opposite to come from appointees made by apparently conservative Presidents. Indeed, just as the term "imperial presidency" came into use increasingly among liberals concerned with Nixon's White House excesses, so did political conservatives view the continuous activism of the Court as an "imperial judiciary." Terms such as "legislation by judiciary," "judicial arrogance," and "government by judiciary" became rallying cries among those who wanted the Supreme Court to narrow its constitutional interpretations.

The election of Ronald Reagan as President in 1980 signaled a conservative revival in the United States. Reagan swept to a landslide victory (which he repeated in 1984, as did George Bush, his eight-year Vice-President and successor to the Oval Office, in 1988) on a platform which forcefully advocated ending "big government" and returning from Washington to the states many powers "expropriated" from them by the "liberal-sponsored malfunction of federalism." Bearing a major responsibility for that "malfunction," according to Reagan and Bush supporters, was the United States Supreme Court.

That stance became very clear in November of 1986 with the publication of a study authorized by President Reagan to examine and evaluate relations between the states and the national government. In a report entitled *The Status of Federal-*

ism in America, the Domestic Policy Council (a Cabinet-level advisory board) asserted that the powers of the national and state governments had shifted radically from what the Framers of the Constitution had intended, much to the detriment of the states. The report also unhesitatingly placed much of the blame on the Supreme Court. For at least fifty years dating back to the New Deal, the document charged, the Court's "erroneous judicial reading" of the Constitution had led to decision after decision which "improperly pre-empted and invalidated the states' legitimate exercise of their sovereign powers," and left them to act merely as "satrapies" and "administrative units" of a "virtually omnipotent national government." The report went on to accuse the Supreme Court of "indifference" to the principle of federalism in some decisions, and of "unprecedented intrusion" into strictly state matters in others. As a consequence of those actions, the report continued, the Supreme Court had "undermined the sovereign decision-making authority of the states" and thereby "acquiesced in improper expansion of Federal power." One Reagan administration spokesman, in a press interview, went as far as to charge the national government with "behaving without legitimate constitutional warrant" during that fifty-year span when it "usurped" state authority. It was about as strong a denunciation of the course of American history as any Americans had ever made.

Accompanying the publication of *The Status of Federalism in America,* Reagan's Attorney-General, Edwin Meese, moved to the forefront of an assault on the Supreme Court. He accused that tribunal of "blatant activism" that dangerously eroded state authority and thereby subverted the intent of the Framers of the Constitution. Supreme Court decisions should be restricted to settling a specific case at hand, Meese argued, and should not be viewed as precedents (or *stare decisis*) which could become part of public or judicial policy. Further, Meese maintained, interpretations of the Constitution should reflect what the Framers intended—"original intent"—not twentieth century social or economic forces about which the men at Philadelphia had absolutely no knowledge.

This assault by Meese and others seemed to be a clear attempt to reduce the role of the national judiciary, and especially of the Supreme Court, as agencies which had made possible the growth of the national government and the transfer to it of many powers which previously had resided in the states.

One immediate outcome (actually it had begun earlier, almost as though in anticipation of the *Status of Federalism* report) was a public assault on the Supreme Court by conservative and right-wing groups, led by Attorney-General Meese. Up to that time (1986), President Reagan had appointed many judges to the federal courts, including two to the Supreme Court. In fact, shortly before the *Status of Federalism* report became public, *Congressional Quarterly* published

THE JUDICIARY

statistics showing that in his first six years as President (and with still two more years to go), Reagan already had appointed almost three hundred new federal judges, enough to leave "an imprint that will be visible long after he has left the White House." Among those appointees were two to the Supreme Court: Sandra Day O'Connor (the first woman ever appointed to the nation's highest tribunal), and Antonin Scalia (the first justice of Italian extraction). Although these appointments delighted "feminist" and "minorities" vested interests, both jurists were chosen also for judicial records which suited Reagan's conservative political philosophy. In addition, when Chief Justice Burger retired—anticipating retirement shortly anyway, he left the Court a little sooner (in 1986) to oversee a nationwide bicentennial commemoration of the Constitution—Reagan elevated Associate Justice William H. Rehnquist to be Chief Justice. Appointed to the Bench in 1971 by President Nixon, Rehnquist was considered by his contemporaries to be the most conservative member of the Court and the nearest to the philosophy espoused by President Reagan. Whether Rehnquist would influence the direction of future Court actions remained to be seen.

It didn't take long, though, for Supreme Court appointments to become issues of major controversy. In 1987 Associate Justice Lewis F. Powell, Jr., retired. Appointed by President Nixon, Powell's views for his sixteen years on the Bench had followed a more middle-of-the-road course than what partisan conservatives had hoped for. To replace Powell, Reagan nominated Robert H. Bork. A very scholarly jurist, Bork championed strongly conservative judicial views which he expressed publicly and widely, and which he demonstrated quite emphatically in judicial posts which he had held earlier. His views seemed to be in complete accord with those posited in the *Status of Federalism* document. Highly volatile confirmation hearings in the Senate resulted in the Bork appointment being rejected by a close vote. Reagan thereupon nominated another conservative, Douglas Ginsburg, but his nomination was quickly withdrawn when a check on his past revealed that as a young man he had occasionally smoked marijuana. Reagan followed those two political fiascoes with yet a third nomination, this time with a "squeaky clean" moderate conservative, Anthony M. Kennedy. His nomination was quickly confirmed, with none of the acrimony of the Bork hearings.

By the time George Bush was elected President in 1988, the long-running liberal versus conservative issue was abetted by additional problems of major and nationwide concern. One was abortion; another was sexism. Both emanated from the emerging role of women in American society. Abortion was an especially divisive issue because it involved morality and religion as much as politics, economics, sociology, and medicine. How they stood on abortion became, indeed, almost a litmus test for candidates for any government post, state or national, elective or appointive.

This was especially true for appointees to the Supreme Court, which both pro-abortion and anti-abortion forces seemed to anticipate would be the ultimate arbiter of the issue. When Associate Justice William J. Brennan, Jr., retired in 1990, President Bush nominated David Souter, an obscure New England judge, whose uncontroversial moderate conservative judicial stance was an official matter of record, but who had no public position on abortion. During the Senate confirmation hearings, Souter adroitly evaded any questions that might give a clue to how he stood on the subject. Accordingly he was quickly and smoothly confirmed.

Not so, however, with the next Bush nominee. In 1991 Associate Justice Thurgood Marshall retired. Appointed in 1967 by President Lyndon B. Johnson, Marshall was the first Black American to sit on the Supreme Court. President Bush nominated Clarence Thomas as his replacement. That Bush nominated a conservative Black jurist to replace the liberal Marshall came as no surprise; many felt, though, that others were much more eminently qualified, and that Bush's nomination was influenced more by political considerations than legal and jurisprudential. As had Souter before him, Thomas evaded all questions seeking to reveal a position on abortion. But suddenly an unexpected issue burst onto the scene: Thomas was accused of sexual harrassment. Despite considerable disquieting and emotional testimony and divisive national concern, the Senate confirmed Thomas by a close vote.

By the end of the Bush administration—he was defeated for re-election in 1992—the national judiciary and especially the Supreme Court had become the center of two seemingly conflicting forces. One was the long-standing and ongoing issue of liberal versus conservative outlook, focusing in the courts on judicial activism versus judicial restraint. In general, liberal elements championed more governmental and judicial activism; conservatives preferred less government and more judicial restraint, with individual people retaining more and more power to make decisions for themselves. The other issue which had pushed to the forefront was the highly volatile question of abortion and abortion rights. It generated totally conflicting signals. On this issue, conservatives—normally favoring judicial restraint—sought exactly the opposite: strong government action and a decisive Supreme Court decision to outlaw abortion. On the other hand, liberals, who normally favored governmental and judicial activism, here strongly supported judicial restraint—for the government and the courts to stay out of the picture—and to leave abortion decisions solely to the individuals concerned; but if there was to be government intervention, it should protect the right of the individual to make that decision.

Thus the national judiciary finds itself today much more involved than it was when it came into being, and perhaps much more than at any time in its two-hundred year history.

Many problems remain to be solved and many questions require answers.

- Has the federal judiciary, and especially the Supreme Court, exceeded its authority in its interpretations of the Constitution as Attorney-General Meese and his supporters suggested? Has the judiciary become too activist? Too politicized?
- Should the Constitution define more clearly the jurisdiction and powers of the federal courts, and especially of the Supreme Court? If so, in what ways?
- Some people have suggested that the federal courts' jurisdiction, and especially that of the Supreme Court, be limited, so that certain types of cases will no longer go to those courts. Do you agree?
- Should we require at least minimum qualifications for federal judges as we do for the President and for members of Congress? If so, what should they be? Should Supreme Court justices require more stringent qualifications than other federal judges?
- Is one Supreme Court sufficient to handle the case load? What about the number of Supreme Court justices?
- Should we continue with separate state and federal court systems, or should they be combined? Or should one or the other be abolished?
- Should federal judges hold office for life or for a specified term? If the latter, should they be eligible for reappointment? Should they be elected instead of appointed?
- What can be done to make our citizenry more familiar with the operation of our federal courts?
- These and other questions concern many American people.

What do you think?

NOTES

1. A lot of *local* jurisprudence in Louisiana has a French flavor, and *local* law in the southwestern border states have a Spanish flavor—but that is local law in contrast with our national law.

2. As Chief Justice, John Marshall has been credited with much of what that "Marshall Court" achieved—and deservedly so because of his legal acumen and influence over the Court. Nevertheless, although overshadowed by Marshall, his colleagues on the Court should not be overlooked. They were by no means mere "rubber stamps" for Marshall. They merit their own place in American legal history. Among them, Justice Joseph Story especially should be noted as one of the greats.

3. It should be kept in mind that the Republican party came into existence for reasons more than just opposition to slavery.

THE AMENDMENTS

The American Constitution, said the great British statesman William Gladstone, is "the most wonderful work ever struck off at a given time by the brain and purpose of man." One reason is that the Constitution is so adaptable to change.

The concept of flexibility may seem plebeian compared with other more visionary principles of our Constitution—principles such as popular sovereignty, limited government, federalism, and checks and balances. Yet the principle of flexibility is no less important. It might, in fact, even be the glue that has kept everything else together for the past two hundred years.

Flexibility—or perhaps the lack of it—has been at the root of many watershed events in history. Not enough flexibility—that is, excessive resistance to change—has caused evils to pile up, until violence and even revolution became the only way to bring about needed change. The American Revolution, the French Revolution, and the Russian Revolution are prime examples in modern history. They all came about because long-standing governments were either unwilling or unable to modify practices and institutions to accommodate societal change. Similar problems of failure of adaptation occurred in recent decades in China, Cuba, South Africa, and Central America, where also bloodshed and violence proved to be the means to solution. (This does not mean that every demand for governmental change is valid and should be accommodated. It seems desirable, though, that a workable mechanism should exist to evaluate legitimate need for change and thereby forestall the necessity of violence.)

Too much flexibility can be as unsatisfactory as too little flexibility. Governments must be stable enough to protect their people from dangers both internal and external. When governments constantly give way to untoward domestic pressures or mob action, the result may be anarchy and tragedy for the people that could be worse than conditions under an unbending tyranny. One need only look at the French Republic of the 1790s (especially the Reign of Terror) or the problems of modern Lebanon in the Middle East.

The Framers of the Constitution experienced both too little and too much flexibility. One of the forces leading to the American Revolution in the first place had been Great Britain's obstinate unwillingness to grant the colonists relief from what the latter considered too much centralized autocratic rule. It took violence—the Revolutionary War—to overcome that lack of flexibility toward needed change. After the Revolutionary War, when the thirteen colonies became independent, they swung to the other extreme, as each insisted on virtually complete freedom of action and state sovereignty, with little or no centralized rule. Withal, they did, at least, recognize the need for some kind of cooperation for survival; and so they organized themselves under the Articles of Confederation.

In so organizing, though, they made what proved to be several serious blunders. They eliminated a strong central government, fearing an American reincarnation of the oppressive British central government. Although a national government did exist in a Congress, that Congress exercised very limited powers. The Articles also excluded national courts and a national chief executive, again for fear they might emulate oppressive British counterparts. But perhaps more pertinent, the creators of the Articles of Confederation clearly intended to de-centralize governmental authority and to place sovereignty in the individual states. So imbued were they with that structure, and so convinced were they that no state should be forced to do anything against its own wishes, that they deliberately sacrificed flexibility for state sovereignty. They incorporated into the Articles a provision that effectively prevented change: any amendment required the consent of all thirteen states. True, that mechanism still allowed change; but realistically, unanimous consent for anything comes very rarely. It was deemed more important that no state have to accept a change it did not approve, regardless of what might be best for all states. State sovereignty carried a higher priority than flexibility.

Within less than a decade, the Founding Fathers became acutely aware of these shortcomings. Efforts to make corrections culminated in the Constitutional Convention in Philadelphia in 1787. Significantly, one of the most important sentiments of that assemblage was a positive attitude toward flexibility and change. Accordingly, during that sweltering summer in the old State House (today called Independence Hall), the Framers set up a government with principles and institutions that suited their needs for their time; but they left it for later generations to adjust to the future.

They did so by providing an amending procedure that could work. It was difficult enough so that future generations could not succumb to mere passing vagaries or temporary pressures or passions; but it was not so difficult as to render the procedure virtually impossible or futile.

We find the mechanism in Article V of the Constitution. It consists of two stages, *proposal* and *ratification*.

Amendments can be *proposed* in one of two ways: (1) by the approval of two-thirds of both Houses of Congress, or (2) by a national convention called by Congress at the request of two thirds of the states.

So far, only the first method has been used successfully. There have been several attempts to use the convention procedure, but they all have failed for lack of sufficient state support. As a result, it is not clear how such a meeting would be convened or exactly what its agenda would be. Specifically, if a convention were called to propose, say, a dual Presidency, could that convention *also* propose (or *instead* propose) an amendment dealing with another issue? Could that convention go so far as to even re-write the Constitution? Legalists and scholars are not at all agreed on answers to those questions. Perhaps that is why this procedure has never been successfully utilized. "By the time you get around to 32 or 33 [of the required 38 states to ratify]," one constitutionalist has stated, "politics becomes more serious and more real." The fear of the unknown may therefore push those who want an amendment toward the two-thirds-of-Congress method; at least there one knows exactly what the proposed amendment will be. Many feel, also—with regard to the convention method—that even if enough states do not endorse a particular proposal, the mere fact of the process being in motion could influence members of Congress to give the matter more favorable attention.

As a matter of fact, even as the convention method for proposing a balanced budget amendment seems recently to have stalled, the demand for a balanced budget has been gaining enough strength in Congress that the first method mentioned in the Constitution—a proposal by two-thirds of the Congress—might lead to such an amendment. The last time the Senate went on record to propose a balanced budget was in 1986, when the vote there fell only one short of the required two-thirds in that house; in 1990, the House fell short by only seven votes. That is getting close to what is required for proposing an amendment.

Once formally proposed, a constitutional amendment can be *ratified* in one of two ways: (1) by the legislatures of three fourths of the states, or (2) by special conventions in three fourths of the states. Only one amendment, the Eighteenth, has been ratified by the special convention method; all others have been ratified by the state legislatures.

One problem over proposed amendments has been the time limit for ratification. The Constitution says nothing about it. The Eighteenth Amendment was the first in which a definite time for ratification (seven years) was fixed. Since then, most proposals (but not all) have set time limits, usually seven years. Several Supreme Court litigations have dealt with the subject. Two especially stand out: *Dillon v. Gloss* (256 U.S. 368 [1921]) and *Coleman v. Miller* (307 U.S. 433 [1939]). The gist of those decisions was that if no time limit is designated, amendments should be ratified within a "reasonable" time. However, the Court added, "reasonable" is a political matter for Congress, not the courts, to decide. Accordingly, when in 1992 a proposal that had been made *in 1789* finally achieved the approval of three-fourths of the states, that proposal was duly certified as the Twenty-Seventh Amendment to the Constitution. (See below for more on that amendment.)

Indeed, at the time the Twenty-Seventh Amendment became part of the Constitution in 1992, *Congressional Quarterly* reported that four old amendments which had been proposed without time limitations still were languishing somewhere in the state legislatures awaiting action. One would change the allocation of membership in the House of Representatives; one would prohibit United States officials from receiving foreign titles of nobility; one would forbid Congress from outlawing slavery; and one would prohibit the exploitation of child labor. The inference was that it was finally time for Congress to clear the slate, so to speak, by legislating all four now as no longer viable proposals.

More than 7,000 suggested amendments have been introduced in Congress in the past two hundred years, but only thirty-four ever received the necessary two-thirds approval to be submitted to the states. Of those, only twenty-seven have been ratified. Considering the vast changes that have taken place since the Constitution was written, it seems most remarkable that so few amendments have been added. More about that later. First, though, a look at those twenty-seven amendments.

The first ten might be considered not actual changes, but rather part of the original Constitution. During the struggle for ratification, opponents of the Constitution—called "antifederalists," although a more appropriate name might have been something like "anti-nationalists" or "anti-centralists"—focused strongly on the lack of a bill of rights. This was not an oversight by the Framers at Philadelphia; they simply had felt that bills of rights already in state constitutions were sufficient and that one in the national Constitution would be superfluous.[1] But in the face of such strong opposition, a remarkable political deal was concluded. Rather than re-convene the Convention to try to re-do the document (which most people feared would lead only to disaster), opponents of the Constitution agreed to vote for it if they were assured that a bill of rights would be enacted once the new government went into effect. That promise was kept. In 1789 twelve amendments were proposed by Congress; two years later, in 1791, ten were ratified and became part of the Constitution.[2] They have been known ever since as our "Bill of Rights."

Every American should read the Bill of Rights carefully, for it deals with what is fundamental to the American way of life. Briefly, its contents are as follows:

The First Amendment guarantees freedom of religion, freedom of speech and the press, and the right of the people peaceably to assembly and to petition the government for redress of grievances.

The Second Amendment deals with the right to keep and bear arms.

The Third Amendment prevents the government from quartering troops in private homes without the consent of the owners.

The Fourth Amendment guarantees us against unreasonable search and seizure.

The Fifth, Sixth, and Seventh Amendments guarantee certain rights in criminal and civil court procedures. They include, among others, no double jeopardy, freedom from self-incrimination, the right to counsel, and the right to confront witnesses. Found here, too, is the right that no person shall be deprived of life, liberty, or property without due process of law.

The Eighth Amendment protects us against excessive bail and against cruel and unusual punishment.

Whereas the first eight amendments deal with specific personal guarantees, the Ninth Amendment points out that our rights are not limited only to those enumerated in the Constitution. There are more, although they are not designated. This is an example of how the principle of flexibility is incorporated even in the Bill of Rights, leaving it for future generations to identify those unspecified rights. Examples of some of those rights, as indicated in later Supreme Court decisions, include the right to engage in political activities and the right to privacy.

The last of the Bill of Rights, the Tenth Amendment, clarifies the federal system of government. Throughout the debates over ratification, many expressed doubts that the Constitution did not clearly enough delineate just how the new federal system was set up—that is, which powers belonged to the new national government and which remained with the states. The Tenth Amendment, therefore, stated that the national government had only those powers which were delegated to it in the Constitution, and all other powers not so delegated were reserved to the states and to the people therein. This clarification, it was hoped, would guarantee an ongoing partnership between the national government and the state governments in running our country, and eliminate any squabbles over which governments had the constitutional power to do just what. Unfortunately things did not work out that way.[3]

Ironically, the Bill of Rights came into being as much for political expediency—that is, to get the Constitution ratified—as to provide certain protections. It was probably the most important political deal ever made in our history. Numerous court decisions later would scrupulously enforce the protections guaranteed in that Bill of Rights.

It would be impossible even to summarize those decisions here, because of the vast number and variety which have affected so many phases of American life. For as society in the United States changed so drastically during the past two hundred years, so too have interpretations of Bill of Rights freedoms changed. The scope and nature of twentieth-century American education have broadened considerably from what they had been earlier. Modern news media and satellite communications have created altogether different and much more complex problems and issues from those faced by the simpler nineteenth-century press. Modern life styles differ markedly from those of earlier days, as do demands upon all citizens merely to survive and compete in the modern world. Yet even as those changes have transpired, interpretations of Bill of Rights freedoms have enabled American society to adjust to those changes, but at the same time to retain those basic freedoms which our Founding Fathers considered so necessary.

Thus even today new issues constantly arise which require diligent scrutiny of the Bill of Rights. Are there, for instance, limitations to freedom of speech? Where is the line between freedom of the press and pornography? What about gun control? Does the Bill of Rights in the Second Amendment protect the right of *any* citizen to own a revolver? What of the controversial issue of separation of church and state? If children open a school day with a brief prayer, is that a violation of the "freedom of religion" guarantee in the Bill of Rights? What constitutes "cruel and unusual" punishment? Is it the seven-year sentence in maximum-security prison for a drug peddler who has destroyed the lives of scores of young people? Or is it the financial burden on the parents of those young people whose taxes pay for food and shelter—and even recreation and entertainment—for that incarcerated pusher for those seven years? Should the death penalty be prescribed for a person who commits numerous and indescribably heinous crimes? How much should procedural due process of law—*i.e.,* "Miranda" rights—protect an individual who voluntarily confesses to felonious criminal activities? How much should a "Fifth Amendment" plea protect a government official whose testimony is vital to national security? Where, indeed, do we draw the line between protecting the welfare and security of the individual and the welfare and security of the community? Is abortion related to the Bill of Rights? These are only a few of the issues we face today which involve basic freedoms guaranteed in the Bill of Rights. Whoever coined the phrase "a *living* Bill of Rights" certainly was correct.

Within a few years after the Bill of Rights was ratified, two more amendments were added to the Constitution. The Eleventh Amendment, ratified in 1799, corrected an oversight by the Framers that was brought to light by the Supreme Court decision in *Chisholm v. Georgia* (2 Dallas 419 [1793]). The Eleventh Amendment protects a state from being sued by a citizen of another state, thereby strengthening the equal relationship of states toward each other as well as clarifying a questionable concept under federalism.

The Twelfth Amendment, ratified in 1804, was really the first adaptation to a societal change, in this case a change in political alignments and relationships. Political parties, or "factions" as they were called at the time of the Constitutional Convention, were not prominent enough at first to affect Presidential elections. Therefore the electoral college system developed by the Framers did not take them into account. By the 1800 election, however, the role of parties had changed dramatically. It led to a tie for the Presidency in the electoral college vote that clearly did not reflect the desires of the voters. The election crisis ended only after thirty-six tie-breaking ballots in the House of Representatives finally saw Thomas Jefferson emerge as President. To prevent a similar fiasco, the Twelfth Amendment came into being, providing for casting electoral votes separately for President and Vice-President, as we still do today.

That, though, oversimplifies how the electoral college actually works. The Framers had anticipated that voters in each state would elect respected and knowledgeable persons as Presidential electors—persons in whom those voters placed enough confidence to entrust the monumental responsibility of choosing a President. But within only a few years after that system was created, political parties came into prominence and, as indicated above, were responsible for the confusion which resulted in the 1800 election. Now, because of the impact of political parties, very complex procedures have developed—but still centered around the Twelfth Amendment.

Our quadrennial Presidential elections actually are fifty separate elections, conducted on the same day within each of the states. Prior to those November elections, political parties in each state, following procedures designated by each state legislature for that state, select delegates to a national convention where collectively—in separate party conventions—they nominate a candidate for their party. Each state, and sometimes even the parties within the same state, choose those delegates their own way—some by primaries, some by caucuses, some by combinations of various and sundry procedures. In the course of selecting those delegates to the national nominating conventions, each party in each state also designates—in different ways, and usually with little or no fanfare or publicity—the appropriate number of persons *of its party* who will cast the electoral votes for *its* state if *its* candidate wins *in that state* in the November election. Each state, according to the Constitution, is entitled to the number of electors equal to the number of its Representatives and Senators. Thus, if a state has ten Representatives and two Senators, it is entitled to twelve Presidential electors. The Democrats of that state will name twelve *Democratic* electors; the Republicans will name twelve *Republican* electors. If the Republican candidate for President wins in that state—the names on the November ballots will be those of the candidates, not of the electors—then the twelve *Republican electors* will do what the Twelfth Amendment authorizes them to do: they will meet at a designated time and place (in the state capital, on the first Tuesday after the first Monday in December following the November election) and cast two ballots. Each will cast one vote for the *Republican* candidate for President—a total of twelve votes; each also will cast one vote for the *Republican* candidate for Vice President—a total of twelve votes.

(Technically, when the voters in November voted, those who voted for the Republican candidates were *really* voting for the twelve Republican electors to be the ones to cast their electoral votes in December, and those who voted for the Democratic candidates were likewise voting for the twelve Democratic electors to be the ones to vote in December. It is probably too true that most voters are not aware that that is what actually is happening.) The electoral votes cast in all fifty states are then counted. The candidate for President who has the majority is elected President, and the candidate for Vice President who has the majority is elected Vice-President. If no candidate has a majority, the Twelfth Amendment directs what is to come next—appropriate elections in the House and/or Senate.

Although many feel that modern communications and technology have rendered that whole electoral college procedure obsolete, the way it operates under the Twelfth Amendment is still the way we elect our President and Vice-President. Many have advocated different ways to nominate the candidates, as well as different ways to elect them. As clumsy and complicated and costly as our present procedures happen to be, the system still works—and it is very likely that no major changes will take place until and/or unless some major crisis develops because of those complexities, and when and if they result in the election of a person or persons contrary to what is clearly the demonstrated desires of the voters.

More than half a century passed before any more amendments were added to the Constitution. Then, in rapid succession, came the Thirteenth, Fourteenth, and Fifteenth Amendments. They were the direct result of the Civil War and are referred to collectively as the "Civil War Amendments." Briefly, the Thirteenth Amendment abolished slavery; the Fourteenth Amendment made all persons born in the United States, including the former slaves, citizens; and the Fifteenth made it illegal to prevent anyone from voting because of race, color, or previous condition of servitude.

The Fourteenth Amendment merits special attention. First of all, though, it should be noted that most of that Amendment is no longer applicable today—it contains many restrictions on supporters of the Confederacy which eventually were removed and of course are no longer operable.

Much more important, however, is Section 1 of the Fourteenth Amendment. First it deals with who are citizens of this country. In 1857, in a highly controversial decision which fueled the sectionalism that erupted into bloody civil war, the Supreme Court in *Dred Scott v. John F. A. Sandford* (19 Howard 393 [1857]) had declared that persons "of African descent," whether free or slave, could not be citizens of a state or of the United States.

The Fourteenth Amendment overturned that ruling and provided instead that "all persons born or naturalized in the United States, and subject to the jurisdiction thereof, are citizens of the United States and of the States wherein they reside."

The Fourteenth Amendment then turned to the rights which those citizens possess, and again dealt with the consequences of earlier Supreme Court action. In 1833 the Court had held in *Barron v. Baltimore* (7 Peters 243 [1833]) that the Bill of Rights applied only to opprobrious acts by the national government but not to those by the state or local governments. The Fourteenth Amendment sought to change that. Indeed, during the debates on that amendment, Congressman John Bingham, one of its principal authors, stated very pointedly that he and others hoped to extend the "sacred bill of rights" against "indecorous" *state* action, to "protect by *national* law the privileges and immunities of all citizens... whenever the same shall be abridged or denied by the unconstitutional acts of any state." Accordingly, the Fourteenth Amendment reads: "No state shall make or enforce any law which shall abridge the privileges or immunities of citizens of the United States; nor shall any State deprive any person of life, liberty, or property, without due process of law" (note the repetition of that important phraseology from the Fifth Amendment); "nor deny to any person within its jurisdiction the equal protection of the laws." Those words became the wellspring from which later flowed many civil rights laws and programs.

But it took almost a hundred years for them to come. For in spite of the intent of those who championed the Fourteenth Amendment, and in spite even of its seemingly clear wording, the Supreme Court for a long time interpreted those words to mean something quite different.

Several factors contributed to the Court's action. The first was the long-existing hazy definition of "civil rights." Civil rights indisputably include such legal rights as the right to vote, to trial by jury, to enter into contracts, to own property, to use the courts, and others. But do civil rights also include social equality as well: the right to live in the same neighborhood, to eat in the same restaurant, to ride in the same railroad car, etc.? One would like to believe that that is what Thomas Jefferson meant by "all men are created equal." But in spite of that ringing phraseology, even Abraham Lincoln maintained that while blacks were human beings entitled to the rights of citizenship and full benefits of the law, that did not include acceptance of "all men" as *social* equals. Did the Fourteenth Amendment change that, then, so that henceforth no state could prohibit one from eating in a certain restaurant or ride in a particular railroad car? Or that businesses could not exclude certain people because of race? Could courts enforce contracts that contained racial discriminatory provisions? Just what did "equal protection of the laws" mean when one individual wanted to use his property one way (segregated) and another individual claimed the right as a citizen of equal access to that property in a different way (integrated)? Unfortunately neither the Fifth Amendment (a prohibition on the federal government) nor the Fourteenth Amendment (a prohibition on the states) actually faced the issue head on with any clear definitions of the meaning of civil rights.

The "fuzziness of civil rights" factor was abetted by a second situation, a change in the direction of the abolitionist movement. Once the Civil War was ended, and especially after the passage of the Thirteenth, Fourteenth, and Fifteenth Amendments, the evangelical ardor of the pre-war abolitionist crusade evaporated almost overnight, and reformers turned their attention to other matters. Historians still do not agree on the reasons why, but once the slaves had been freed and granted rights of citizenship and suffrage, they suddenly were left on their own to compete for a new place in American society. Their general lack of education and of marketable economic skills—because of the constrictions of slavery—were in themselves an enormous obstacle to lifting themselves from the throes of slave life. That was compounded by infamous and shameful racial prejudice, an abominable xenophobic disease which afflicts mankind all over the world but which is especially detestable in a free democratic society. That prejudice and racism proved to be an important and disastrous factor in the history of the Fourteenth Amendment.

A third factor which affected the history and development of the Fourteenth Amendment was the transformation of the United States after the Civil War from a rural agricultural society to one that became more and more urban and industrial. The post-Civil War era experienced a veritable explosion of a new industrialism and a consuming nation-wide determination for economic and material growth and expansion. Known popularly as the "Gilded Age," the last few decades of the nineteenth century saw unprecedented economic growth as the Industrial Revolution reached the United States in full force. Our population expanded by leaps and bounds as millions of immigrants flocked to our shores from Europe, crowding into the eastern cities, flooding into the open plains of the midwest, and filling the western frontier which for so long had beckoned more and more settlers. A new multi-cultural and multi-ethnic society inexorably replaced the old, as huge industries and metropolitan urban centers gradually displaced the small-town and small-farm way of life.

All these changes affected the nature of the litigations which came into the courts. They also influenced the attitudes of jurists in how they viewed legal relationships, especially in how they reordered their own legal and political priorities.

The consequences could be seen markedly in two kinds of cases which came before the Supreme Court. The first category consisted of suits dealing with economic regulation, and is best exemplified by the *Slaughterhouse Cases* (16 Wallace 36 [1873]), only a few years following the ratification of the Fourteenth

Amendment. As far back as 1819, in *Dartmouth College v. Woodward* (4 Wheaton 515 [1819]), the strong pro-property Chief Justice John Marshall had proclaimed the legal principle that a corporation was an "artificial person," entitled to the same legal protections as any human citizen. In 1873 the Court in *Slaughterhouse* went further: if a business was a corporation and therefore a "person" and also a "citizen," that business was duly protected by the Fourteenth Amendment against certain state interference. Intended to safeguard and guarantee the rights of newly freed slaves, the Fourteenth Amendment became instead a vehicle to protect and to promote growing big business. As the court broadened the *Slaughterhouse* interpretation, big business found the Fourteenth Amendment one of its greatest boons. One of those broader interpretations merits special mention, *Hurtado v. California* (110 U.S. 516 [1884]), in which the Court asserted bluntly that the Fourteenth Amendment did not extend the Bill of Rights prohibitions to the states. Not until forty years later, in *Gitlow v. New York* (268 U.S. 652 [1925]) did the Court finally reverse itself and allow that the Fourteenth Amendment did indeed extend the Bill of Rights restrictions against the states. Meanwhile, though, for several decades, the Fourteenth Amendment sustained and even shielded the growth of big business from state interference; while at the same time many states continued discriminatory civil rights practices toward their black citizens.

Along with those litigations dealing with business and economic regulation, another group based on the Fourteenth Amendment involved civil rights of black citizens. The actual number of cases in the latter category was relatively few. And those few floundered on the fuzzy "civil rights *versus* social equality" distinction pointed out earlier. The result was a sordid record of blatant state-sanctioned racial discriminatory practices, including such things as disqualifying blacks from sitting on juries, restricting them from living in certain neighborhoods, and even denying them the right to vote. Indeed, the shameful segregation that so many associate with some parts of the South (as well, it should be pointed out, with some parts of the North) in the late nineteenth and early twentieth centuries was fostered and abetted in no small part by the Supreme Court's interpretations of the Fourteenth Amendment. Two of the most infamous were in the *Civil Rights Cases* (109 U.S. 3 [1883]) and *Plessy v. Ferguson* (163 U.S. 537 [1896]) decisions. In the former, the Court declared unconstitutional the Civil Rights Act of 1875 which prohibited racial discrimination by proprietors of hotels, theaters, and railways. The Court declared that such practices were *private* matters not within the purview of the Fourteenth Amendment. In the *Plessy* case the Court upheld the "separate but equal" doctrine, thereby putting a stamp of approval on racial segregation in institutions of all sorts, including schools, railroads, and even drinking and toilet facilities—as long as separate facilities—and "equal," however that term was interpreted—were available for the black populace.

Black Americans were not the only group wronged by narrow interpretations of the Fourteenth Amendment. The Supreme Court dealt severe blows also to rights of women. In 1873, in *Bradwell v. Illinois* (16 Wallace 131 [1873]), the Court rejected the claim of a woman to practice law, denying that occupational choice was a woman's right protected by the Fourteenth Amendment's "privileges and immunities" clause. Of wider impact was *Minor v. Happersett* (21 Wallace 163 [1875], declaring that states could restrict voting to men only, the Court holding that women's suffrage also was not a right protected by the Fourteenth Amendment. That changed later, of course, but it took an amendment to the Constitution to do it. As for other women's rights, many remained limited until the 1960s and beyond, precipitating a very spirited movement for an "equal rights" amendment to guarantee equality for women in all aspects of American life.

World War II proved to be a watershed in the struggles to do something about all sorts of discrimination. Blacks, women, Hispanics, Orientals, native American Indians, and other minorities had served bravely in the armed forces. Many had labored diligently in the work force on the home front. And America had been urbanized and industrialized long enough to realize some of its injustices of the past. In 1954, accordingly, in *Brown v. the Board of Education of Topeka* (349 U.S. 294 [1954]), a unanimous Court reversed the *Plessy* decision as a violation of the Fourteenth Amendment. That was followed a decade later by Congress passing the Civil Rights Act of 1964, the Voting Rights Act of 1965, and other legislation of a similar vein. The door was opened finally, though not without considerable resistance, to ending segregation and discrimination in many areas of American life. New interpretations of the Fourteenth Amendment finally brought to fruition what had been its intent when ratified a century earlier. In fact, not only were rights of black citizens recognized, but so were those of other minority groups, not only racial and ethnic, but also such groups as the aged, the sick, the indigent, and the mentally and physically impaired. Nevertheless, it seems that no sooner was one aggrieved group accomodated than another appeared; this is one of the prices a free and constantly changing people must pay, apparently, until some utopian society is finally attained.

Following the Civil War Amendments, no further changes were made in the Constitution for about fifty years. The early twentieth century was the height of the Progressive period, epitomized by Presidents Theodore Roosevelt, William Howard Taft, and Woodrow Wilson. Between 1913 and 1920 four amendments were ratified. Three related directly to expansion of democracy, both politically and economically. The Sixteenth Amendment legalized the income tax and

THE AMENDMENTS

opened a hitherto untapped source of revenue for many new government programs. The Seventeenth Amendment provided for the election of United States Senators by direct election of the voters instead of by the state legislatures. And the Nineteenth Amendment, as indicated above, gave women the right to vote, culminating a struggle for the women's franchise which had begun a century earlier in Jacksonian times.

Along with those three Progressive amendments came the Eighteenth Amendment, the "Prohibition" Amendment. Anti-drink elements had been active in America from the time liquor first was distilled here—way back in the early colonial days—but World War I proved to be their greatest boon. The fact that alcohol and grain were both essential for the war effort abetted the moral crusade against "John Barleycorn." Pushed by the Anti-Saloon League, one of the most powerful pressure groups in American history, the Prohibition Amendment became part of the Constitution in 1918. But it created more problems than it solved, for apparently morals cannot be legislated in a free society. Bootlegging spread and "home hooch" proliferated. Much worse, though, was the widespread negative attitude toward prohibition laws; they were openly ridiculed, defied, and ignored. Bootleggers delivered illegal liquor directly to the offices of Congressmen and Senators. President Warren Harding regularly served whiskey at White House poker parties. Combined with other factors which produced the "Roaring Twenties," widespread disregard toward the Eighteenth Amendment created an atmosphere conducive to crime and gangsterism. Not surprising as a sign of the times was that one of the most widely known symbols of the 1920s was the criminal Al Capone.

The advent of Franklin D. Roosevelt and the New Deal in 1933 brought a change. Specifically, two more amendments were quickly ratified. The Twentieth, known as the "Lame Duck" Amendment, moved up the inauguration of the President and the convening of Congress from March to January. The Framers had built in a four month span between election and inauguration to allow plenty of time for counting ballots and breaking ties. Sometimes that delay allowed an incumbent (or a "lame duck") to stay on well after the electorate had indicated its preference for someone else. That was especially true after the 1932 election, with the country floundering in the Great Depression and President Hoover unable to do much. Furthermore, by the 1930s communication and transportation had so improved that the time could be shortened. In fact, many feel today that the transition period might be reduced even more because of further improvements in communications technology.

The Twenty-First Amendment came in 1933 on a wave of enthusiasm that matched the fervor of the earlier drive for the Eighteenth Amendment. Many people associated much of the nation's social and economic malaise with Prohibition, just as earlier they had connected it with speakeasies and bootlegging. Not to be overlooked, either, was that legalizing the brewing industry also meant jobs for countless unemployed. The result was the Twenty-First Amendment which repealed the Eighteenth. "Happy Days Are Here Again" symbolized in song the repeal of Prohibition as much as it did the politics of Franklin D. Roosevelt.

One of the most provocative episodes of the New Deal period centered, incidentally, on the Supreme Court. It was the so called "Court Packing" proposal to re-structure that body. Because of adverse rulings by the Court, Roosevelt feared that the "nine old men," as he beratingly dubbed them, might stand in the way of the New Deal program. Arguing that the Justices were overburdened with excessive case-loads, the President proposed increasing the size of the Supreme Court from nine to fifteen, adding fifty judges to the lower federal courts, and streamlining the judicial procedure to speed the litigation of cases involving constitutional issues. Though Roosevelt stressed the need to make the Court more efficient and responsive, most saw this as a blatant move by the President to appoint judges favorable to his views and thereby ensure the implementation of his programs. Despite Roosevelt's enormous popularity—he had just been overwhelmingly re-elected in 1936—the country and Congress rejected the President's proposal, refusing, as many contemporaries expressed it, "to fiddle with the Constitution" just to achieve political ends.

As a matter of fact, the next amendment to be ratified, the Twenty-Second, might even be construed as anti-Roosevelt. True, Roosevelt was an unusually popular President and was elected an unprecedented four times; but such popularity inevitably breeds resentment and even fuels reaction. Furthermore, much of Roosevelt's political leadership of the 1930s changed to personal charisma in the 1940s, as a result of the country's reticence to change leaders during World War II. With the war over, however, the Twenty-Second Amendment was proposed and ratified, providing that no one could be elected President to more than two terms. Although historians are pretty much agreed that this amendment came about as a reaction to the Roosevelt experience, it is also clear that this amendment made into law what had been a two-term tradition dating back to George Washington.

The decade of the 1960s saw a tumultuous civil rights movement that witnessed just about everything from protest marches to assassinations to constitutional amendments. This is not the place to review the deplorable history of what happened to the civil rights of America's black population after the Civil War. Suffice it to say that it took a hundred years for those rights to finally come to fruition, and it began in the aftermath of World War II. Among the first steps were measures by President Harry S. Truman to desegregate America's armed forces, a process completed under his successor Dwight D. Eisenhower. Of equal importance was the breaking of the color line in professional baseball, with the great Jackie Robinson becoming the first black player in the Big Leagues. (Black athletes had been prominent in other sports—*i.e.,* Jack Johnson and Joe Louis in boxing, Jesse Owens in track—but baseball, after all, is considered the "national" pastime.) Perhaps the most significant in a series of important events was the landmark 1954 Supreme Court decision in *Brown v. the Board of Education of Topeka* (349 U.S. 294 [1954]), which declared racial segregation in public schools to be illegal.

Other developments in this civil rights crusade included the passage of two amendments to the United States Constitution. The Twenty-Third Amendment permitted the District of Columbia, overwhelmingly black, to cast electoral votes for President and Vice-President, just as did the states. The Twenty-Fourth Amendment outlawed the poll tax in Presidential elections, a device many states had used for a long time to prevent blacks and other minorities from voting.

Crises in the 1950s and 1960s were not confined to civil rights. On more than one occasion they centered around Presidential succession. President Kennedy was assassinated; Presidents Eisenhower and Johnson experienced serious illness and surgery. Conflicting views and interpretations about both temporary and permanent succession led to the Twenty-Fifth Amendment.

That amendment came just in time, for in the 1970s Vice-President Spiro T. Agnew and President Richard M. Nixon both resigned from office in disgrace. This was not the first time the Vice-Presidency was vacant. John C. Calhoun had resigned in 1832 over differences with President Andrew Jackson. Seven other Vice-Presidents had died in office. None, however, had been replaced, because there had been no compulsion to do so, nor did the Constitution provide for a replacement in that office if it became vacant. On the other hand, the office of the President had become vacant eight times as a result of death, four of them—Lincoln, Garfield, McKinley, and Kennedy—by assassination. In each case the Vice-President immediately succeeded to the Presidency, but leaving the office of Vice-President vacant.

Widespread confusion and conjecture during the illnesses of President Eisenhower (1950s) and President Johnson (1960s) led to the need for clarification. The result was the Twenty-Fifth Amendment. It explained circumstances and procedures by which a Vice-President could succeed to the Presidency, either temporarily or permanently, when factors other than the President's death led to the Chief Executive being considered "incapacitated" and unable to perform his duties. The amendment also provided for filling the vacant Vice-President's office when the latter was elevated to the Presidency, or if the office became vacant for any other reason.

The Twenty-Fifth Amendment had been in place but a few years when its provisions became critical. In 1973 Vice-President Agnew resigned rather than face almost certain impeachment when confronted by irrefutable evidence of ongoing criminal behavior, both before and after he assumed office. The honest and "squeaky clean" Gerald R. Ford was appointed to fill the office. (Ford was a veteran Congressman from Michigan, and at the time was the Republican Floor Leader in the House of Representatives.) While that scenario was unfolding, one of the most convulsive crises in twentieth-century American history was unraveling, the "Watergate Affair." In the background of all of this was the divisive war in Vietnam. Events reached a climax in 1974. Faced with almost certain impeachment for numerous abuses of his office, President Nixon resigned, the first person ever to abdicate the Presidency. The mechanism established in the new Twenty-Fifth Amendment made possible a remarkably smooth transition which saved the country from a devastating trauma. Vice-President Ford became President; he, in turn, appointed Governor Nelson A. Rockefeller of New York to be Vice-President. One of our most dangerous constitutional crises was over. The nation and the Constitution were still intact; and the new Twenty-Fifth Amendment had played a decisive role.

Midst all the other crises in the 1960s and 1970s was the very unpopular war in Vietnam. Many grievances emerged, including: "If I'm old enough to fight and die for my country, I'm also old enough to vote." In 1971, accordingly, the Twenty-Sixth Amendment came into existence, lowering the voting age to eighteen. With the voting age lowered, of course, many more Americans acquired the opportunity to be a part of the democratic decision-making process. Whether they do, however, depends upon their individual willingness to participate. Of course, that applies to everyone, not just the eighteen-to-twenty-one age group.

Since the passage of the Twenty-Sixth Amendment in 1971, at least four issues loomed as subjects for potential constitutional amendments. They dealt with women's rights, a balanced budget, prayer in the public schools, and abortion. But in 1992 another matter suddenly emerged: the compensation of members of Congress and specifically the question of mid-term raises.

The morphology of that amendment is quite singular. Congress has the authority to establish the salaries of its own members, as it does that of the President. One difference, though, exists. The President's salary cannot be increased during his current term; any increase must await either a second term or a successor. No such constitutional limitation applies to Congress, and so salary increases can be voted to go into effect immediately or at any time during the

THE AMENDMENTS

current term. Among the amendments which James Madison proposed in 1789, ten were duly ratified and became the first ten amendments to the Constitution—our Bill of Rights. One which did not receive the necessary ratification by three-fourths of the states would have changed the salary situation in Congress to be the same as for the President; that is, no salary increase could go into effect until the next term of Congress. But having failed ratification, that proposal seemed to have become a dead issue.

Two hundred years later, in the summer of 1991, the Senate voted itself an increase of $23,200 to bring Senate salaries up to the level of salaries in the House—$129,500 per year. Although few disagree that being a member of Congress is very costly, for some time our national legislators had come under considerable criticism over various devices some used to augment their salaries and even to build financial coffers for political purposes. The timing of this 1991 increase triggered an outpouring of strong concern. The country was in the midst of serious economic difficulties; and widespread unemployment and increasing job layoffs contrasted starkly with the Senate voting itself what to many seemed an outrageous "money grab." Demands to limit the terms of members of Congress, and especially to limit their salaries, were loudly pronounced all over the country—even if it took a Constitutional amendment to do it. That the following year—1992—was an election year merely added to the tension.

Suddenly the country became aware that a salary limitation amendment actually was "in the pipeline," so to speak. It was, incredibly, the one that had been proposed by James Madison way back in 1789—two hundred years earlier!—that Congressional salary increases could not take effect in mid-term but had to wait until the next term of Congress. No time limit had ever been placed on that proposed amendment. Accordingly, after the first ten—the Bill of Rights—had been ratified, this proposal merely languished in the state legislatures. During the entire nineteenth century, only one state legislature ratified it—Ohio, in 1873. It wasn't until the 1970s—a full century later—that any more states took similar action, influenced unquestionably by a growing national concern, especially among conservative groups, over the increasing costs of our national government. In truth, though, even those who ratified this old amendment were not quite sure how effective or valid that ratification was, considering that this proposal had been lying around for such a long time. The Senate action in the summer of 1991 aroused a new interest in the old "lost amendment," and states which had done nothing before now found reason to act. On May 7, 1992, Michigan became the thirty-eighth state since 1789 to ratify Madison's proposal. It now had the approval of three-fourths of the states.

The question, of course, was whether an amendment proposed in 1789 could remain viable for so long. Constitutionalists were divided, but most felt that the key factor was that no time limit had been set in the proposal. (Most proposed amendments in later years normally included a time limit, usually seven years.) Indeed, a Supreme Court decision, *Coleman v. Miller* (307 U.S. 433 [1939]), declared that if a proposed amendment contained no time limit for ratification, a "reasonable" time should be allowed, and what was "reasonable" should be left for Congress to determine. The closest Congress came to defining "reasonable" was in the 1980s, when an "equal rights for women" amendment failed to receive the approval of three-fourths of the states within a prescribed seven-year time limit; Congress then extended that time limit for another three years. (The proposal still failed to be ratified.)

Two events in 1992 made the 1789 Madison proposal the Twenty-Seventh Amendment to the Constitution. First was the action by the Archivist of the United States. Pursuant to Section 106b, Title 1 of the United States Code (1988 Edition), he is the person authorized to proclaim that a proposed amendment has received the approval of three-fourths of the states and has been duly ratified to become a part of the Constitution. Some felt that Archivist Don W. Wilson might hold off on this amendment and wait for Congress to act first, using *Coleman v. Miller* as the basis. Instead, Wilson, himself a professional historian, concluded that the Madison proposal had met the requisites for ratification prescribed in the Constitution. On May 18, 1992, he officially certified it as the Twenty-Seventh Amendment and ordered it duly printed as such in the *Federal Register*, in which are published official documents, proclamations, etc. of the United States Government.

The second event occurred a few days later. It was resolutions passed by both houses of Congress approving the Archivist's action and also proclaiming the amendment as duly ratified. When Congress acted, however, the Senator who introduced the resolution indicated that its purpose was really two-fold. One was to endorse the Archivist's action. The other purpose, however, had something of an ominous separation-of-powers ring to it: it was to indicate that *Congress* had the final say on whether ratification had been achieved. In this case, since both the Archivist and Congress agreed, the question remained moot.

One might wonder, though, if either the Archivist or the Congress had disagreed on the vialibity and validity of the old Madison proposal and the ensuing ratification procedures, what, then, would be the legal status of that proposed amendment? Or, for that matter, the status of any other proposal with a similar morphology? For in fact there are at least four more amendment proposals without time limitations languishing somewhere in the state legislatures. One is the last of the original 1789 Madison proposals, which would change the allocation of members of the House of Representatives; one proposed in 1810 which would prohibit United States officials from receiving foreign titles of nobility; one proposed in 1861 which would forbid Congress from outlawing slavery; and one proposed in 1924 which would prohibit the exploitation of child labor. To allay any problems over the time limit question, steps have been taken in Congress to invalidate those amendment proposals and wipe them off the slate. That does not mean, however, that others would not take their place.

Thus the Constitution has been amended only twenty-seven times in two hundred years. If we consider the first ten—the Bill of Rights—as tantamount to being part of the original document, that leaves only seventeen changes. Two of those—the one providing for Prohibition and the one providing for its repeal—balance each other out. That leaves only fifteen actual changes to the Constitution in the past two hundred years. Most have dealt with either clarifying or expanding citizenship or voting rights or election procedures, and thus reflect the continued concern for the democratic process and civil rights.

Considering the tremendous changes of the past two hundred years in American society, how has the Constitution survived with so few amendments? Certainly more changes must have been necessary. Earlier we alluded to the importance of flexibility and how the Framers were satisfied that they had built that principle into the Constitution with the amendment procedure. What they did not foresee was that there would be other ways of adapting to change that would be just as effective as amendment. We generally refer to those other ways as "informal" amendments in contrast with the twenty-seven "formal" amendments. Ironically, most of those "informal" amendments probably would never have made it had they been proposed as formal amendments. Yet they have been just as binding as if they had come about that way.

They number many more than the formal amendments. Indeed, it would be very difficult to count them or to make some sort of numerical list of them. Furthermore, they came about in many different ways, most without publicity or fanfare; in fact, often we are not even aware until later that they even exist—many sort of "just happened."

Scholars of American history and government generally classify those informal amendments under five headings: (1) court decisions; (2) Presidential actions; (3) Congressional actions; (4) customs and tradition; and (5) political party practices. We shall look at a few examples of each.

First, *court decisions*. Early in our history, in 1803, in the landmark case of *Marbury v. Madison* (1 Cranch 137 [1803]), the Supreme Court asserted the doctrine of judicial review and the power to declare a law of Congress unconstitutional. From that base, the Court emerged as the final interpreter of the law. In fact, one of the most meaningful truisms of American life is the statement attributed to Chief Justice Charles Evans Hughes: "The Constitution is what the judges say it is." Different Courts have interpreted the words of the Constitution or of a law differently, according to changing times and changing circumstances, and differing judicial philosophies. Thus, for instance, as indicated above, in 1896, in *Plessy v. Ferguson* (163 U.S. 537 [1896]), the Court interpreted the "equal protection of the laws" provision of the Fourteenth Amendment to allow segregated facilities for blacks as long as they were "separate but equal." In 1954, in *Brown v. the Board of Education of Topeka* (349 U.S. 294 [1954]), the Court reversed its *Plessy* interpretation and outlawed racial segregation of any kind in the public schools as unequal and therefore unconstitutional. That decision opened the door for more actions which desegregated one institution after another, from swimming pools to theaters to restaurants to hotels. American society has changed notably because of that one decision. No formal constitutional amendment was necessary to desegregate society; the Court's decision was enough.

Unfortunately *attitudes* such as bigotry and xenophobia cannot be legislated or changed by court decisions. They can change the *outward manifestations* of those attitudes, such as by outlawing segregation, but changing attitudes themselves is much more difficult. Of course, this is not by any means an exclusively American problem; it exists all over the world. But that is no consolation.

Our history is replete with societal changes brought about by Court interpretations either of the Constitution or of laws. They include, for instance, interpretations which dealt with hours and conditions of work, with the meaning of "due process of law" in the treatment of accused criminals, with the treatment accorded the sick and the indigent, and with activities of students in schools. The wording of the law or of the Constitution may remain the same; what often changes is the Court's interpretation of what that wording means as society changes. Yet those new interpretations are as binding as though they were a formal part of the Constitution or of the law.

Presidential executive action is another method of informal amendment to the Constitution. For instance, when President William Henry Harrison died in 1841, Vice-President John Tyler succeeded to the office according to the Constitution. This was the first time this had happened. But what were his powers? The Constitution does not say. Was he only "acting" President, or did he assume the full status of his deceased predecessor? Questions existed even about his title: was he now "President Tyler" or was he still "Vice-President Tyler," but merely acting as President? After consulting with others, Tyler determined that he was in fact President in title and in power, just as though he had been elected to that office in the first place. His ruling was accepted, and it has applied to every later Vice-

THE AMENDMENTS

President who succeeded to the Presidency—just as though it explicitly stated so in the Constitution.

Another example of informal amendment through Presidential action is the executive agreement. The Constitution empowers the President to make treaties with foreign countries, but those treaties must be ratified by two-thirds of the Senate. After the devastating experience Woodrow Wilson had with the Treaty of Versailles following World War I, twentieth-century Presidents have found the device of "executive agreements" easier to make and much easier to implement, and without the hassle of Senatorial interference. The Constitution says absolutely nothing about the executive agreement; it is a power Presidents have conveniently inferred from the term "executive power" in the Constitution. Yet a Presidential executive agreement is just as binding as if authorized in the original Constitution, in a formal amendment, or in a law of Congress.

Not only the courts and the Presidents, but *Congressional action* has also changed the Constitution through informal amendment, by basic legislation or by other action. For instance, the Constitution provides for a Congress, but it says very little about how it should operate, leaving that to Congress itself. That is precisely what Congress did, setting up the complex system of committees and seniority so vital in how we make governmental decisions which affect all of us every day. Those procedures are as inviolable as though stipulated in the Constitution; yet periodically they are modified or even rescinded by Congressional action. No Constitutional amendment is required.

Another example equating Congressional legislation with amendment: We already have alluded to the powerful role of the Supreme Court. Yet the number of justices on the Court is determined by Congress. Legislation changing that number could very easily alter the prevailing judicial philosophy of the Court and the legal interpretations that emanate from there, simply by changing the Court's majority. (Recall Franklin D. Roosevelt's attempt to do so.) Clearly that is tantamount to amending the Constitution. Yet Congress alone can do this, as it has on several occasions. And that Congressional action is as binding as a formal amendment.

A fourth type of informal amendment is *custom and tradition*. The Constitution says nothing about the President's cabinet; all it states is that the President may require in writing the opinions of the heads of the departments. (The Constitution does not even provide for departments; the Framers simply assumed, based upon experiences under state governments and under the Articles of Confederation, that any chief executive would have to have departments through which to carry out his various executive functions.) At first Washington did just that, requesting the advice of the department heads in writing, just as provided for in the

Constitution. He soon found it more convenient to meet with them in person. Thus was born the Cabinet, and it has continued ever since, based upon nothing more than the custom established by the first President. As Presidents requested and Congress created more departments—again the Constitution says nothing about how many departments—those department heads traditionally sat in as additional Cabinet members. As a matter of fact, the term "Cabinet" was not even used in law until the 1920s, when Congress passed a law dealing with salaries of Cabinet members.

Another example of the importance of custom. The Constitution requires that a member of the House of Representatives must be a resident of the state he or she represents. Early in our history—in the colonial days, in fact—we developed the custom that legislative representatives must reside actually in the district represented—we call that "geographic" representation. Someone living in northern California, for instance, could—according to the Constitution—run for a Congressional district in southern California; but his or her chance of being elected is virtually nil, because custom demands that the candidate live in the district to be represented. It may not be in the Constitution, but the custom is just as strong.

Practices by political parties comprise another category of informal amendments to the Constitution. A good example is the national convention to nominate candidates for President and Vice-President. The Constitution provides for the Electoral College to choose those officials, but says nothing about the candidates from whom they should choose. At first no formal nominating procedures existed; voters elected known and knowledgeable people to be Electors, and had sufficient trust and confidence in them to choose competent persons for President and Vice-President. The Electors would vote for two people. It was taken for granted, by general consensus, that all would vote for George Washington, who would then become President, and that John Adams would be the second choice of enough Electors that he would be Vice-President. That is exactly what happened in the first two elections. By the 1796 election, however, party influences began to be felt. The outcome was that Adams was elected President and Thomas Jefferson Vice-President. Though they represented different "factions," as parties were called then, they were such outstanding personalities that not too many were overly disturbed by what was showing up as a weakness in the election system.

But by the 1800 election, political parties had become prominent enough that party caucuses informally named both the Presidential and Vice-Presidential candidates for their party, and voters and Electors cast their ballots accordingly. This generated the election crisis of 1800. All the Democratic-Republican (as the Jeffersonian party was called then) Electors voted for both Jefferson and Aaron Burr, thereby creating an unexpected tie. Although most Electors intended

THE AMENDMENTS

Jefferson as President and Burr as Vice-President, the tie threw the election into the House of Representatives, which was controlled by the opposition Federalist party. After considerable behind-the-scene politicking and thirty-six grueling ballots, the House finally elected Jefferson to be President. Shortly thereafter the Twelfth Amendment changed the procedure to avoid a similar debacle. Electors still voted for two persons, but now they designated which they wanted for President and which they wanted for Vice-President.

But the Twelfth Amendment still had no effect on how candidates were nominated; it was still by party caucus. In the 1830s, during the Jacksonian period, national nominating conventions came into being, ostensibly giving the broad party membership the nominating power. (Behind-the-scene back-room politicking still played a major role.) We still have national conventions today, augmented by a variety of state caucuses, conventions, primaries, and other methods to determine convention membership. These procedures differ from state to state and from party to party, and they even change from election to election. None of this is found in the Constitution. The complicated and often confusing process is controlled by states and by political parties—yet it is as binding as if it were a formal part of the Constitution, in either the original body or in the amendments.

We have examined one of the most valuable attributes of our Constitution—its flexibility and its adaptability to change. The Constitution can be modified in a number of ways. One is to change its actual wording by formal amendment. Another way—in fact the most common way—is to adapt needed changes through so-called "informal" processes: court interpretations, executive action, Congressional action, custom, or party practice. All are equally effective and binding.

The past two hundred years have shown us several truisms about change and our Constitution. One is that nothing in the Constitution is totally immune from change. No matter how sacrosanct something may seem, if the people want to change it they will do so. That change may come about in any of several ways, but it will come, formally or informally.

Our history has shown us that some changes are much more difficult to accomplish than others. Issues such as slavery and prohibition are quite different from voting qualifications and dates of inauguration.

Our history has shown us that some changes have been mistakes, despite enthusiastic support for those changes. Our history shows us also that we can correct those mistakes.

Do some changes lend themselves more to the formal amendment process? Are others better brought about through an informal procedure?

If moral issues, whose values should prevail? For that matter, should we even attempt to codify moral issues? (Note that prohibition was a moral issue—and so was slavery.)

What are some of the changes being proposed today? Based on the history of Constitutional flexibility, how might they best be achieved?

What about another Constitutional Convention to re-examine the whole Constitution? Is that feasible?

What do you think?

NOTES

1. After the colonies had declared their independence in 1776, they drew up constitutions to accommodate their new status as independent states. Connecticut and Rhode Island merely continued their old colonial charters, but changed the locus of sovereignty from England to themselves. Others drew up new constitutions. All, however, adopted bills of rights. Six—Connecticut, Rhode Island, Georgia, South Carolina, New Jersey, and New York—incorporated those protective provisions as component parts of their state constitutions. The other states adopted separate bills of rights as addenda to their constitutions. An excellent account of the origins of the national Bill of Rights is Robert Allen Rutland, *The Birth of the Bill of Rights, 1776-1791* (Revised Edition), Boston: Northeastern University Press, 1983.

2. The two which were rejected dealt with a mechanism for apportioning the House of Representatives and with salaries of members of Congress. Neither, it should be noted, dealt with personal rights. The salary proposal eventually became the Twenty-Seventh Amendment—see below for more on that.

3. The original draft of the Tenth Amendment provided that the federal government could exercise only those powers that were "expressly" delegated to it. That word was excluded from the amendment as finally ratified. That exclusion became a central point later in numerous constitutional arguments over "liberal" versus "strict" construction of the Constitution, as well as in controversies over whether the federal government or state governments possessed the legal authority to enact certain legislation. See essay on Federalism.

APPENDIX A
Articles of Confederation
March 1, 1781

Whereas the Delegates of the United States of America, in Congress assembled, did, on the 15th day of November, in the Year of Our Lord One thousand Seven Hundred and Seventy seven, and in the Second Year of the Independence of America, agree to certain articles of Confederation and perpetual Union between the States of Newhampshire, Massachusetts-bay, Rhodeisland and Providence Plantations, Connecticut, New York, New Jersey, Pennsylvania, Delaware, Maryland, Virginia, North-Carolina, South-Carolina, and Georgia in the words following, viz. "Articles of Confederation and perpetual Union between the states of Newhampshire, Massachusetts-bay, Rhodeisland and Providence Plantations, Connecticut, New-York, New-Jersey, Pennsylvania, Delaware, Maryland, Virginia, North-Carolina, South-Carolina and Georgia."

Article I. The Stile of this confederacy shall be "The United States of America."

Article II. Each state retains its sovereignty, freedom, and independence, and every Power, Jurisdiction and right, which is not by this confederation expressly delegated to the United States, in Congress assembled.

Article III. The said states hereby severally enter into a firm league of friendship with each other, for their common defence, the security of their Liberties, and their mutual and general welfare, binding themselves to assist each other, against all force offered to, or attacks made upon them, or any of them, on account of religion, sovereignty, trade, or any other pretence whatever.

Article IV. The better to secure and perpetuate mutual friendship and intercourse among the people of the different states in this union, the free inhabitants of each of these states, paupers, vagabonds and fugitives from justice excepted, shall be entitled to all privileges and immunities of free citizens in the several states; and the people of each state shall have free ingress and regress to and from any other state, and shall enjoy therein all the privileges of trade and commerce, subject to the same duties, impositions and restrictions as the inhabitants thereof respectively, provided that such restriction shall not extend so far as to prevent the removal of property imported into any state, to any other state, of which the Owner is an inhabitant; provided also that no imposition, duties or restriction shall be laid by any state, on the property of the united states, or either of them.

If any Person guilty of, or charged with treason, felony, or other high misdemeanor in any state, shall flee from Justice, and be found in any of the united states, he shall, upon demand of the Governor or executive power, of the state from which he fled, be delivered up and removed to the state having jurisdiction of his offence.

Full faith and credit shall be given in each of these states to the records, acts and judicial proceedings of the courts and magistrates of every other state.

Article V. For the more convenient management of the general interests of the united states, delegates shall be annually appointed in such manner as the legislature of each state shall direct, to meet in Congress on the first Monday in November, in every year, with a power reserved to each state, to recall its delegates, or any of them, at any time within the year, and to send others in their stead, for the remainder of the Year.

No state shall be represented in Congress by less than two, nor by more than seven Members; and no person shall be capable of being a delegate for more than three years in any term of six years; nor shall any person, being a delegate, be capable of holding any office under the united states, for which he, or another for his benefit receives any salary, fees or emolument of any kind.

Each state shall maintain its own delegates in a meeting of the states, and while they act as members of the committee of the states.

In determining questions in the united states in Congress assembled, each state shall have one vote.

Freedom of speech and debate in Congress shall not be impeached or questioned in any Court, or place out of Congress, and the members of congress shall be protected in their persons from arrests and imprisonments, during the time of their going to and from, and attendance on congress, except for treason, felony, or breach of the peace.

Article VI. No state, without the Consent of the united states in congress assembled, shall send any embassy to, or receive any embassy from, or enter into any conference, agreement, alliance or treaty with any King prince or state; nor shall any person holding any office of profit or trust under the united states, or any of them, accept of any present, emolument, office or title of any kind whatever from any king, prince or foreign state; nor shall the united states in congress assembled, or any of them, grant any title of nobility.

No two or more states shall enter into any treaty, confederation or alliance whatever between them, without the consent of the united states in congress assembled, specifying accurately the purposes for which the same is to be entered into, and how long it shall continue.

No state shall lay any imposts or duties, which may interfere with any stipulations in treaties, entered into by the united states in congress assembled, with any king, prince or state, in pursuance of any treaties already proposed by congress, to the courts of France and Spain.

No vessels of war shall be kept up in time of peace by any state, except such number only, as shall be deemed necessary by the united states in congress assembled, for the defence of such state, or its trade; nor shall any body of forces be kept up by any state, in time of peace, except such number only, as in the judgment of the united states, in congress assembled, shall be deemed requisite to garrison the forts necessary for the defence of such state; but every state shall always keep up a well regulated and disciplined militia, sufficiently armed and accoutred, and shall provide and constantly have ready for use, in public stores, a due number of field pieces and tents, and a proper quantity of arms, ammunition and camp equipage.

No state shall engage in any war without the consent of the united states in congress assembled, unless such state be actually invaded by enemies, or shall have received certain advice of a resolution being formed by some nation of Indians to invade such state, and the danger is so imminent as not to admit of a delay till the united states in congress assembled can be consulted: nor shall any state grant commissions to any ships or vessels of war, nor letters of marque or reprisal, except it be after a declaration of war by the united states in congress assembled, and then only against the kingdom or state and the subjects thereof, against which war has been so declared, and under such regulations as shall be established by the united states in congress assembled, unless such state be infested by pirates, in which case vessels of war may be fitted out for that occasion, and kept so long as the danger shall continue, or until the united states in congress assembled, shall determine otherwise.

Article VII. When land-forces are raised by any state for the common defence, all officers of or under the rank of colonel, shall be appointed by the legislature of each state respectively, by whom such forces shall be raised, or in such manner as such state shall direct, and all vacancies shall be filled up by the State which first made the appointment.

Article VIII. All charges of war, and all other expences that shall be incurred for the common defence or general welfare, and allowed by the united states in congress assembled, shall be defrayed out of a common treasury, which shall be supplied by the several states in proportion to the value of all land within each state, granted to or surveyed for any Person, as such land and the buildings and improvements thereon shall be estimated according to such mode as the united states in congress assembled, shall from time to time direct and appoint.

The taxes for paying that proportion shall be laid and levied by the authority and direction of the legislatures of the several states within the time agreed upon by the united states in congress assembled.

Article IX. The united states in congress assembled, shall have the sole and exclusive right and power of determining on peace and war, except in the cases mentioned in the sixth article—of sending and receiving ambassadors—entering into treaties and alliances, provided that no treaty of commerce shall be made whereby the legislative power of the respective states shall be restrained from imposing such imposts and duties on foreigners as their own people are subjected to, or from prohibiting the exportation or importation of any species of goods or commodities, whatsoever—of establishing rules for deciding in all cases, what captures on land or water shall be legal, and in what manner prizes taken by land or naval forces in the service of the united states shall be divided or appropriated—of granting letters of marque and reprisal in times of peace—appointing courts for the trial of piracies and felonies committed on the high seas and establishing courts for receiving and determining finally appeals in all cases of captures, provided that no member of congress shall be appointed a judge of any of the said courts.

The united states in congress assembled shall also be the last resort on appeal in all disputes and differences now subsisting or that hereafter may arise between two or more states concerning boundary, jurisdiction or any other cause whatever; which authority shall always be exercised in the manner following. Whenever the legislative or executive authority or lawful agent of any state in controversy with another shall present a petition to congress stating the matter in question and praying for a hearing, notice thereof shall be given by order of congress to the legislative or executive authority of the other state in controversy, and a day assigned for the appearance of the parties by their lawful agents, who shall then be directed to appoint by joint consent, commissioners or judges to constitute a court for hearing and determining the matter in question: but if they cannot agree, congress shall name three persons out of each of the united states, and from the list of such persons each party shall alternately strike out one, the petitioners beginning, until the number shall be reduced to thirteen; and from that number not less than seven, nor more than nine names as congress shall direct, shall in the presence of congress be drawn out by lot, and the persons whose names shall be so drawn or any five of them, shall be commissioners or judges, to hear and finally determine the controversy, so always as a major part of the judges who shall hear the cause shall agree in the determination: and if either party shall neglect to attend at the day appointed, without showing reasons, which congress shall judge sufficient, or being present shall refuse to strike, the congress shall proceed to nominate three persons out of each state, and the secretary of congress shall strike in behalf of such party absent or refusing; and the judgment and sentence of the court to be appointed, in the manner before prescribed, shall be final and conclusive; and if any of the parties shall refuse to submit to the authority of such court, or to appear

APPENDIX A

or defend their claim or cause, the court shall nevertheless proceed to pronounce sentence, or judgment, which shall in like manner be final and decisive, the judgment or sentence and other proceedings being in either case transmitted to congress, and lodged among the acts of congress for the security of the parties concerned: provided that every commissioner, before he sits in judgment, shall take an oath to be administered by one of the judges of the supreme or superior court of the state, where the cause shall be tried, "well and truly to hear and determine the matter in question, according to the best of his judgment, without favour, affection or hope of reward:" provided also, that no state shall be deprived of territory for the benefit of the united states.

All controversies concerning the private right of soil claimed under different grants of two or more states, whose jurisdictions as they may respect such lands, and the states which passed such grants are adjusted, the said grants or either of them being at the same time claimed to have originated antecedent to such settlement of jurisdiction, shall on the petition of either party to the congress of the united states, be finally determined as near as may be in the same manner as is before prescribed for deciding disputes respecting territorial jurisdiction between different states.

The united states in congress assembled shall also have the sole and exclusive right and power of regulating the alloy and value of coin struck by their own authority, or by that of the respective states—fixing the standard of weights and measures throughout the united states—regulating the trade and managing all affairs with the Indians, not members of any of the states, provided that the legislative right of any state within its own limits be not infringed or violated—establishing or regulating post-offices from one state to another, throughout all the united states, and exacting such postage on the papers passing thro' the same as may be requisite to defray the expences of the said office—appointing all officers of the land forces, in the service of the united states, excepting regimental officers—appointing all the officers of the naval forces, and commissioning all officers whatever in the service of the united states—making rules for the government and regulation of the said land and naval forces, and directing their operations.

The united states in congress assembled shall have authority to appoint a committee, to sit in the recess of congress, to be denominated "A Committee of the States," and to consist of one delegate from each state; and to appoint such other committees and civil officers as may be necessary for managing the general affairs of the united states under their direction—to appoint one of their number to preside, provided that no person be allowed to serve in the office of president more than one year in any term of three years; to ascertain the necessary sums of money to be raised for the service of the united states, and to appropriate and apply the same for defraying the public expences—to borrow money, or emit bills on the credit of the united states, transmitting every half year to the respective states an account of the sums of money so borrowed or emitted,—to build and equip a navy—to agree upon the number of land forces, and to make requisitions from each state for its quota, in proportion to the number of white inhabitants in such state; which requisition shall be binding, and thereupon the legislature of each state shall appoint the regimental officers, raise the men and cloath, arm and equip them in a soldier like manner, at the expence of the united states; and the officers and men so cloathed, armed and equipped shall march to the place appointed, and within the time agreed on by the united states in congress assembled: But if the united states in congress assembled shall, on consideration of circumstances judge proper that any state should not raise men, or should raise a smaller number than its quota, and that any other state should raise a greater number of men than the quota thereof, such extra number shall be raised, officered, cloathed, armed and equipped in the same manner as the quota of such state, unless the legislature of such state shall judge that such extra number cannot be safely spared out of the same, in which case they shall raise officer, cloath, arm and equip as many of such extra number as they judge can be safely spared. And the officers and men so cloathed, armed and equipped, shall march to the place appointed, and within the time agreed on by the united states in congress assembled.

The united states in congress assembled shall never engage in a war, nor grant letters of marque and reprisal in time of peace, nor enter into any treaties or alliances, nor coin money, nor regulate the value thereof, nor ascertain the sums and expences necessary for the defence and welfare of the united states, or any of them, nor emit bills, nor borrow money on the credit of the united states, nor appropriate money, nor agree upon the number of vessels of war, to be built or purchased, or the number of land or sea forces to be raised, nor appoint a commander in chief of the army or navy, unless nine states assent to the same: nor shall a question on any other point, except for adjourning from day to day be determined, unless by the votes of a majority of the united states in congress assembled.

The congress of the united states shall have power to adjourn to any time within the year, and to any place within the united states, so that no period of adjournment be for a longer duration than the space of six Months, and shall publish the Journal of their proceedings monthly, except such parts thereof relating to treaties, alliances or military operations, as in their judgment require secrecy; and the yeas and nays of the delegates of each state on any question shall be entered on the Journal, when it is desired by any delegate; and the delegates of a state, or any of them, at his or their request shall be furnished with a transcript of the said Journal, except such parts as are above excepted, to lay before the legislatures of the several states.

Article X. The committee of the states, or any nine of them, shall be authorized to execute, in the recess of congress, such of the powers of congress as the united states in congress assembled, by the consent of nine states, shall from time to time think expedient to vest them with; provided that no power be delegated to the said committee, for the exercise of which, by the articles of confederation, the voice of nine states in the congress of the united states assembled is requisite.

Article XI. Canada acceding to this confederation, and joining in the measures of the united states, shall be admitted into, and entitled to all the advantages of this union: but no other colony shall be admitted into the same, unless such admission be agreed to by nine states.

Article XII. All bills of credit emitted, monies borrowed and debts contracted by, or under the authority of congress, before the assembling of the united states, in pursuance of the present confederation, shall be deemed and considered as a charge against the united states, for payment and satisfaction whereof the said united states, and the public faith are hereby solemnly pledged.

Article XIII. Every state shall abide by the determinations of the united states in congress assembled, on all questions which by this confederation are submitted to them. And the Articles of this confederation shall be inviolably observed by every state, and the union shall be perpetual; nor shall any alteration at any time hereafter be made in any of them; unless such alteration be agreed to in a congress of the united states, and be afterwards confirmed by the legislatures of every state.

And Whereas it hath pleased the Great Governor of the World to incline the hearts of the legislatures we respectively represent in congress, to approve of, and to authorize us to ratify the said articles of confederation and perpetual union. Know Ye that we the undersigned delegates, by virtue of the power and authority to us given for that purpose, do by these presents, in the name and in behalf of our respective constituents, fully and entirely ratify and confirm each and every of the said articles of confederation and perpetual union, and all and singular the matters and things therein contained: And we do further solemnly plight and engage the faith of our respective constituents, that they shall abide by the determinations of the united states in congress assembled, on all questions, which by the said confederation are submitted to them. And that the articles thereof shall be inviolably observed by the states we respectively represent, and that the union shall be perpetual. In Witness whereof we have hereunto set our hands in Congress. Done at Philadelphia in the state of Pennsylvania the ninth day of July, in the Year of our Lord one Thousand seven Hundred and Seventy-eight, and in the third year of the independence of America.

APPENDIX B
Constitution of the United States

We the people of the United States, in Order to form a more perfect Union, establish Justice, insure domestic Tranquility, provide for the common defence, promote the general Welfare, and secure the Blessings of Liberty to ourselves and our Posterity, do ordain and establish this Constitution for the United States of America.

ARTICLE 1.

Section 1. All legislative Powers herein granted shall be vested in a Congress of the United States, which shall consist of a Senate and House of Representatives.

Section 2. The House of Representatives shall be composed of Members chosen every second Year by the People of the several States, and the Electors in each State shall have the Qualifications requisite for Electors of the most numerous Branch of the State Legislature.

No person shall be a Representative who shall not have attained to the Age of twenty five Years, and been seven Years a Citizen of the United States, and who shall not, when elected, be an Inhabitant of that State in which he shall be chosen.

Representatives and direct Taxes shall be apportioned among the several States which may be included within this Union, according to their respective Numbers, which shall be determined by adding to the whole Number of free Persons, including those bound to Service for a Term of Years, and excluding Indians not taxed, three fifths of all other Persons. The actual Enumeration shall be made within three Years after the first Meeting of the Congress of the United States, and within every subsequent Term of ten Years, in such Manner as they shall by Law direct. The Number of Representatives shall not exceed one for every thirty Thousand, but each State shall have at Least one Representative; and until such enumeration shall be made, the State of New Hampshire shall be entitled to chuse three, Massachusetts eight, Rhode-lsland and Providence Plantations one, Connecticut five, New-York six, New Jersey four, Pennsylvania eight, Delaware one, Maryland six, Virginia ten, North Carolina five, South Carolina five, and Georgia three.

When vacancies happen in the Representation from any State, the Executive Authority thereof shall issue Writs of Election to fill such Vacancies.

The House of Representatives shall chuse their Speaker and other Officers; and shall have the sole Power of Impeachment.

Section 3. The Senate of the United States shall be composed of two Senators from each State, chosen by the Legislature thereof, for six Years; and each Senator shall have one Vote.

Immediately after they shall be assembled in Consequence of the first Election, they shall be divided as equally as may be into three Classes. The Seats of the Senators of the first Class shall be vacated at the Expiration of the second Year, of the second Class at the Expiration of the fourth Year, and of the third Class at the Expiration of the sixth Year, so that one third may be chosen every second Year; and if Vacancies happen by Resignation, or otherwise, during the Recess of the Legislature of any State, the Executive thereof may make temporary Appointments until the next Meeting of the Legislature, which shall then fill such Vacancies.

No Person shall be a Senator who shall not have attained to the Age of thirty Years, and been nine Years a Citizen of the United States, and who shall not, when elected, be an Inhabitant of that State for which he shall be chosen.

The Vice President of the United States shall be President of the Senate, but shall have no Vote, unless they be equally divided.

The Senate shall chuse their other Officers, and also a President pro tempore, in the Absence of the Vice President, or when he shall exercise the Office of President of the United States.

The Senate shall have the sole Power to try all Impeachments. When sitting for that Purpose, they shall be on Oath or Affirmation. When the President of the United States is tried, the Chief Justice shall preside: And no Person shall be convicted without the Concurrence of two thirds of the Members present.

Judgment in Cases of Impeachment shall not extend further than to removal from Office, and disqualification to hold and enjoy any Office of honor, Trust or Profit under the United States: but the Party convicted shall nevertheless be liable and subject to Indictment, Trial, Judgment and Punishment, according to Law.

Section 4. The Times, Places and Manner of holding Elections for Senators and Representatives, shall be prescribed in each State by the Legislature thereof; but the Congress may at any time by Law make or alter such Regulations, except as to the Places of chusing Senators.

The Congress shall assemble at least once in every Year, and such Meeting shall be on the first Monday in December, unless they shall by Law appoint a different Day.

Section 5. Each House shall be the Judge of the Elections, Returns and Qualifications of its own Members, and a Majority of each shall constitute a Quorum to do Business; but a smaller Number may adjourn from day to day, and may be authorized to compel the Attendance of absent Members, in such Manner, and under such Penalties as each House may provide.

APPENDIX B

Each House may determine the Rules of its Proceedings, punish its Members for disorderly Behaviour, and, with the Concurrence of two thirds, expel a Member.

Each House shall keep a Journal of its Proceedings, and from time to time publish the same, excepting such Parts as may in their Judgment require Secrecy; and the Yeas and Nays of the Members of either House on any question shall, at the Desire of one fifth of those Present, be entered on the Journal.

Neither House, during the Session of Congress, shall, without the Consent of the other, adjourn for more than three days, nor to any other Place than that in which the two Houses shall be sitting.

Section 6. The Senators and Representatives shall receive a Compensation for their Services, to be ascertained by Law, and paid out of the Treasury of the United States. They shall in all Cases, except Treason, Felony and Breach of the Peace, be privileged from Arrest during their Attendance at the Session of their respective Houses, and in going to and returning from the same; and for any Speech or Debate in either House, they shall not be questioned in any other Place.

No Senator or Representative shall, during the Time for which he was elected, be appointed to any civil Office under the Authority of the United States, which shall have been created, or the Emoluments whereof shall have been increased during such time; and no Person holding any Office under the United States, shall be a Member of either House during his Continuance in Office.

Section 7. All Bills for raising Revenue shall originate in the House of Representatives; but the Senate may propose or concur with Amendments as on other Bills.

Every Bill which shall have passed the House of Representatives and the Senate, shall, before it become a Law, be presented to the President of the United States; If he approve he shall sign it, but if not he shall return it, with his Objections to that House in which it shall have originated, who shall enter the Objections at large on their Journal, and proceed to reconsider it. If after such Reconsideration two thirds of that House shall agree to pass the Bill, it shall be sent, together with the Objections, to the other House, by which it shall likewise be reconsidered, and if approved by two thirds of that House, it shall become a Law. But in all such Cases the Votes of both Houses shall be determined by yeas and Nays, and the Names of the Persons voting for and against the Bill shall be entered on the Journal of each House respectively. If any Bill shall not be returned by the President within ten days (Sundays excepted) after it shall have been presented to him, the Same shall be a Law, in like Manner as if he had signed it, unless the Congress by their Adjournment prevent its Return in which Case it shall not be a Law.

Every Order, Resolution, or Vote to which the Concurrence of the Senate and House of Representatives may be necessary (except on a question of Adjournment) shall be presented to the President of the United States; and before the Same shall take Effect, shall be approved by him, or being disapproved by him, shall be repassed by two thirds of the Senate and House of Representatives, according to the Rules and Limitations prescribed in the Case of a Bill.

Section 8. The Congress shall have Power To lay and collect Taxes, Duties, Imposts and Excises, to pay the Debts and provide for the common Defence and general Welfare of the United States; but all Duties, Imposts and Excises shall be uniform throughout the United States;

To borrow Money on the credit of the United States;

To regulate Commerce with foreign Nations, and among the several States, and with the Indian Tribes;

To establish an uniform Rule of Naturalization, and uniform Laws on the subject of Bankruptcies throughout the United States;

To coin Money, regulate the Value thereof, and of foreign Coin, and fix the Standard of Weights and Measures;

To provide for the Punishment of counterfeiting the Securities and current Coin of the United States;

To establish Post Offices and post Roads;

To promote the Progress of Science and useful Arts, by securing for limited Times to Authors and Inventors the exclusive Right to their respective Writings and Discoveries;

To constitute Tribunals inferior to the supreme Court.

To declare War, grant Letters of Marque and Reprisal, and make Rules concerning Captures on Land and Water;

To raise and support Armies, but no Appropriation of Money to that Use shall be for a longer Term than two Years;

To provide and maintain a Navy;

To make Rules for the Government and Regulation of the land and naval Forces;

To provide for calling forth the Militia to execute the Laws of the Union, suppress Insurrections and repel Invasions;

To provide for organizing, arming, and disciplining, the Militia, and for governing such Part of them as may be employed in the Service of the United States, reserving to the States respectively, the Appointment of the Officers, and the Authority of training the Militia according to the discipline prescribed by Congress;

APPENDIX B

To exercise exclusive Legislation in all Cases whatsoever, over such District (not exceeding ten Miles square) as may, by Cession of particular States, and the Acceptance of Congress, become the Seat of the Government of the United States, and to exercise like Authority over all Places purchased by the Consent of the Legislature of the State in which the Same shall be, for the Erection of Forts, Magazines, Arsenals, dock-Yards, and other needful Buildings;—And

To make all Laws which shall be necessary and proper for carrying into Execution the foregoing Powers, and all other Powers vested by this Constitution in the Government of the United States, or in any Department or Officer thereof.

Section 9. The Migration or Importation of such Persons as any of the States now existing shall think proper to admit, shall not be prohibited by the Congress prior to the Year one thousand eight hundred and eight, but a Tax or duty may be imposed on such Importation, not exceeding ten dollars for each Person.

The Privilege of the Writ of Habeas Corpus shall not be suspended, unless when in Cases of Rebellion or Invasion the public Safety may require it.

No Bill of Attainder or ex post facto Law shall be passed.

No Capitation, or other direct, Tax shall be laid, unless in Proportion to the Census or Enumeration herein before directed to be taken.

No Tax or Duty shall be laid on Articles exported from any State.

No Preference shall be given by any Regulation of Commerce or Revenue to the Ports of one State over those of another: nor shall Vessels bound to, or from, one State, be obliged to enter, clear, or pay Duties in another.

No Money shall be drawn from the Treasury, but in Consequence of Appropriations made by Law; and a regular Statement and Account of the Receipts and Expenditures of all public Money shall be published from time to time.

No Title of Nobility shall be granted by the United States: And no Person holding any Office of Profit or Trust under them, shall, without the Consent of the Congress, accept of any present, Emolument, Office, or Title, of any kind whatever, from any King, Prince, or foreign State.

Section 10. No State shall enter into any Treaty, Alliance, or Confederation; grant Letters of Marque and Reprisal; coin Money; emit Bills of Credit; make any Thing but gold and silver Coin a Tender in Payment of Debts; pass any Bill of Attainder, ex post facto Law, or Law impairing the Obligation of Contracts, or grant any Title of Nobility.

No State shall, without the Consent of the Congress, lay any Imposts or Duties on Imports or Exports, except what may be absolutely necessary for executing its inspection Laws: and the net Produce of all Duties and Imposts, laid by any State on Imports or Exports, shall be for the Use of the Treasury of the

United States; and all such Laws shall be subject to the Revision and Control of the Congress.

No State shall, without the Consent of Congress, lay any Duty of Tonnage, keep Troops, or Ships of War in time of Peace, enter into any Agreement or Compact with another State, or with a foreign Power, or engage in War, unless actually invaded, or in such imminent Danger as will not admit of delay.

ARTICLE II.

Section 1. The executive Power shall be vested in a President of the United States of America. He shall hold his Office during the Term of four Years, and, together with the Vice President, chosen for the same Term, be elected as follows:

Each State shall appoint, in such Manner as the Legislature thereof may direct, a Number of Electors, equal to the whole Number of Senators and Representatives to which the State may be entitled in the Congress: but no Senator or Representative, or Person holding an Office of Trust or Profit under the United States, shall be appointed an Elector.

The Electors shall meet in their respective States, and vote by Ballot for two Persons, of whom one at least shall not be an Inhabitant of the same State with themselves. And they shall make a List of all the Persons voted for, and of the Number of Votes for each; which List they shall sign and certify, and transmitted sealed to the Seat of the Government of the United States, directed to the President of the Senate. The President of the Senate shall, in the Presence of the Senate and House of Representatives, open all the Certificates, and the Votes shall then be counted. The Person having the greatest Number of Votes shall be the President, if such Number be a Majority of the whole Number of Electors appointed; and if there be more than one who have such Majority, and have an equal Number of Votes, then the House of Representatives shall immediately chuse by Ballot one of them for President; and if no Person have a Majority, then from the five highest on the List the said House shall in like Manner chuse the President. But in chusing the President, the Votes shall be taken by States, the Representation from each State having one Vote; a quorum for this Purpose shall consist of a Member or Members from two thirds of the States, and a Majority of all the States shall be necessary to a Choice. In every Case, after the Choice of the President, the Person having the greatest Number of Votes of the Electors shall be the Vice President. But if there should remain two or more who have equal Votes, the Senate shall chuse from them by Ballot the Vice President.

The Congress may determine the Time of chusing the Electors, and the Day on which they shall give their Votes; which Day shall be the same throughout the United States.

No Person except a natural born Citizen, or a Citizen of the United States, at the time of the Adoption of this Constitution, shall be eligible to the Office of President; neither shall any Person be eligible to that Office who shall not have attained to the Age of thirty five Years, and been fourteen Years a Resident within the United States.

In Case of the Removal of the President from Office, or of his Death, Resignation, or Inability to discharge the Powers and Duties of the said Office, the Same shall devolve on the Vice President, and the Congress may by Law provide for the Case of Removal, Death, Resignation or Inability, both of the President and Vice President, declaring what Officer shall then act as President, and such Officer shall act accordingly, until the Disability be removed, or a President shall be elected.

The President shall, at stated Times, receive for his Services, a Compensation, which shall neither be increased nor diminished during the Period for which he shall have been elected, and he shall not receive within that Period any other Emolument from the United States, or any of them.

Before he enter on the Execution of his Office, he shall take the following Oath or Affirmation:—"I do solemnly swear (or affirm) that I will faithfully execute the Office of President of the United States, and will to the best of my Ability, preserve, protect and defend the Constitution of the United States."

Section 2. The President shall be Commander in Chief of the Army and Navy of the United States, and of the Militia of the several States, when called into the actual Service of the United States; he may require the Opinion, in writing, of the principal Officer in each of the executive Departments, upon any Subject relating to the Duties of their respective Offices, and he shall have Power to grant Reprieves and Pardons for Offences against the United States, except in Cases of Impeachment.

He shall have Power, by and with the Advice and Consent of the Senate, to make Treaties, provided two thirds of the Senators present concur; and he shall nominate, and by and with the Advice and Consent of the Senate, shall appoint Ambassadors, other public Ministers and Consuls, Judges of the supreme Court, and all other Officers of the United States, whose Appointments are not herein otherwise provided for, and which shall be established by Law: but the Congress may by Law vest the Appointment of such inferior Officers, as they think proper, in the President alone, in the Courts of Law, or in the Heads of Departments.

The President shall have Power to fill up all Vacancies that may happen during the Recess of the Senate, by granting Commissions which shall expire at the End of their next Session.

Section 3. He shall from time to time give to the Congress Information of the State of the Union, and recommend to their Consideration such Measures as he shall judge necessary and expedient; he may, on extraordinary Occasions, convene both Houses, or either of them, and in Case of Disagreement between them, with Respect to the Time of Adjournment, he may adjourn them to such Time as he shall think proper; he shall receive Ambassadors and other public Ministers; he shall take Care that the Laws be faithfully executed, and shall Commission all the Officers of the United States.

Section 4. The President, Vice President and all civil Officers of the United States, shall be removed from Office on Impeachment for, and Conviction of, Treason, Bribery, or other high Crimes and Misdemeanors.

ARTICLE III.

Section 1. The judicial Power of the United States, shall be vested in one supreme Court, and in such inferior Courts as the Congress may from time to time ordain and establish. The Judges, both of the supreme and inferior Courts, shall hold their Offices during good Behaviour, and shall, at stated Times, receive for their Services, a Compensation, which shall not be diminished during their Continuance in Office.

Section 2. The judicial Power shall extend to all Cases, in Law and Equity, arising under this Constitution, the Laws of the United States, and Treaties made, or which shall be made, under their Authority;—to all Cases affecting Ambassadors, other public Ministers and Consuls;—to all Cases of admiralty and maritime Jurisdiction; to Controversies to which the United States shall be a Party; to Controversies between two or more States; between a State and Citizens of another State; between Citizens of different States, between Citizens of the same State claiming Lands under Grants of different States, and between a State, or the Citizens thereof, and foreign States, Citizens or Subjects.

In all Cases affecting Ambassadors, other public Ministers and Consuls, and those in which a State shall be Party, the supreme Court shall have original Jurisdiction. In all the other Cases before mentioned, the supreme Court shall have appellate Jurisdiction, both as to Law and Fact, with such Exceptions, and under such Regulations as the Congress shall make.

The Trial of all Crimes, except in Cases of Impeachment, shall be by Jury; and such Trial shall be held in the State where the said Crimes shall have been committed; but when not committed within any State, the Trial shall be at such Place or Places as the Congress may by Law have directed.

Section 3. Treason against the United States, shall consist only in levying War against them, or in adhering to their Enemies, giving them Aid and Comfort. No Person shall be convicted of Treason unless on the Testimony of two Witnesses to the same overt Act, or on Confession in open Court.

The Congress shall have Power to declare the Punishment of Treason, but no Attainder of Treason shall work Corruption of Blood, or Forfeiture except during the Life of the Person attained.

ARTICLE IV.

Section 1. Full Faith and Credit shall be given in each State to the public Acts, Records, and judicial Proceedings of every other State. And the Congress may by general Laws prescribe the Manner in which such Acts, Records and Proceedings shall be proved, and the Effect thereof.

Section 2. The Citizens of each State shall be entitled to all Privileges and Immunities of Citizens in the several States.

A Person charged in any State with Treason, Felony, or other Crime, who shall flee from Justice, and be found in another State, shall on Demand of the executive Authority of the State from which he fled, be delivered up, to be removed to the State having Jurisdiction of the Crime.

No Person held to Service or Labour in one State, under the Laws thereof, escaping into another, shall, in Consequence of any Law or Regulation therein, be discharged from such Service or Labour, but shall be delivered up on Claim of the Party to whom such Service or Labour may be due.

Section 3. New States may be admitted by the Congress into this Union; but no new State shall be formed or erected within the Jurisdiction of any other State; nor any State be formed by the Junction of two or more States, or Parts of States, without the Consent of the Legislatures of the States concerned as well as of the Congress.

The Congress shall have Power to dispose of and make all needful Rules and Regulations respecting the Territory or other Property belonging to the United States; and nothing in this Constitution shall be so construed as to Prejudice any Claims of the United States, or of any particular State.

Section 4. The United States shall guarantee to every State in this Union a Republican form of Government, and shall protect each of them against Invasion; and on Application of the Legislature, or of the Executive (when the Legislature cannot be convened) against domestic Violence.

ARTICLE V.

The Congress, whenever two thirds of both Houses shall deem it necessary, shall propose Amendments to this Constitution, or, on the Application of the Legislatures of two thirds of the several States, shall call a Convention for proposing Amendments, which, in either Case, shall be valid to all Intents and Purposes, as Part of this Constitution, when ratified by the Legislatures of three fourths of the several States, or by Conventions in three fourths thereof, as the one or the other Mode of Ratification may be proposed by the Congress; Provided that no Amendment which may be made prior to the Year One thousand eight hundred and eight shall in any Manner affect the first and fourth Clauses in the Ninth Section of the first Article; and that no state, without its Consent, shall be deprived of its equal Suffrage in the Senate.

ARTICLE VI.

All Debts contracted and Engagements entered into, before the Adoption of this Constitution, shall be as valid against the United States under this Constitution, as under the Confederation.

This Constitution, and the Laws of the United States which shall be made in Pursuance thereof; and all Treaties made, or which shall be made, under the Authority of the United States, shall be the supreme Law of the Land; and the Judges in every State shall be bound thereby, any Thing in the Constitution or Laws of any State to the Contrary notwithstanding.

The Senators and Representatives before mentioned, and the Members of the several State Legislatures, and all executive and judicial Officers, both of the United States and of the several States, shall be bound by Oath or Affirmation, to support this Constitution; but no religious Test shall ever be required as a Qualification to any Office or public Trust under the United States.

ARTICLE VII.

The Ratification of the Conventions of nine States, shall be sufficient for the Establishment of this Constitution between the States so ratifying the Same.

Done in Convention by the Unanimous Consent of the States present the Seventeenth Day of September in the Year of our Lord one thousand seven hundred and Eighty seven and of the Independence of the United States of America the Twelfth. In witness whereof We have hereunto subscribed our Names:

APPENDIX B

Attest: WILLIAM JACKSON
　　　　Secretary

	G[o] WASHINGTON-Presid[t] and deputy from Virginia
New Hampshire	John Langdon
	Nicholas Gilman
Massachusetts	Nathaniel Gorham
	Rufus King
Connecticut	W[m] Sam[l] Johnson
	Roger Sherman
New York	Alexander Hamilton
New Jersey	Wil: Livingston
	David Brearley
	W[m] Paterson.
	Jona: Dayton
Pennsylvania	B Franklin
	Thomas Mifflin
	Rob[t] Morris
	Geo. Clymer
	Tho[s] FitzSimons
	Jared Ingersoll
	James Wilson
	Gouv Morris
Delaware	Geo: Read
	Gunning Bedford jun
	John Dickinson
	Richard Bassett
	Jaco: Broom
Maryland	James M[c]Henry
	Dan of S[t] Tho[s] Jenifer
	Dan[l] Carroll
Virginia	John Blair
	James Madison Jr.
North Carolina	W[m] Blount
	Rich[d] Dobbs Spaight
	Hu Williamson

WE THE PEOPLE

South Carolina	J. Rutledge
	Charles Cotesworth Pinckney
	Charles Pinckney
	Pierce Butler
Georgia	William Few
	Abr Baldwin

AMENDMENTS TO THE CONSTITUTION

Articles in Addition to, and Amendment of the Constitution of the United Slates of America, proposed by Congress, and ratified by the Legislatures of the several States, pursuant to the fifth Article of the original Constitution.

AMENDMENT I.

Congress shall make no law respecting an establishment of religion, or prohibiting the free exercise thereof; or abridging the freedom of speech, or of the press; or the right of the people peaceably to assemble, and to petition the Government for a redress of grievances.

AMENDMENT II.

A well regulated Militia, being necessary to the security of a free State, the right of the people to keep and bear Arms, shall not be infringed.

AMENDMENT III.

No Soldier shall, in time of peace be quartered in any house, without the consent of the Owner, nor in time of war, but in a manner to be prescribed by law.

AMENDMENT IV.

The right of the people to be secure in their persons, houses, papers, and effects, against unreasonable searches and seizures, shall not be violated, and no Warrants shall issue, but upon probable cause, supported by Oath or affirmation, and particularly describing the place to be searched, and the persons or things to be seized.

AMENDMENT V.

No person shall be held to answer for a capital, or otherwise infamous crime, unless on a presentment or indictment of a Grand Jury, except in cases arising in the land or naval forces, or in the Militia, when in actual service in time of War or public danger; nor shall any person be subject for the same offence to be twice put in jeopardy of life or limb; nor shall be compelled in any criminal case to be a witness against himself, nor be deprived of life, liberty, or property, without due process of law; nor shall private property be taken for public use, without just compensation.

AMENDMENT VI.

In all criminal prosecutions, the accused shall enjoy the right to a speedy and public trial, by an impartial jury of the State and district wherein the crime shall have been committed, which district shall have been previously ascertained by law, and to be informed of the nature and cause of the accusation; to be confronted with the witnesses against him; to have compulsory process for obtaining witnesses in his favor, and to have the Assistance of Counsel for his defence.

AMENDMENT VII.

In Suits at common law, where the value in controversy shall exceed twenty dollars, the right of trial by jury shall be preserved, and no fact tried by a jury, shall be otherwise re-examined in any Court of the United States, than according to the rules of the common law.

AMENDMENT VIII.

Excessive bail shall not be required, nor excessive fines imposed, nor cruel and unusual punishments inflicted.

AMENDMENT IX.

The enumeration in the Constitution, of certain rights, shall not be construed to deny or disparage others retained by the people.

AMENDMENT X.

The powers not delegated to the United States by the Constitution, nor prohibited by it to the States, are reserved to the States respectively, or to the people. [The first ten amendments went into effect December 15, 1791.]

AMENDMENT XI.

The Judicial power of the United States shall not be construed to extend to any suit in law or equity, commenced or prosecuted against one of the United States by Citizens of another State, or by Citizens or Subjects of any Foreign State. [January 8, 1798.]

AMENDMENT XII.

The Electors shall meet in their respective states, and vote by ballot for President and Vice-President, one of whom, at least, shall not be an inhabitant of the same state with themselves; they shall name in their ballots the person voted for as President, and in distinct ballots the person voted for as Vice-President, and they shall make distinct lists of all persons voted for as President, and of all persons voted for as Vice-President, and of the number of votes for each, which lists they shall sign and certify, and transmit sealed to the seat of the government of the United States, directed to the President of the Senate;—The President of the Senate shall, in the presence of the Senate and House of Representatives, open all the certificates and the votes shall then be counted;—The person having the greatest number of votes for President, shall be the President, if such number be a majority of the whole number of Electors appointed; and if no person have such majority, then from the persons having the highest numbers not exceeding three on the list of those voted for as President, the House of Representatives shall choose immediately, by ballot, the President. But in choosing the President, the votes shall be taken by states, the representation from each state having one vote; a quorum for this purpose shall consist of a member or members from two-thirds of the states, and a majority of all the states shall be necessary to a choice. And if the House of Representatives shall not choose a President whenever the right of choice shall devolve upon them, before the fourth day of March next following, then the Vice-President shall act as President, as in the case of the death or other constitutional disability of the President.—The person having the greatest number of votes as Vice-President, shall be the Vice-President, if such number be a majority of the whole number of Electors appointed, and if no person have a majority, then from the two highest numbers on the list, the Senate shall choose the Vice-President; a quorum for the purpose shall consist of two-thirds of the whole number of Senators, and a majority of the whole number shall be necessary to a choice. But no person constitutionally ineligible to the office of President shall be eligible to that of Vice-President of the United States. [September 25, 1804.]

AMENDMENT XIII.

Section 1. Neither slavery nor involuntary servitude, except as a punishment for crime whereof the party shall have been duly convicted, shall exist within the United States, or any place subject to their jurisdiction.

Section 2. Congress shall have power to enforce this article by appropriate legislation. [December 18, 1865.]

AMENDMENT XIV.

Section 1. All persons born or naturalized in the United States, and subject to the jurisdiction thereof, are citizens of the United States and of the State wherein they reside. No State shall make or enforce any law which shall abridge the privileges or immunities of citizens of the United States; nor shall any State deprive any person of life, liberty, or property, without due process of law; nor deny to any person within its jurisdiction the equal protection of the laws.

Section 2. Representatives shall be apportioned among the several States according to their respective numbers, counting the whole number of persons in each State, excluding Indians not taxed. But when the right to vote at any election for the choice of electors for President and Vice President of the United States, Representatives in Congress, the Executive and Judicial officers of a State, or the members of the Legislature thereof, is denied to any of the male inhabitants of such State, being twenty-one years of age, and citizens of the United States, or in any way abridged, except for participation in rebellion, or other crime, the basis of representation therein shall be reduced in the proportion which the number of such male citizens shall bear to the whole number of male citizens twenty-one years of age in such State.

Section 3. No person shall be a Senator or Representative in Congress, or elector of President and Vice President, or hold any office, civil or military, under the United States, or under any State, who, having previously taken an oath, as a member of Congress, or as an officer of the United States, or as a member of any State legislature, or as an executive or judicial officer of any State, to support the Constitution of the United States, shall have engaged in insurrection or rebellion against the same, or given aid or comfort to the enemies thereof. But Congress may by a vote of two-thirds of each House, remove such disability.

Section 4. The validity of the public debt of the United States, authorized by law, including debts incurred for payment of pensions and bounties for services in suppressing insurrection or rebellion, shall not be questioned. But neither the

United States nor any State shall assume or pay any debt or obligation incurred in aid of insurrection or rebellion against the United States, or any claim for the loss or emancipation of any slave; but all such debts, obligations and claims shall be held illegal and void.

Section 5. The Congress shall have power to enforce, by appropriate legislation, the provisions of this article. [July 28, 1868.]

AMENDMENT XV.

Section 1. The right of citizens of the United States to vote shall not be denied or abridged by the United States or by any State on account of race, color or previous condition of servitude.

Section 2. The Congress shall have power to enforce this article by appropriate legislation. [March 30, 1870.]

AMENDMENT XVI.

The Congress shall have power to lay and collect taxes on incomes, from whatever source derived, without apportionment among the several States, and without regard to any census or enumeration. [February 25, 1913.]

AMENDMENT XVII.

The Senate of the United States shall be composed of two senators from each State, elected by the people thereof, for six years; and each Senator shall have one vote. The electors in each State shall have the qualifications requisite for electors of the most numerous branch of the State legislature.

When vacancies happen in the representation of any State in the Senate, the executive authority of such State shall issue writs of election to fill such vacancies: *Provided,* That the legislature of any State may empower the executive thereof to make temporary appointments until the people fill the vacancies by election as the legislature may direct.

This amendment shall not be so construed as to affect the election or term of any senator chosen before it becomes valid as part of the Constitution. [May 31, 1913.]

AMENDMENT XVIII.

After one year from the ratification of this article, the manufacture, sale, or transportation of intoxicating liquors within, the importation thereof into, or the exportation thereof from the United States and all territory subject to the jurisdiction thereof for beverage purposes is hereby prohibited.

The Congress and the several States shall have concurrent power to enforce this article by appropriate legislation.

This article shall be inoperative unless it shall have been ratified as an amendment to the Constitution by the legislatures of the several States, as provided in the Constitution, within seven years from the date of the submission thereof to the States by Congress. [January 29, 1919.]

AMENDMENT XIX.

The right of the citizens of the United States to vote shall not be denied or abridged by the United States or by any State on account of sex.

The Congress shall have power by appropriate legislation to enforce the provisions of this article. [August 26, 1920.]

AMENDMENT XX.

Section 1. The terms of the President and Vice-President shall end at noon on the twentieth day of January, and the terms of Senators and Representatives at noon on the third day of January, of the years in which such terms would have ended if this article had not been ratified; and the terms of their successors shall then begin.

Section 2. The Congress shall assemble at least once in every year, and such meeting shall begin at noon on the third day of January, unless they shall by law appoint a different day.

Section 3. If, at the time fixed for the beginning of the term of the President, the President-elect shall have died, the Vice-President-elect shall become President. If a President shall not have been chosen before the time fixed for the beginning of his term, or if the President-elect shall have failed to qualify, then the Vice-President-elect shall act as President until a President shall have qualified; and the Congress may by law provide for the case wherein neither a President-elect nor a Vice-President-elect shall have qualified, declaring who shall then act as President, or the manner in which one who is to act shall be selected, and such person shall act accordingly until a President or Vice-President shall have qualified.

Section 4. The Congress may by law provide for the case of the death of any of the persons from whom the House of Representatives may choose a President whenever the right of choice shall have devolved upon them, and for the case of the death of any of the persons from whom the Senate may choose a Vice President whenever the right of choice shall have devolved upon them.

Section 5. Sections 1 and 2 shall take effect on the 15th day of October following the ratification of this article.

Section 6. This article shall be inoperative unless it shall have been ratified as an amendment to the Constitution by the legislatures of three-fourths of the several States within seven years from the date of its submission. [February 6, 1933.]

AMENDMENT XXI.

Section 1. The eighteenth article of amendment to the Constitution of the United States is hereby repealed.

Section 2. The transportation or importation into any State, Territory or possession of the United States for delivery or use therein of intoxicating liquors, in violation of the laws thereof, is hereby prohibited.

Section 3. This article shall be inoperative unless it shall have been ratified as an amendment to the Constitution by convention in the several States, as provided in the Constitution, within seven years from the date of the submission thereof to the States by the Congress. [December 5, 1933.]

AMENDMENT XXII.

Section 1. No person shall be elected to the office of the President more than twice, and no person who has held the office of President, or acted as President, for more than two years of a term to which some other person was elected President shall be elected to the office of the President more than once. But this Article shall not apply to any person holding the office of President when this Article was proposed by the Congress, and shall not prevent any person who may be holding the office of President, or acting as President, during the term within which this Article becomes operative from holding the office of President or acting as President during the remainder of such term.

Section 2. This article shall be inoperative unless it shall have been ratified as an amendment to the Constitution by the legislatures of three-fourths of the several States within seven years from the date of its submission to the States by the Congress. [February 27, 1951.]

AMENDMENT XXIII.

Section 1. The District constituting the seat of government of the United States shall appoint in such manner as the Congress may direct:

A number of electors of President and Vice-President equal to the whole number of Senators and Representatives in Congress to which the District would be entitled if it were a State, but in no event more than the least populous State; they shall be in addition to those appointed by the States, but they shall be considered, for the purposes of the election of President and Vice-President, to be electors appointed by a State; and they shall meet in the District and perform such duties as provided by the twelfth article of amendment.

Section 2. The Congress shall have the power to enforce this article by appropriate legislation. [March 29, 1961.]

AMENDMENT XXIV.

Section 1. The right of citizens of the United States to vote in any primary or other election for President or Vice President, for electors for President or Vice President, or for Senator or Representative in Congress, shall not be denied or abridged by the United States or any State by reason of failure to pay any poll tax or other tax.

Section 2. The Congress shall have power to enforce this article by appropriate legislation. [January 23, 1964.]

AMENDMENT XXV.

Section 1. In case of the removal of the President from office or of his death or resignation, the Vice President shall become President.

Section 2. Whenever there is a vacancy in the office of Vice President, the President shall nominate a Vice President who shall take office upon confirmation by a majority vote of both Houses of Congress.

Section 3. Whenever the President transmits to the President pro tempore of the Senate and the Speaker of the House of Representatives his written declaration that he is unable to discharge the powers and duties of his office, and until he transmits to them a written declaration to the contrary, such powers and duties shall be discharged by the Vice President as Acting President.

Section 4. Whenever the Vice President and a majority of either the principal officers of the executive departments or of such other body as Congress may by law provide, transmit to the President pro tempore of the Senate and the Speaker of the House of Representatives their written declaration that the President is unable to discharge the powers and duties of his office, the Vice President shall immediately assume the powers and duties of the office as Acting President.

Thereafter, when the President transmits to the President pro tempore of the Senate and the Speaker of the House of Representatives his written declaration that no inability exists, he shall resume the powers and duties of his office unless the Vice President and a majority of either the principal officers of the executive departments or of such other body as Congress may by law provide, transmit within four days to the President pro tempore of the Senate and the Speaker of the House of Representatives their written declaration that the President is unable to discharge the powers and duties of his office. Thereupon Congress shall decide the issue, assembling within forty-eight hours for that purpose if not in session. If the Congress, within twenty-one days after receipt of the latter written declaration, or, if Congress is not in session, within twenty-one days after Congress is required to assemble, determines by two-thirds vote of both Houses that the President is unable to discharge the powers and duties of his office, the Vice President shall continue to discharge the same as Acting President; otherwise, the President shall resume the powers and duties of his office. [February 10, 1967.]

AMENDMENT XXVI.

Section 1. The right of citizens of the United States, who are eighteen years of age or older, to vote shall not be denied or abridged by the United States or by any State on account of age.

Section 2. The Congress shall have power to enforce this article by appropriate legislation [June 30, 1971.]

AMENDMENT XXVII.

No law, varying the compensation for the services of the Senators and Representatives, shall take effect, until an election of Representatives shall have intervened. [May 18, 1992.]

BIBLIOGRAPHY

Any bibliography dealing with the development of our Constitution necessarily includes thousands of items. Still it would be incomplete, because additional materials continue to be published as we commemorate the Constitution's bicentennial. The following are just a few suggestions.

Many general constitutional histories contain extensive bibliographies. Among the best is Alfred H. Kelly, Winfred A. Harbison, and Herman Belz, *The American Constitution: Its Origins and Development.* Already in its seventh edition (New York: W. W. Norton, 1991), earlier editions also include excellent bibliographies. Of comparable scholarship is Melvin I. Urofsky, *A March of Liberty: A Constitutional History of the United States* (New York: Alfred A. Knopf, 1988). An accompanying volume of documents edited by Professor Urofsky contains valuable primary materials.

Though not as extensive in either textual detail or in bibliographical materials, other general constitutional histories are valuable reading and provide excellent surveys of the birth of the Constitution and its development. They include: Forrest McDonald, *A Constitutional History of the United States* (New York: Franklin Watts, 1982), and Broadus and Louise P. Mitchell, *A Biography of the Constitution of the United States* (New York: Oxford University Press, 1964). Equally valuable, though not as up-to-date, is Carl Brent Swisher, *American Constitutional Development* (Boston: Houghton Mifflin Company, 1954).

Basic to the reader are accounts of what transpired at the Constitutional Convention in Philadelphia. Max Farrand (ed.), *The Records of the Federal Convention of 1787* (New Haven: Yale University Press, 1937 edition, 4 volumes, and later editions and revisions) remains the fullest account, based on the notes of James Madison and others. A one-volume paper edition, *Notes of Debates in the Federal Convention of 1787 Reported by James Madison* (New York: W. W. Norton, 1987 and later editions) is an invaluable item for any collection of Constitutional materials. Outstanding accounts of the Convention include Catherine Drinker Bowen, *Miracle at Philadelphia* (Boston: Little Brown, 1966); Carl Van Doren, *The Great Rehearsal* (New York: Viking, 1969); James Lincoln Collier and Christopher Collier, *Decision at Philadelphia* (New York: Random House/Reader's Digest Press, 1985); and Clinton Rossiter, *1787: The Grand Convention* (New York: Macmillan, 1986).

A number of bibliographical guides are very beneficial. They are readily available and well organized, so that searchers can identify materials topically and chronologically. One of the best is Kermit L. Hall (ed.), *A Comprehensive Bibliography of American Constitutional and Legal History,* 5 volumes (Millwood, N.Y.: Kraus Thompson International, 1984). Two volumes in the "Goldentree Bibliographies" series published by Harlan Davison, Inc., Arlington Heights, Illinois, are very good: E. James Ferguson (ed.), *Confederation, Constitution, and Early National Period, 1781-1815;* and Alpheus T. Mason and D. Grier Stephenson, Jr. (eds.), *American Constitutional Development.* Also available is Stephen M. Millett (ed.), *A Selected Bibliography of American Constitutional History* (Santa Barbara, California: ABC-Clio Press, 1975). ABC-Clio Press has published a very usable annotated bibliographical series, the "ABC-Clio Research Guides." An excellent addition to that series (1986) is Suzanne R. Ontiveros (ed.), *The Dynamic Constitution: A Historical Bibliography.* Other useful volumes in the same series include Robert U. Goehlert (ed.), *Congress and Law-Making;* and Robert U. Goehlert and Fenton S. Martin (eds.), *The Presidency: A Research Guide.*

No attempt to understand the Constitution could suffice without a careful reading of *The Federalist Papers* authored by James Madison, Alexander Hamilton, and John Jay. A number of excellent editions are available, with most including scholarly commentaries.

Not confined to constitutional history, a bibliographical *MUST* for all students of history is Oscar Handlin *et al* (eds.), *Harvard Guide to American History* (Belknap Press of Harvard University Press, 1960, later paperback editions edited by Frank Freidel *et al*). Check also in the Reference Division of your library for additional bibliographies.

More specific listings, even very selective, would necessitate a very lengthy roster, much too tedious for the student to go through. In lieu thereof is a *brief* bibliography suggested by the Commission on the Bicentennial of the United States Constitution. Many more excellent works are available.

Bancroft, George, *History of the Formation of the Constitution of the United States of America.* 2 vols. New York: D. Appleton and Co., 1884.

Berger, Raoul, *Congress v. The Supreme Court.* Boston: Harvard University Press, 1969. (Also in Bantam paper edition.)

Berns, Walter, *The Writing of the Constitution of the United States.* Washington: American Enterprise Institute, 1985.

BIBLIOGRAPHY

Bloom, Sol, *The Story of the Constitution*. Washington: National Archives and Record Administration, 1986.

Bowen, Catherine Drinker, *Miracle at Philadelphia*. Boston: Little Brown, 1966. Later edition, Boston: Atlantic Monthly Press, 1986.

Bradford, M. E., *Remembering Who We Are: Observations of a Southern Conservative*. Athens, Ga.: University of Georgia Press, 1985.

Bradford, M. E., *A Worthy Conspiracy: Brief Lives of the Framers of the United States Constitution*. Marlborough, New Hampshire: Plymouth Rock Foundation, 1983.

Collier, James Lincoln, and Christopher Collier, *Decision in Philadelphia: The Constitutional Convention of 1787*. New York: Random House/Reader's Digest Press, 1985.

Corwin, Edward S., T*he "Higher Law" Background of American Constitutional Law*. Ithaca: Cornell University Press, 1955.

Cullop, Floyd G., *The Constitution of the United States*. New York: New American Library, 1984.

Diamond, Martin, *The Founding of the Democratic Republic*. Itaska, Illinois: F. E. Peacock Publishers, 1981.

Dietz, Gottfried, *The Federalist: A Classic on Federalism and Free Government*. Baltimore: The Johns Hopkins Press, 1960.

Epstein, David F., *The Political Theory of "The Federalist."* Chicago: University of Chicago Press, 1984.

Elliot, Jonathan (ed.), *The Debates in the Several State Conventions on the Adoption of the Federal Constitution*. 5 volumes. Philadelphia: J. B. Lippincott, 1901.

Farrand, Max, *The Framing of the Constitution of the United States*. New Haven: Yale University Press, 1913.

Farrand, Max (ed.), *The Records of the Federal Convention of 1787*. 4 volumes. New Haven: Yale University Press, 1937.

Fisher, Louis, *Politics of Shared Powers*. Washington: Congressional Quarterly Press, 1981.

Friendly, Fred W. and Martha J. J. Elliot., *The Constitution: That Delicate Balance.* New York: Random House, 1984.

Frisch, Morton J. (ed.), *Selected Writings and Speeches of Alexander Hamilton.* Washington: American Enterprise Institute, 1985.

Hamilton, Alexander, James Madison, and John Jay, *The Federalist Papers.* With Introduction by Clinton Rossiter. New York: New American Library, 1961. (Several other publications and editions available from other presses.)

Hayer, F. A., *The Constitution of Liberty.* Chicago: University of Chicago Press, 1960.

Jensen, Merrill, John K. Kaminski, and Gaspare S. Saladino (eds.), *The Documentary History of the Ratification of the Constitution and the Bill of Rights.* Madison: University of Wisconsin Press, multi-volume project, 1976-1984.

Kelly, Alfred H., Winfred A. Harbison, and Herman Belz, *The American Constitution.* 7th Edition. New York: W. W. Norton, 1991.

Kurland, Philip B. and Ralph Lerner (eds.), *The Founders' Constitution.* 5 volumes. Chicago: University of Chicago Press, 1986.

Levy, Leonard W. (ed.), *Essays on the Making of the Constitution.* 2nd Edition. New York: Oxford University Press, 1982.

Madison, James, *Notes of Debates in the Federal Convention of 1787.* Introduction by Adrienne Koch. Athens, Ohio: Ohio University Press, 1966, and later editions.

McDonald, Forrest, *E. Pluribus Unum: The Formation of the American Republic. 1776-1790.* Indianapolis: Liberty Press, 1979.

McDonald, Forrest, *Novus Ordo Seclorum: The Intellectual Origins of the Constitution.* Lawrence, Kansas: University of Kansas Press, 1985.

McDonald, Forrest, *We the People: The Economic Origins of the Constitution.* Chicago: University of Chicago Press, 1975.

McDowell, Gary L, *Curbing the Courts: The Constitution and the Limits of Judicial Power.* Baton Rouge: Louisiana State University Press, 1986.

McDowell, Gary, and Ralph Rossom, *Taking the Constitution Seriously: Essays on the Constitution and Constitutional Law.* Dubuque, Iowa: Kendall-Hunt, 1981.

BIBLIOGRAPHY

McLauglin, Andrew C., *The Confederation and the Constitution, 1783-1789.* New York: Collier Books, 1967.

McKenna, George, *A Guide to the Constitution: That Delicate Balance.* New York: Random House, 1984.

Meyers, Marvin (ed.), *The Minds of the Founder: Sources of the Political Thought of James Madison.* Hanover, N. H.: University Press, 1982.

Pyle, Christopher H. and Richard M. Pious, *The President, Congress, and the Constitution.* New York: The Free Press,

Rakove, Jack N., *The Beginnings of National Politics: An Interpretive History of the Continental Congress.* New York: Alfred A. Knopf, 1979.

Rossiter, Clinton, *1787: The Grand Convention.* New York: Macmillan, 1966.

Storing, Herbert J., *What the Anti-Federalists Were For.* Chicago: University of Chicago Press, 1981.

Storing, Herbert J. (ed.), *The Complete Anti-Federalists.* 7 volumes. Chicago: University of Chicago Press, 1981.

Story, Joseph, *Familiar Expositions of the Constitution of the United States.* N.p., 1840.

United States National Archives, *The Foundation of the Union.* Washington: The National Archives, 1970.

Van Doren, Carl, *The Great Rehearsal.* New York: Viking Press, 1969.

Warren, Charles, *The Making of the Constitution.* New York: Barnes and Noble, 1967.

Wood, Gordon, *The Creation of the American Republic, 1776-1787.* New York: W. W. Norton, 1969.

Wood, Gordon (ed.), *Documentary History of the Constitution.* 5 volumes. Washington, D. C.: Department of State, 1894-1905.

INDEX

Abortion, 26, 29-30, 119-121
Adams, John, 7, 81, 146
Adams, John Quincy, 64-65
Agnew, Spiro T., 66, 139, 140
Afghanistan, 91
"Age of Jackson," 21
Albany Plan of Union, 6
Alien and Sedition Acts, 18
Amendments, time limits, 127-128
American Revolution, 101
Antifederalists, 128
Anti-incumbency, 43, 47, 48
Anti-Saloon League, 137
Appellate jurisdiction, 102
Appendix to *Congressional Record,* 54
Apportionment, 40
Archivist of the United States, 142
Areopagitica, 53
Arms Export Control Act (1985), 67, 95
Articles of Confederation, 6, 7, 36-37, 38, 77, 101, 125-126, 151-158
"At large" elections, 41, 42
Australia, 7

Baker v. Carr (1962), 40, 116
Bank bill veto, 60, 78
Bank, national, 12, 18
Barbary pirates, 84
Barron v. Baltimore (1833), 133
Bedford, Gunning, 38
Belknap, William, 52
Benton, Thomas Hart, 65
Berger, Victor L., 55
Berlin Blockade, 92
Berlin Wall, 28, 96

"Big Business," 21, 113-114
Bill of Rights, 10, 128-130
Bingham, John, 133
Blount, William, 56
Board of Trade, 102
Bonham's Case, Dr. (1610), 110
Booth, John Wilkes, 87-88
Bork, Robert H., 119
Bradwell v. Illinois (1873), 136
Brandeis, Louis Dembitz, 114
Brennan, William J., Jr., 120
"Broad" interpretation of Constitution, 12
Brown v. Board of Education of Topeka (1954), 25, 116, 144, 136, 139
Buchanan, James, 65
Budget, 76
"Bundle of Compromises," 38
Burger, Warren E., 103, 117, 119
Burgesses, House of, 35
Burr, Aaron, 146
Bush, George, 27-28, 30, 60, 66, 67, 68, 70, 76, 85, 96, 97, 104, 117, 119

Cabinet, Presidential, 145-146
Calhoun, John C., 19, 65, 139
California, 3
Cambodia, 67, 96
Canada, 3, 157
Capone, Al, 137
Carter, Jimmy, 25, 66, 69, 96
Censure, 56
Census, Bureau of the, 40
Central America, 67
Champion v. Casey (1792), 110

Charles River Bridge v. Warren Bridge
    (1837), 21, 111
Chase, Samuel, 104
Checks and balances, 51, 59, 62, 78
Chisholm v. Georgia (1793), 106, 130
Christian Science Monitor, 105
Church and state, 26
Circuit Courts, United States, 107
Civil rights, 93, 133
Civil Rights Act of 1875, 135
Civil Rights Act of 1964, 116, 136
Civil Rights Cases (1883), 135
Civil War, 5, 19, 84, 87, 111-113
"Civil War Amendments," 132
Claiborne, Harry E., 44, 45, 50-51
Clay, Henry, 65
Clayton Anti-Trust Act, 22
Cleveland, Grover, 84
Clinton, Bill, 30, 70, 80, 97
Coal Strike of 1902, 89
Coke, Sir Edward, 110
Cold War, 27, 28, 91, 96
Coleman v. Miller (1939), 58, 127, 142
Colonial law, 102
"Committee of the States," 155, 157
Concord, Battle of, 5
Concurrent jurisdiction, judicial, 108
Concurrent powers, governmental, 9
Confederated form of government, 3, 4
Congress of the Articles of Confederation, 6
Congressional Apportionment Act, 42
Congressional-Presidential relations, 65-70
Congressional Quarterly, 127
"Congressional Reconstruction," 66
Congressional Record, 54
"Congressional veto," 61
Connecticut Compromise, 39
"Conservatives," 24
Constitutional Convention, 12, 16, 37, 106, 108
"Containment" policy, 96

"Contra" forces, 68, 96
Coolidge, Calvin, 79
Corporations, 135
"Court of Appeals," 107
Court of Military Appeals, 108
"Court packing scheme," 115, 138
Coverdell, Paul, 48
Cuban Missile Crisis, 92
Customs Courts, 108

Dartmouth College v. Woodward (1819), 110, 135
Declaration of Independence, 3
Declared wars, 85
Delegated powers, 11
Delegates, territorial, 40
Denied powers, 10
"Deputy" representation, 36
Desegregation, 25
"Desert Storm," 68, 85, 97
Dillon v. Gloss (1921), 127
District Courts, United States, 107
District of Columbia, 139
"Diversity of citizenship," 105
Domestic Policy Council, 27, 118
Douglas, William O., 44, 116
Dred Scott v. John F. A. Sanford (1857), 78, 110, 111, 112, 132

Educational tests (for voting), 53
Eighteenth Amendment, 127, 137
Eisenhower, Dwight D., 16, 25, 76, 79, 80, 82, 84, 94, 116, 139
"Elastic clause," 13
Election of 1992, 30
Electoral College, 131-132, 146
Eleventh Amendment, 106, 130
Ellsworth, Oliver, 106, 109
Emancipation Proclamation, 87
Employment Act of 1946, 25, 93
Enlightenment, Age of, 37, 89
Enumerated powers, 12
Escobedo v. Illinois (1964), 116

INDEX

"Essex Junto," 18
Exclusive powers, 10
"Executive agreement," 92-93, 145
Executive orders, 75
Ex Parte McCardle (1869), 106
Expressed powers, 12
Expulsion from Congress, 56

"Fair Deal," 25, 93
"Farewell Adress," 89, 90
Faubus, Orval, 25
"Federal question," 105
Federal Register, 58, 142
Federal Reserve Act, 20, 22
Federalism, 3, 63-64, 129
Federalist No. 70, 78
Ferraro, Geraldine, 82
Fifteenth Amendment, 53
Fifth Amendment, 116, 133
Fillmore, Millard, 65
"Fireside chats," 77
First Continental Congress, 5, 6, 36
Fisher, Louis, 70
Fletcher v. Peck (1810), 110
Flexibility principle, 79, 125-126, 129, 147
"For cause," 104
Ford, Gerald R., 25, 51, 64, 65, 66, 67, 96, 140
Ford, Henry, 55
Foreign policy, 89 ff.
Fourteenth Amendment, 132-136
Fowler, Wyche, 48
Fox, Charles James, 7
"Franking" privilege, 59
Franklin, Benjamin, 6, 38
"Free World," 91
French and Indian War, 6

Garfield, James A., 65, 139
General Assembly (U.N.), 5
"Geographic" representation, 36, 45, 146
"Gerrymandering," 40

Gibbons v. Ogden (1824), 110
"Gilded Age," 113, 134
Ginsburg, Douglas, 119
Gitlow v. New York (1925), 135
Gladstone, William, 125
Global village, 90
"Good behavior," 104
"Granger Cases" (1877), 113
Grant, Ulysses S., 82
Great Britain, 3
"Great Communicator," 82
"Great Compromise," 39
Great Depression, 23, 66, 90, 115
"Great Society," 25, 93
Grenada, 67, 92, 96
"Gridlock," 60, 70
Gulf War, 68 (*see also* "Desert Storm")

Habeas Corpus Act of 1867, 106
Hamilton, Alexander 12, 15, 78, 81, 84
"Happy Days Are Here Again," 138
Harding, Warren E., 65, 137
Harrington, James, 37
Harrison, Benjamin, 65
Harrison, William H., 65, 80, 81, 144
Hartford Convention, 18
Hastings, Alcee, 44, 45, 50-51
Hayden, Carl, 48
Hayes, Rutherford B., 65
Hawaii, 3
Holmes, Oliver Wendell, Jr., 14, 114
Hoover, Herbert, 79, 81
House of Representatives, 40-45
Hughes, Charles Evans, 144
Hurtado v. California (1884), 135
Hussein, Saddam, 68, 95
Hylton v. United States (1796), 110

Impeachment, 26, 44, 50-52, 56, 78, 94, 104, 140
"Imperial Judiciary," 117
"Imperial Presidency," 66, 95
Implied powers, 12

Independence (from Great Britain), 5
Independence Hall, 126
Industrial Revolution, 20, 88, 89, 134
Industrialization, 21
"Informal" amendments, 143
Intelligence Authorization Assistance Act (1986), 67, 95
International Court of Justice, 5
Interstate commerce, 22
Interstate Commerce Act, 22, 114
Intolerable Acts, 5
Iran, 67, 92, 96
"Irangate," 67, 96
Iraq, 68, 95
Iron Curtain, 28
Isolationism, 89

Jackson, Andrew, 19, 60, 65, 66, 78, 86, 139
"Jacksonian Democracy," 21, 86
Jay, John, 109
Jefferson, Thomas, 65, 81, 84, 85, 88-89, 131, 133, 146
"Jeffersonian Democracy," 20, 86
"John Wilkes Affair," 55
Johnson, Andrew, 44-45, 64, 88
Johnson, Jack, 139
Johnson, Lyndon B., 16, 25, 26, 64, 65, 76, 94, 139
Judicial review, 51, 78, 109-110
Judiciary Act of 1789, 78, 105, 106-109
Jurisdiction of federal courts, 105-106

Kennedy, Anthony M., 119
Kennedy, John F., 16, 25, 65, 76, 80, 82, 84, 94, 139
Kennedy, Robert, 94
King, Martin Luther, Jr., 94
Kirkpatrick v. Preisley (1969), 40
Korea, 91, 92, 97
Kuwait, 68, 95

LaFollette, Robert, 65
"Laissez faire," 24

"Lame Duck Amendment," 54, 137
Law, English, 102
Leadership principle, Presidency, 79
League of Nations, 90
Lebanon, 67, 92, 96
"Legislative courts," 108
"Legislative veto," 61
Lexington, Battle of, 5
"Liberal" interpretation of Constitution, 12
"Liberals," 24
Libya, 96
Limited government, 63-64
Lincoln, Abraham, 19, 65, 84, 87, 133, 139
"Line-item veto," 60, 61-62
Literacy tests, for voting, 53
Locke, John, 37
Lodge, Henry Cabot, 55
"Log-rolling," 46
"Loose" interpretation of Constitution, 12
Lords of Trade, 102
"Lost Amendment" (27th Amendment), 141
Louis, Joe, 139
Louisiana Purchase, 18, 86

Madison, James, 37, 64, 141
Maine elections, 54
"Manifest Destiny," 88, 90
Marbury v. Madison (1803), 51, 78, 109, 110, 143
"Marshall Court," 109, 121
Marshall, John, 15, 109, 135
Marshall, Thomas R., 55
Marshall, Thurgood, 120
Mayaguez, 67, 96
Maysville Veto, 19, 78
McCarthy, Joseph R., 56, 59
McCulloch v. Maryland (1819), 15, 110-111
McKinley, William, 65, 82, 139

INDEX

Medicare, 15
"Men of virtue," 47
Mercantilism, 8, 102
Meese, Edwin, 27-28, 118
Middle East, 67-92
Milton, John, 53
Minor v. Happersett (1875), 136
Miranda v. Arizona (1966), 116
"Miranda rights," 26
Missouri Compromise, 18, 78
Money bills, 63
"Money grab," 141
Monroe Doctrine, 86-87, 90
Monroe, James, 115
Montesquieu, 37
Munn v. Illinois (1877), 113

Napoleon Bonaparte, 35, 86
"Narrow" interpretation of Constitution, 12
Nast, Thomas, 21
National Emergencies Act, 95
"National" representation, 36
National Security Act, 67, 95
"Natural born" citizen, 81
"Necessary and proper" clause, 12, 22, 111
Newberry, Truman H., 55
"New Deal," 23, 66, 91, 93, 115
New England Confederation, 6
"New Freedom," 22
"New Frontier," 25
New Jersey Plan, 39
"New Republicanism," 25, 93
"Nine Old Men," 115, 138
Nineteenth Amendment, 53, 137
Ninth Amendment, 15, 129
Nixon, Richard M., 25, 26, 44, 45, 51, 52, 60, 65, 66, 67, 94, 95, 117, 139
Nixon, Walter L., 44, 45, 50-51, 104
Nominating Conventions, 145-147
Noriega, Manuel, 97
"Normalcy," 23, 90

Norris, George W., 65
"Nullification," 18, 19
Nuclear armaments, 67, 91

O'Connor, Sandra Day, 27, 119
"One-man-one-vote," 40, 116
Original jurisdiction, 102
"Original intent," 27, 118
"Overriding" a veto, 60
Owens, Jesse, 139

Panama, 28, 67, 92, 97
Parliament, 3, 35, 36
Paterson, William 39
"Peace dividend," 28
Perot, H. Ross, 30, 98
Persian Gulf, 28, 67, 68, 92, 95
Pickering, John, 104
Pickering, Timothy, 18
Pierce, Franklin, 65
Plessy v. Ferguson (1896), 116, 135, 144
"Pocket veto," 61
Political Action Committees (PACs), 57
"Political availability," 82
Polk, James K., 64, 86
Poll tax, 53, 139
"Pork," 62
Powell, Adam Clayton, 55
Powell, Lewis F., Jr. 119
Powers of Congress, 12
President, 75 *ff.*
   as chief executive, 75
   as chief of state, 75
   as ceremonial head, 75
   in legislative process, 75-76
   in judicial process, 76
   as chief administrator, 76
   as commander-in-chief, 76
   as chief diplomat, 77
   nomination, 83
   election, 83
President (under Articles of Confederation), 6

WE THE PEOPLE

President Pro Tempore, 49
Presidential leadership, 75
Presidential powers, 75-77
"Presidential Reconstruction," 66
Presidential Succession Act of 1948, 43
Presidential veto, 59-62
Presidential war powers, 60-61, 68-69
Privacy, right to, 26
Privy Council, 102
Procedural due process, 130
"Pro-choice," 29-30
Progressivism, 21, 89, 114
Prohibition, 137
"Proletariat" government, 22
"Pro-life," 29-30
Proposal of amendments, 126-127
Provinces (Canadian), 3
Pure Food and Drug Acts, 22

Qualifications, federal judges, 104
Qualifications, President, 80-82
Qualifications, Representatives, 42
Qualifications, Senators, 48-49

"Radical Republicans," 88
Randolph, Edmund, 39
Ratification of amendments, 127-128
Rayburn, Sam, 65
Reagan, Ronald, 23, 26-28, 47, 60, 66-67, 76, 80, 82-83, 96, 97, 104, 117
Reconstruction, 65, 88, 111-113
Rehnquist, William H., 105, 119
Reign of Terror, 35, 125
Representative government, 36
Residual powers, 11
Resolutions, Congressional, 62
Revolutionary War, 125
Reynolds v. Sims (1964), 40, 116
"Riding circuit," 107
Ritter, Halsted, 50
"Roaring Twenties," 23, 115, 137
Roberts, Brigham H., 55
Robinson, Jackie, 139

Robinson, Joseph T., 65
Rockefeller, John D., 21
Rockefeller, Nelson A., 140
Roosevelt, Franklin D., 23, 65, 82, 90, 107, 115, 138
Roosevelt, Theodore, 65, 80, 82, 89, 114
Rotation in office, 86
Rousseau, 37
"Rule of Reason," 114
Russian Revolution, 35

Saddam Hussein, 68, 95
Salaries, Congressional, 56-59, 140-141
"Salary grab" of 1991, 157
Scalia, Antonin, 27, 119
Schlesinger, Arthur, Jr., 94
Second Continental Congress, 3, 5, 6, 36
Segregation, 16
Senate, 45-52
"Separate but equal," 116, 135
Separation of powers, 59, 78
Seventeenth Amendment, 48-49, 53, 137
Sexism, 119-120
Sherman Anti-Trust Act, 22, 114
Sidney, Algernon, 37
Sixth Amendment, 116
Sixteenth Amendment, 136-137
Slaughterhouse Cases (1873), 113, 134-135
Smith, Al, 82
Socialism, 24
Souter, David, 120
Sovereignty, 3, 6
Soviet Union, 67, 91, 96
Spanish-American War, 90
Speaker of the House, 43
Special session of Congress, 76
Spoils system, 86
"Square Deal," 22
Stamp Act Congress, 6
Stare decisis, 118
"Star Wars," 96
State of the Union Address, 75

INDEX

State sovereignty, 126
"States' Rights Doctrine," 19
"Status of Federalism in America, The," 27, 117-118
"Stewardship" principle of Presidency, 79
Story, Joseph, 122
"Stream of Commerce," 114
"Strict" interpretation of Constitution, 12
"Sun belt" states, 40
Supreme Court of United States, 27-28
"Supreme law of the land," 9, 108-109

Taft, Robert A., 65
Taft, William H., 84, 89, 114
Taney, Roger B., 21, 111-112
Tax Court, 108
Tax programs, 76
Tennessee Valley Authority (TVA), 24
Tenth Amendment, 3, 11, 15, 105, 109
Term limitations, 43, 55
Terrorism, 67, 84, 92
Texas, 3
Texas v. White (1869), 19, 109
Third World nations, 35, 91
Thirteenth Amendment, 19
Thomas, Clarence, 120
Time limitations, amendments, 141-142
"Times have changes" principle, 80
Trade treaties, 7
Truman, Harry S, 15, 25, 60, 65, 85, 94, 96, 97, 139
Twelfth Amendment, 130-132, 147
Twentieth Amendment, 54, 137
Twenty-First Amendment, 137-138
Twenty-Second Amendment, 82, 138
Twenty-Third Amendment, 139
Twenty-Fourth Amendment, 53, 116, 139
Twenty-Fifth Amendment, 66, 139-140
Twenty-Sixth Amendment, 53, 140
Twenty-Seventh Amendment, 57-58, 141-143

Two-term tradition, 82, 138
Tyler, John, 65, 85, 86, 144
Unitary form of government, 3, 4
United Nations, 3, 5, 85, 91
United States v. Curtiss-Wright Corporation (1936), 75
Urbanism, 21
U. S. News & World Report, 76, 104

Van Buren, Martin, 65, 86
Veto, presidential, 59-62
Vietnam, 26, 60, 66, 67, 85, 91, 92, 94, 140
Virginia and Kentucky Resolutions, 18
Virginia Plan, 39
"Virtual" representation, 36, 45
Versailles, Treaty of, 55, 56, 78, 90
Voice votes, 63
Voltaire, 37
Voting in Congress, 45-47
Voting qualifications, 53
Voting restrictions, 53
Voting Rights Act of 1965, 53, 116, 136

Wage and hour regulation, 14
Wallace, George, 25
War of 1812, 18
War Powers Act, 60-61, 67, 95
Ware v. Hylton (1796), 110
Warren, Earl, 25, 116
Washington, George, 17, 65, 83-84, 146
"Watergate Affair," 26, 66, 94, 140
Webster, Daniel, 11, 65
Wesberry v. Sanders (1960), 40, 116
Whiskey Rebellion, 84
Whitten, Jamie L., 43
Wilson, Don W., 142
Wilson, Woodrow, 20, 55, 65, 78, 84, 89, 90, 114, 145
Women's rights, 26
World Court, 5
World War I, 23
World War II, 25, 66, 90, 138